EAST ASIAN HISTORICAL MONOGRAPHS

General Editor: WANG GUNGWU

POLITICS IN A PLURAL SOCIETY

POLITICS IN
A PLURAL SOCIETY

A STUDY OF NON-COMMUNAL
POLITICAL PARTIES IN WEST MALAYSIA

R.K. VASIL

Published for the Australian
Institute of International Affairs

KUALA LUMPUR   SINGAPORE
OXFORD UNIVERSITY PRESS
LONDON   NEW YORK
1971

Oxford University Press, Ely House, London, W.I.
GLASGOW NEW YORK TORONTO MELBOURNE WELLINGTON
CAPE TOWN SALISBURY IBADAN NAIROBI DAR ES SALAAM LUSAKA ADDIS ABABA
BOMBAY CALCUTTA MADRAS KARACHI LAHORE DACCA
KUALA LUMPUR SINGAPORE HONG KONG TOKYO
Bangunan Loke Yew, Kuala Lumpur
© *Australian Institute of International Affairs 1971*

PRINTED BY PRINTERS AND CONVERTERS (PTE) LTD SINGAPORE

FOR DEEPA

PREFACE

PARTY politics in Malaysia has been largely a matter of mobilizing communal backing. Hence the existence of non-communal political parties may seem paradoxical or quixotic. Yet many such parties have been formed from time to time and a study of these can be just as revealing about political processes in Malaysia as a study of the avowedly communal ones. One could even say that a study of these parties can shed more light on the viability of the political system, the extent of integration of the different racial groups and their relations with one another.

Recent events in the country have proved that the Alliance, which is no more than a coalition of the communal bodies of the three major communities, is only a transitional phenomenon. In the past it had been able to alleviate the fundamental communal contradiction, but it is doubtful if it can solve the problems and create a new Malaysian nation. The Alliance, based on the idea of Malay supremacy in the government and administration of the country as a counter-weight to Chinese economic and commercial power, has put little emphasis on the creation of an integrated new society. Until recently it had been possible for the Alliance to maintain a position of political supremacy of the Malays, by and large, without seriously endangering communal harmony and straining constitutional democracy, because of the great personal influence of its leader, Tunku Abdul Rahman. The Tunku had also been successful in imposing a moderating influence on the Malays and making them make minor concessions to the non-Malays so as not to upset the whole arrangement. But recent events have made it obvious that the old arrangement is no longer workable and that the whole situation is in the melting pot. New solutions have to be worked out to resolve the basic contradiction between the demands of the Malays for a position of political supremacy and of the non-Malays for immediate equality of civic rights.

This makes the non-communal political parties of even more vital significance in the plural society of Malaysia. The future resolution of the contradiction and the establishment of an integrated new nation should substantially depend on the existence and working of non-communal political parties.

This book is based on a doctoral dissertation presented to the Department of History, University of Malaya, Kuala Lumpur in early 1968. It is a result of two years of research in Malaysia, from May 1963 to May 1965, and is largely based on primary material, unpublished party documents and personal interviews. The study was completed in 1967, well before the formation of two new non-communal political parties, the Gerakan Rakyat Malaysia and the Democratic Action Party, and the crucial 1969 general elections in the country. It is for this reason that the important political developments in Malaysia since 1967 have been considered only in the postscript.

I am indebted to the Government of Malaysia for granting me a Commonwealth Fellowship which enabled me to stay in the country for two years and undertake the research. A substantial part of the writing of the book was done at the Australian National University, Canberra, during a period of six months in 1965. I am grateful to Professor J.D.B. Miller, Head of the Department of International Relations of the University, who kindly offered me a Visiting Fellowship. My debt is particularly great to Professor Wang Gungwu, Australian National University (formerly Head of the Department of History, University of Malaya), who acted as the supervisor for the dissertation, and J.A.C. Mackie (Centre of South East Asian Studies, Monash University, Australia), who not only read the entire manuscript and made many useful comments but helped me in many ways.

In Malaysia I am indebted to a very large number of people without whose help and generosity this work would not have been completed. This includes people in the various political parties, trade unions and newspapers. I am sure they would undertstand the reason I am not identifying them individually. However, I would like to make a special mention of D.R. Seenivasagam and Ooi Thiam Siew, both of whom unfortunately have passed away, and Tan Kai Hee and Lim Kit Siang, both presently under detention by the Malaysian Government (the former since early 1965). To all of them I owe a special debt of gratitude. I would also like to thank three great Malaysians, Dr. Tan Chee Khoon, Dr. Lim Chong Eu and V. Veerappen, whose friendships have been an immense personal gain to me from my contact with Malaysia. I am saying this, fully conscious of the fact that these three have played an important part in the story told in this book. I must also thank Dato Syed Jaafar Albar whose friendship and frankness gave me a real understanding of Malay feelings. I know he would strongly disagree with many things that I have said in the book but only hope that he would not doubt my integrity and honesty.

Finally, let me thank Professors Norman Harper and Brian Beddie for their kind interest. I am especially grateful to Professor Hedley Bull for all his help in arranging the publication of the book on behalf of the Australian Institute of International Affairs and to the Institute for its generous financial assistance.

Victoria University   R. K. VASIL
Wellington, New Zealand
June 1970

CONTENTS

TABLES

I

COMMUNALISM AND THE POLITICAL PROCESS IN WEST MALAYSIA

Communal and Political Setting

THIS is a study of the non-communal political parties in West Malaysia,[1] past and present. The parties included are: the Independence of Malaya Party and the Party Negara; the Labour Party, the Party Raayat and the Socialist Front; the People's Progressive Party and the United Democratic Party; and the parties of personage like the National Association of Perak, the Malayan Party and the National Convention Party. These are included because, even though they may not have remained entirely non-communal political parties in a strict sense, they were launched by their founders as genuinely non-communal political parties. When formed they allowed full membership to all the people of the country irrespective of their racial origin. Their constitutions today, even after the parties have changed considerably in their character, proclaim them to be non-communal. And, as far as their aims and objects are concerned, they were not committed to protect or promote the interests of any one racial group only, nor did they base their appeal on purely communalistic lines.

In comparison, both the United Malays National Organisation (UMNO) and the Malayan Chinese Association (MCA), the two major communal parties, allow full membership only to Malays and Chinese respectively.[2] Further, they are committed essentially

---

[1] This study excludes the non-communal political parties in Sabah and Sarawak. The racial situation in these areas and the political experience of the people there have not been the same as that in Malaya. Also, political parties there are of very recent origin; they came into existence only around 1963, the year when Malaysia was formed.

[2] However, persons belonging to other racial groups are allowed to become associate members. But this does not permit them to hold any official position in the parties or have the right to vote.

to protect the position and interests of their own respective communities. For example, the constitution of the UMNO proclaims the following to be its major aims and objects.

1. To safeguard and preserve the Constitution of the Federation of Malaya, particularly the provisions relating to the Muslim Religion, Malay language and custom, the dignity and prestige of Their Highnesses the Malay Rulers and the special privileges of the Malays.
2. To promote the advancement of Islam and to foster its growth as the *modus vivendi* for all Muslims living in the Federation of Malaya.
3. To take such steps as may be necessary for the welfare and advancement of its members, the Malays particularly and the citizens of the Federation of Malaya generally.[3]

Similarly, the constitution of the MCA lays down the following, among others, as the objects of the Association:

1. To foster, safeguard, advance and secure the political, social, educational, cultural, economic and other interests of its members by legitimate and constitutional means.
2. To consider, assist and deal with problems affecting its members as a whole.
3. To preserve and sustain the use and study of the Chinese language.[4]

As will be seen later such provisions are not found in the constitutions of parties which have been considered non-communal for the purposes of this study.

It is intended to study the non-communal parties in relation,

---

[3] *Undang-Undang Tubuh* (Constitution), United Malays National Organisation, 16 and 17 April 1960, pp. 1-2 of the English version.

[4] *Constitution of the Malaysian Chinese Association*, 12 November 1963, pp. 2-3. The constitution of the association as adopted on 12 June 1949, when the organization was founded, mentioned the following as its main object:

> To foster and safeguard the social, political, cultural and economic welfare of *the Malayan Chinese* by legitimate and constitutional means. (Emphasis added.)

In the later constitution quoted above 'the Malayan Chinese' was replaced by 'its members' which hardly makes any difference since only people 'of Chinese descent' are eligible for the membership of the association.

first, to the broad framework of the communal situation in the country, and second, to the pattern of politics of the Alliance Party, which has been the ruling party since 1955, two years before the country became independent. The latter is of particular significance because it is mainly against the communal political parties forming the Alliance that the non-communal ones have to compete for electoral support and power. The political climate in the country, in which the non-communal parties have to function, has been set by the racial situation and the rule by the three communal parties for more than a decade.

The Communal Framework

Malaysia is an example of a multi-racial society *par excellence:* its population consists of Malays, Chinese, Indians (and some other smaller groups), representing the three major racial groups of Southern and Eastern Asia. These three groups differ very sharply from each other in religion, culture, language, customs, food-habits and dress. Not many countries in the world have more different peoples living together within a single political system.

According to a mid-1967 estimate the Malays (including other indigenous groups) accounted for 50 per cent of the population, the Chinese 37 per cent, Indians and Pakistanis 11 per cent, and others 2 per cent.[5] The size of the minority communities is of great significance. They are not minority groups in the sense one thinks of Chinese minorities in Indonesia, Thailand and the Philippines. They constitute about 49.9 percent of the total population in Malaysia.

The regional variation in the racial composition of the population is important. Malays mostly live in the rural areas, 'notably in the two rice-bowl areas of Kedah and Kelantan and in other rice-growing areas in the west coast States such as Krian (Perak)',[6] and on the east coast. Of the 2.6 million urban population of Ma-

[5] Malaysia, *Buku Rasmi Tahunan* (Official Year Book), 1966, Kuala Lumpur, Government Press, 1968, p. 29.

[6] T.G. McGee 'Population: A Preliminary Analysis', in Wang Gungwu (editor), *Malaysia, A Survey*, London, Pall Mall Press, 1964, p. 68.

laya in 1957 only 0.6 million were Malays. Over 1.7 million of them were Chinese, and 0.3 million others.[7]

The non-Malays are primarily concentrated in the port cities of Penang and Malacca and other urban areas in the west coast States of Johore, Perak, Selangor and Negri Sembilan. These people have generally lived apart. During the period of the British rule the different racial groups hardly came together. The immigrant peoples were made to feel that they were aliens and did not belong to Malaya. No attempts were made to bring them together. The process of integration of these people into a new Malayan nation was seriously hampered. All Malays are Muslims whereas most Chinese are Buddhists or Christians and Indians predominantly Hindus. As a result intermarriages among the different racial groups have been tabooed.[8]

Further, the differences in the economic position of the Malays and the Chinese have aggravated the difficulties and have had a serious impact on the politics of the country. The table below gives a rough measure of this economic gap.

TABLE 1

APPROXIMATE AGGREGATE INDIVIDUAL INCOMES BY RACE, 1957

	Malays	Chinese	Indians	Total*
Aggregate individual incomes ($m.)	1,125	1,975	475	3,675
Percentage of total	30	54	13	100
Population (m.)	3.13	2.33	0.7	6.28
Average annual income per head ($)	359	848	691	585
Average annual income per adult male ($)	1,433	3,264	2,013	2,128

Household Budget Survey, Report of the Inland Revenue Department, 1958; and Census of Malaya, 1957, quoted in T.H. Silcock and E.K. Fisk, *The Political Economy of Independent Malaya*, Singapore, Eastern University Press, 1963, p. 3.
*Includes Europeans and others.

[7] Hamzah Sendut, 'Urbanisation', ibid. p. 89.

[8] In the case of Muslims inter-marriage is prohibited by their religion. Tunku Abdul Rahman, the Prime Minister of Malaysia and the President of the Alliance, told the author that integration and assimilation of the non-Malays is not possible because inter-marriages are very restricted due to the differences in religion. Also, he pointed out that the Chinese have a very long tradition behind them and 'they are very proud of it', which makes their integration very difficult. Kuala Lumpur, March 1965.

The relative position of the different racial groups in the share of national wealth is obvious. However, it is not really so important whether the Chinese own a large part of the wealth. The important point is that most of the Malays and their leaders believe this to be true and this determines their attitude towards non-Malays, the Chinese in particular.

To the Malays, therefore, it is imperative that they must have a pre-eminent position in the administration and government of the country in order to offset the dominant non-Malay control over the economic and commercial life. Speaking before the Central General Committee of the Malayan Chinese Association on 12 July 1959, at the height of a crisis in the Alliance, Tan Siew Sin, one of the small group of Chinese leaders acceptable to the UMNO, the President of the MCA since 1961, conceded: 'Regarding Sino-Malay relationship there was a fear that because of the economic power of the Chinese, the Malays would be completely swamped and to avoid this it was necessary for the Malays to retain their political power'.[9] Later, at the time of the 1964 general elections he was to put forward the same view more explicitly:

> We have to accept that the Chinese are economically stronger than the Malays. The Malays, therefore, feel that in order to counterbalance their weak economic position they have got to have political power. They feel that with this political power or special position they could cope with the other races politically and economically.[10]

More recently, Tun Haji Abdul Razak bin Hussein, the Deputy Prime Minister of Malaysia, in an interview with the author on the New Zealand Broadcasting Corporation, said:

> It is true at the moment that political power is in the hands of the Malaysians and economic power is in the hands of the Chinese. That is why we must try and balance things out. That is why we are doing our best to try and give the Malays a little bit of a share in the economic life to enable them to feel safe in the country. After all they were the original settlers.[11]

[9] *Minutes of a Central General Committee Meeting held on 12 July 1959,* Kuala Lumpur, p. 13 (mimeographed).
[10] *The Straits Times,* 6 March 1964.
[11] In April 1967.

Combined with this is the deep-rooted feeling that the Malays alone are the *bumiputra*, the sons of the soil, and as such, have certain special rights over the country. On 30 June 1952, a few months after the UMNO and the MCA had successfully contested the municipal elections in Kuala Lumpur, which had laid the foundation of the present Alliance, Tunku Abdul Rahman, the Prime Minister of Malaysia declared: 'Malaya is for the Malays and it should not be governed by a mixture of races'.[12] The Malays must safeguard their rights over this land 'which is ours for the benefit of our future generations'. More recently, in an interview with *The Asia Magazine*, the Tunku said:

> It is understood by all that this country by its very name, its traditions and character is Malay. The indigenous people are Malays and while they on the whole have been left behind in the economic and professional fields, others have been helped along by the understanding and tolerance of the Malays to be successes in whatever fields they are in. In any other country where aliens try to dominate economic and other fields, eventually there is bitter opposition from the indigenous people. But not with the Malays. Therefore, in return, they must appreciate the position of the Malays who have been given land in Malay reservations and jobs in the Government.
>
> Without those where would they go? They can't go into business which is in the hands of the non-Malays. And anyhow these businessmen quite naturally employ their own people. Therefore, if Malays are driven out of everything, however tolerant they may be, there is a limit. Resentment would build up and there would be trouble, and those who had found prosperity would also suffer. [13]

The Malays have a great fear of being 'reduced to the status of Red Indians striving to live in the wastelands of America'.

[12] *The Straits Times*, 1 July 1952. In fact, the Tunku had started making these extreme statements immediately after assuming the Presidency of the UMNO in late August 1951. The Tunku was so extreme that Raja Ayoub bin Raja Haji Bok, Chairman of the Kuala Lumpur branch of the UMNO, was forced to warn on 13 September 1951 that the Tunku would be blocking all chances of UMNO's success in the municipal elections in Kuala Lumpur, where a large part of the electorate was non-Malay, if he went on making 'Malaya for the Malays' statements. Ibid. 14 September 1951. The UMNO youth leader at the time, Mohammad Sopiee, branded the Tunku's policy as 'narrow racialism' and 'explosive'.

[13] On 30 August 1964.

The two supreme features of the Malays' approach to politics in Malaysia are: first, that the unity of the Malays has to be maintained at all costs; and second, that the UMNO must have a dominant position within the Alliance so as to have control over the government and administration of the country. Both these are fundamental from the point of view of the Malays. But both have had a very significant impact on the working of non-communal political parties.

The unity of the Malays is of the greatest importance. Malays who have ever dared to go out of the ranks of the Malays have been called traitors to the Malay cause. In fact, they become outcasts within the Malay community. There is the case of Dato Onn bin Jaafar, father of Malay nationalism and the founder of the UMNO. Soon after he left the UMNO, its new President, Tunku Abdul Rahman, said that Dato Onn, by leaving the UMNO and forming the non-communal IMP, had sold away Malay rights and heritage to other races.[14] One could also cite the example of Dato Zainal Abidin bin Haji Abas, at one time the Chairman of the United Democratic Party. Dato Zainal, coming from Perak, had been a very prominent Malay for over two decades. He, along with his mentor, Dato Onn, was one of the founders of the UMNO in 1946 and was also its first General Secretary. Later, in 1951, he left the UMNO with Dato Onn and joined the IMP. He later accepted the chairmanship of the United Democratic Party. But today, because of his politics, he is completely alienated from the Malay community. In the 1964 general elections, he contested for Parliament from his home constituency, Parit in Perak, where he was not only defeated by an UMNO candidate but lost his deposit. When Aziz Ishak, a top-ranking leader of the UMNO and a senior member of the Cabinet, dared to cross swords with Tunku Abdul Rahman, he was eased out of the UMNO. Once he was out of the UMNO he was hounded, and during the 1964 general elections all kinds of charges were laid against him and his political party, the National Convention Party. Not long after the elections he was arrested under the Internal Security Act on the unproved and unpressed charge of working with the Indonesians.

[14] *The Straits Times*, 1 July 1952.

The present delimitation of constituencies for the Malaysian Parliament gives a strong weightage in favour of the Malay electorate. This is based on the delimitation made for the purposes of the elections for the Federal Legislative Council in 1955. At that time the country was divided into fifty-two constituencies on the basis of a near-equal distribution of population. This delimitation was far from perfect and the Election Commission of the independent Federation of Malaya had the following to say about it:

> ... the Constituency Delineation Commission of the day had made use, *faute de mieux*, of an estimate of population prepared in 1953, and based on the 1947 census figures. This estimate did not take into account the redistribution of population brought about by the circumstances of the Emergency, and the actual population figures of the various constituencies in consequence varied considerably. [15]

It further stated that as the constituencies 'had been based on population figures only, without taking into account the variation in the percentage of citizens in each constituency, even greater discrepancy was to be found between the figures of registered electors'.

The Constitution of the Federation of Malaya, before it was amended in 1962, had provided that for the purpose of the 1959 elections (the first after independence) 'the Federation shall be divided into constituencies by dividing into two constituencies each of the constituencies delimited for the purpose of elections to the Federal Legislative Council [in 1955] ....' [16] But at the same time, under Article 116, it had charged the Election Commission to delimit the country into 100 federal constituencies on the basis of the near-equality of registered voters rather than

---

[15] Federation of Malaya, Election Commission, *Report on the Parliamentary and State Elections, 1959*, Kuala Lumpur, Government Press, 1960, p. 2. For example, the Ulu Selangor constituency had a total of 7,835 voters while another constituency, Kelantan Timor, had 46,221 voters. See Federation of Malaya, *Report on the First Election of Members to the Legislative Council of the Federation of Malaya*, Kuala Lumpur, Government Press, 1955.

[16] Article 171 (1) of the Federal Constitution, *Malayan Constitution Documents*, 2nd edition, Vol. I, Kuala Lumpur, Government Press, 1962, p. 135.

population.[17] This new delimitation, according to the Constitution, was to be used for the elections after 1959. As a result the Election Commission, after the completion of the 1959 general elections, betook itself to the task of dividing the country into 100 constituencies and its report was published in 1960.[18] But it aroused strong fears among the leaders of the UMNO, the senior partner in the ruling Alliance, who were afraid that this would give the non-Malays a greater measure of political power. There would be a larger number of constituencies where the Malays would not form a majority of the voters. Consequently, the Constitution was amended under the Constitution (Amendment) Act, 1962 and the new delimitation of constituencies was discarded. The country reverted to the 104 constituencies of the 1959 general elections and the 1964 general elections were held in 104 Parliamentary constituencies.[19]

Later, at the time of the formation of Malaysia, Singapore, with its predominantly non-Malay population, was allocated only

[17] Article 116 (4), repealed in 1962, had provided:

Each State shall be divided into constituencies in such a manner that each constituency contains a number of electors as nearly equal to the electoral quota of the State as may be after making due allowance for the distribution of the different communities and for differences in density of population and the means of communication; but the allowance so made shall not increase or reduce the number of electors in any constituency to a number differing from the electoral quota by more than fifteen per cent.

'Electoral quota' here refers to the number obtained by dividing the number of electors in the State by the total number of constituencies alloted to the State.

[18] *Federation of Malaya, Election Commission Report on the Delimitation of Parliamentary and State Constituencies, under the Provisions of the Constitution of the PTM, 1960*, Kuala Lumpur, Government Press, 1960.

[19] This resulted in a great variation in the size of the constituencies in the 1964 general elections. The extent of the variation can be seen in the following table:

No. of Voters	No. of constituencies, 1964 elections	No. of constituencies in delimitation by Election Commission, 1960
10,000 - 15,000	2	—
15,000 - 20,000	9	4
20,000 - 25,000	38	75
25,000 - 30,000	31	21
30,000 and over	24	—
	104	100

15 out of 159 seats in the Malaysian Parliament (9.3 per cent of the total) when it accounted for 16.7 per cent of the total population. This under-representation was accepted by Lee Kuan Yew in return for greater power over education and labour policy than enjoyed by the other States of the Federation.

The Alliance and its Pattern of Politics

The Alliance is a freak of history. But it has altered the course of Malaysian history. It started as an alliance of two communal organizations, the United Malays National Organisation and the Malayan Chinese Association, both distrustful of each other. The two communal organizations had nothing in common, except their upper-class leadership. In fact, each of them was committed primarily to protect the community it represented from the other.[20]

It came into being at the beginning of 1952 as a temporary alliance between the Selangor State branch of the MCA and the Kuala Lumpur branch of the UMNO, with the sole aim of jointly contesting the Kuala Lumpur municipal elections in February 1952.[21] It was done without the prior knowledge of the national

[20] It was something like the Hindu Mahasabha and the All India Muslim League, the communal organizations of the Hindus and the Muslims respectively, joining hands in the pre-Independence period to fight against the non-communal Indian National Congress.

[21] The following were the incidents that led to this event.

Sir Henry Lee, a very prosperous tin miner and the most powerful leader of the Chinese community in the State of Selangor, was the President of the Selangor state branch of the Malayan Chinese Association at the time of the formation of the IMP. At the inaugural meeting of the IMP on 16 September 1951 at the Hotel Majestic in Kuala Lumpur, Sir Henry Lee was ignored and was not invited by the organisers to sit on the platform where were seated the representatives (many of whom were very much less known than Sir Henry Lee) of the various organizations which had supported the formation of the IMP. He was also not asked to address the meeting. Sir Henry, a power to reckon with in Selangor, was visibly hurt. Also, he had not been consulted by Dato Onn bin Jaafar prior to the formation of the IMP, while the latter had consulted almost every other important leader in the country. It seems that Sir Henry was so badly hurt that he took it upon himself to see that the IMP failed.

Soon after this, at the Miners' Club in Kuala Lumpur, Sir Henry happened to meet Yahya bin Dato Abdul Razak, Chairman of the UMNO Election Sub-Committee for the Kuala Lumpur branch, who had his own minor mining in-leadership of the two organizations. The common objective of the two disparate communal organizations was to defeat the Independence of Malaya Party, a party which could pose a serious threat to them. The IMP had earlier been established by Dato Onn on 16 September 1951 when the UMNO rejected his plan to open its membership to non-Malays and convert it into a non-communal national party.

The new arrangement proved a great success in the Kuala Lumpur municipal elections. The UMNO and the MCA[22] were able to capture nine of the twelve seats for which elections were held; the MCA won six and the UMNO three seats. The IMP was able to secure only two seats and, as will be seen later, this proved to be the beginning of the end for the IMP. The UMNO-MCA candidates won by large majorities and the IMP was badly beaten.

This unexpected success of the joint effort spurred the national leadership of the two parties to use the idea in the subsequent elections. And in all the elections after the one in Kuala Lumpur it was unbeaten. This is how the foundation of the Alliance was laid. The idea worked so well that the substantial opposition to it

---

terests and who knew Sir Henry. The UMNO, earlier, in the middle of May 1951, had decided not to contest the Kuala Lumpur municipal elections but to support candidates worthy of its support (*The Straits Times*, 18 May 1951). But later, in early July, it changed its mind and decided to field a few candidates of its own (Ibid. 5 July 1951). Right from the time of its formation the UMNO never had adequate funds. As the Chairman of the Election Sub-Committee, Dato Yahya's main job was to raise funds for fighting the elections. Collection of funds was thus foremost in his mind when he happened to meet Sir Henry in the Miners' Club. It was this meeting which provided the basis of cooperation between the UMNO and the MCA. Sir Henry, with the aim of defeating the IMP in the coming Kuala Lumpur elections, seized the opportunity and told Dato Yahya that the financially powerful MCA would be glad to provide funds to the UMNO to contest the elections on the condition that the two parties did not fight against each other and only fielded joint candidates. Dato Yahya, without realizing the potential and consequences of the arrangement which was to be effected only at the local level and which was to be temporary in nature, readily agreed and did not consider it necessary to consult the Kuala Lumpur branch of the UMNO. On 9 January 1952, when the announcement was made it surprised Datin Puteh Maria, the Chairman of the Kuala Lumpur branch of the UMNO, who immediately called an emergency meeting of the branch executive and protested that she had not been consulted prior to the announcement (Ibid. 10 January 1952).

[22] At this time the name Alliance was not used. The joint nominees were fielded as UMNO-MCA candidates.

from within the UMNO, by those who were distrustful of the Chinese, was weakened and the Alliance became a permanent one. Paradoxically, it was those leaders of the Malays who believed that the land of the Malays 'should not be governed by a mixture of races' who were to be the promoters of the Alliance. But the basis on which the Alliance was to be accepted by the UMNO was to become clear later, after it had to operate within the framework of an independent polity. Also, the leaders of the MCA, many of whom had earlier committed themselves to the IMP idea and had worked for it, saw in the Alliance a way of sharing political power without having to lose the independent identity of the MCA, the organization established to protect the Chinese and their interests.

Very soon the success of the arrangement was to attract the Malayan Indian Congress, the communal organization of the third largest racial group, the Indians. On 17 October 1954, the Executive Committee of the MIC, after a heated debate, decided to link up with the UMNO-MCA Alliance.[23]

The Alliance was initially conceived as a mutually beneficial election device. Instead of campaigning against each other, the member parties cooperated with each other. They divided the constituencies among themselves, by and large, on the basis of the racial origin of a majority of the voters in the constituency. And during the elections they helped each other; the organizational facilities of each member party were used for the jointly agreed candidates.

It very successfully contested the first elections for the Federal Legislative Council in 1955, when it was able to win fifty-one of the fifty-two seats for which elections were held. Its candidates again won with very comfortable majorities.

This was the honeymoon period of the Alliance, rather of the UMNO and the MCA. The Malay fear of the Chinese had not been borne out in a serious way: the British were still there to protect them against the Chinese. Also, the main preoccupation was with obtaining independence. UMNO had initially demanded that 90 per cent of the Alliance candidates for the Federal Legislative Council election should be Malays. Tunku Abdul Rahman, con-

[23] *The Straits Times*, 18 October 1954.

scious of the danger if the demand was conceded, threatened to resign his position as the President of the UMNO if the organization stuck to its demand. And to force the issue, on 4 June 1955 at the UMNO General Assembly in Kuala Lumpur, he demanded and secured a vote of confidence in his leadership and the Alliance with the MCA.[24] The final allotment gave the UMNO 35 seats, the MCA 15 seats and the MIC 2. It should be noted that at this time the racial composition of the electorate was as follows: Malays 84.2 per cent, Chinese 11.2 per cent and Indians and others 4.6 per cent. The Malays were willing, though not without a strong protest, to give the Chinese about 30 per cent of the seats when the latter constituted only 11.2 per cent of the electorate. This is important and it should be noted that this was possible only in 1955 when the country was not independent. The same issue was to lead to a very serious crisis in the Alliance in 1959 at the time of the federal elections, the first after independence, and for some time threatened the very existence of the Alliance.[25] The same Tunku Abdul Rahman, who had threatened to resign the Presidency of the UMNO in 1955 if the Chinese were not given a reasonable number of seats, when confronted in 1959 with an MCA demand for about 40 seats out of a total of 104, reacted very violently.

The organization of the Alliance at this time was very loose and the relationship of the three member parties was not clearly defined. In a leading article *The Straits Times* said on 12 July 1956:

> A curious feature of the Alliance is that it exists by virtue of a gentleman's agreement between three political parties — the UMNO, the MCA and the MIC. This political marriage has never been regularized to define the precise relationship between these partners. To press the analogy, the partners never became one. Each retained its identity and its freedom of action. The Alliance has been no more than a voluntary subordination of the identities of the individual parties for cooperative action in the common objective of winning independence and fighting the elections last year.

After the great victory of the Alliance in the 1955 elections and the smooth working thus far, several leaders, both of the UMNO

[24] Ibid. 5 June 1955.
[25] See pp. 27-31 below.

and the MCA, stated that the Alliance would soon be converted into a national political party. The Secretary-General of the MCA declared on 30 June 1955 that 'it was only a question of time before the partners of the Alliance were amalgamated into one national group, giving up their communal charàcteristics'.[26] Khir Johari, the Publicity Chief of the UMNO and the closest confidant of Tunku Abdul Rahman, said that 'some years from now the three political bodies [forming the Alliance] would wind up into one — a truly national organization, whose members would be Malayans and whose interests would be for the country as a whole without any emphasis on any particular race'.[27] However, as we shall see later, this was not to happen. The Alliance was to remain a coalition of communal parties representing the different racial groups.

The MCA, initially, because of its superior organization and financial power had at least secured an equal position with the UMNO in the Alliance. Also, as long as elections were held at the municipal level only, the MCA was able to assert equality with the UMNO, for very large sections of the electorate in these cities and towns were Chinese. Even though large numbers of Chinese had not acquired citizenship they constituted a sizeable part of the electorate (based on a restricted franchise) in urban centres like Kuala Lumpur, Ipoh, Seremban, George Town (Penang), and Malacca. But this situation was to change drastically from about the time of the first national elections for the state legislatures and the Federal Legislative Council, in 1955, when 84.2 per cent of the voters were Malays and the Chinese constituted only 11.2 per cent of the total. The MCA had to accept gratefully fifteen seats out of a total of fifty-two for the Federal Legislative Council that it was allocated. Even these were given to them only after Tunku Abdul Rahman threatened to resign the Presidency of the UMNO if it would not give a fair number of seats to the MCA. What is more, once the Alliance emerged as the chief representative of Malayan national aspirations, the UMNO, representing the *bumiputra*, asserted itself as the senior and dominant partner. Realizing that in any negotiations for inde-

[26] *The Straits Times*, 1 July 1955.
[27] Ibid. 12 June 1957.

pendence with the British it was the Malays who had to play the leading role, the MCA and the MIC, as representatives of the immigrant non-Malay communities, accepted this secondary role. And beginning with this, the MCA got caught in a vicious circle, since the more it gave in to the UMNO the more it lost support among the Chinese; and the smaller its base in the Chinese community the less significant became its bargaining power with the UMNO in the Alliance. In future, whenever it was to make demands on behalf of the Chinese community it was to be told by the UMNO leaders in the Alliance: How can you demand all these for the Chinese when you can't get their support? Deliver the Chinese vote for the Alliance and then make demands on their behalf.[28] It now became an important feature of UMNO strategy to keep the MCA weak enough (in terms of popular Chinese support) so as to make it dependent on the UMNO and not enable it to make excessive demands on behalf of the Chinese community and at the same time popular enough among the Chinese to deliver the necessary votes, in addition to the larger UMNO vote, to retain the Alliance in power.

The first important occasion when the MCA was not able to assert equality with the UMNO and was compelled to accept a secondary position in the Alliance was at the time of constitution-drafting in Malaya in late 1956 and early 1957. The MCA was forced, at this crucial time, to make substantial concessions to the UMNO with regard to issues of vital interest to the Chinese community. The pressure felt by the MCA was well expressed by Tan Siew Sin (the present President of the Association), at the meeting of its Central Working Committee on 7 April 1957 held to discuss the changes in the recommendations of the Reid Constitutional Commission being demanded by the UMNO, when he said that while he appreciated 'the force of the argument' of those who were opposed to these changes he felt that 'if we insist . . . we may well have to part company from UMNO. This the MCA cannot afford to do.'[29]

[28] This argument was effectively used by the UMNO during the 1964 general elections to hold in check MCA demands.

[29] *Minutes of Central Working Committee Meeting*, 7 April 1957.

Earlier, in 1956, at the time of the deliberations regarding the Alliance memorandum to the Reid Constitutional Commission, it was obvious that the rank and file of the Chinese community and many of the leaders of the MCA, both at the national and state levels, were extremely concerned about the future Constitution of the country. The feelings were fully expressed by no less a person than Tan Siew Sin when he was constrained to write in a personal letter to Dr. Lim Chong Eu (later to be the President of the MCA and an adversary of Tan Siew Sin) on 27 September 1956:

> Briefly my views can be summarised thus: In the present stage of the country's development, we must face the fact that communalism exists in a big way. Even the Malays, with their overwhelming voting strength want their 'special rights' written into the Constitution. Some of them are not satisfied with their present plums, i.e. the majority of posts, and the best of them too, in the public service, [and] they want to extend this highly discriminatory form of legislation into industry and commerce. 'Warta Negara' talks about the necessity for making the Malays the 'master race' of Malaya. This presumably means that non-Malays are to be reduced to the status of hewers of wood and drawers of water. Shades of Hitler! Others want Malaya to join up with Indonesia. I myself have heard this from the lips of one or two UMNO officials. It is unnecessary for me to tell you what this idea, seriously pursued, will lead to. It is difficult to assess the strength of these various forms of racial fanaticism but, at the same time, one cannot blame the Chinese and other non-Malays for being slightly nervous, to say the least! The non-Malays, therefore, have to be communal merely to ensure their survival.
>
> A Malayan nation does not exist at the moment and may never will [sic], the way things are going. Such being the case, to my mind, the MCA must uphold Chinese interests, first, last and all the time.[30]

Lau Pak Khuan, an ex-President of the MCA in Perak and the most powerful Chinese leader in the State, warned that unless the following four points were submitted by the MCA in its joint memorandum (with the UMNO) to the Reid Constitutional Commission, the Perak Chinese would break away from the MCA and submit their own views directly to the Commission:

---

[30] A photo-copy of the original with this writer. *Warta Berita,* now defunct, was then a prominent Malay language newspaper.

1. Equal citizenship rights for Indians and Chinese. They should be accorded the same rights as the Malays.
2. Those born in Malaya, irrespective of race or parentage, and those who have lived in this country during the last five years and are loyal to this country should be given citizenship rights.
3. Responsibilities and privileges of the citizens of independent Malaya should be equal.
4. Multi-lingualism should be adopted, with the languages of the various races regarded as official. [31]

Even the MCA was forced to admit that its leadership of the Chinese community had been threatened by the controversy over the important issue of *jus soli*.[32] The Chief Executive Secretary of the MCA, T. H. Tan, reporting on a meeting of the MCA leaders in Malacca, wrote to the Alliance National Council that it had decided that 'the MCA, as the political representative of the Chinese, must support the principle of *jus soli*'. On 7 July 1956, the MCA Central Working Committee 'decided that the MCA members of the Alliance Ad Hoc Political Committee should demand unconditional *jus soli*'.[33] The powerful Federation of Chinese Guilds and Associations warned in mid-1956 that 'the overwhelming majority of the Chinese in the country, were against three main features of the proposed Alliance memorandum to the Reid Commission. It maintained that the Chinese wanted

1. Chinese to be one of the official languages.
2. *Jus soli* to be applied unconditionally.
3. No additional privileges be accorded to the Malays. They had no objection to the continuation of privileges already being enjoyed by the Malays. [34]

However, these demands of the Chinese community were, by and large, ignored by the MCA. It was forced to give in to the UMNO on several important issues. Chinese was not accorded the status of an official language. The Constitution accepted by the MCA made Malay the sole official language of the country. The

[31] *The Straits Times*, 29 March 1956.

[32] Ibid. 17 April 1956.

[33] *Minutes of MCA Central Working Committee Meeting*, 7 July 1956.

[34] *The Straits Times*, 25 August 1956.

Malays were given more privileges than they had enjoyed before under the Federation of Malaya Agreement of 1948. Under the new Constitution a proportion of posts in the public services, permits to engage in trade or business, government scholarships, etc., were to be reserved for the Malays.[35] More, the time limit of fifteen years demanded by the non-Malay communities for these special privileges for the Malays, which was unacceptable to the UMNO, was given up. The new Constitution provided that it 'shall be the responsibility of the Yang di-Pertuan Agong [the Head of State] to safeguard the special position of the Malays . . . .'[36] Also against the recommendation of the Reid Commission, Islam was designated the official religion of the new federation.

With regard to the key provisions relating to the special position of the Malays, it is widely maintained in Malaysia that when the MCA and the MIC insisted on a fifteen-year limit, they were told by UMNO leaders (Tun Abdul Razak's name is specially mentioned) that a fifteen-year limit was not necessary, because for all they knew these provisions may not any more be necessary after a few years. And, therefore, the best course was to leave it to the Yang di-Pertuan Agong who would review the situation from time to time to decide if they were still necessary. The following is what Ong Yoke Lin, who was the sole MCA representative on the Government's official working party which had finalized the changes in the Reid Commission recommendations and had determined the Constitution of Independent Malaya, told a meeting of the Central Working Committee of the MCA on 4 May 1957,

> That the White Paper which the Government proposes to issue will include a note that it will be in the interests of all concerned that the Yang di-Pertuan Agong should review the provisions of this Article [Special position of the Malays] from time to time.[37]

[35] See Article 153 (2) of the Constitution, *Malayan Constitutional Documents*, op. cit. p. 117.

[36] Further, Article 38 (5) of the Constitution provides that the Conference of Rulers 'shall be consulted before any change in policy affecting administrative action under Article 153 is made' (Ibid. p. 49).

[37] *Minutes of Central Working Committee Meeting of the Malayan Chinese Association*, 4 May 1957. Also see 'Draft on Special Position of Malays' enclosed with the Minutes.

It was only on this basis that the provisions relating to the Malay special position were accepted by the MCA Central Working Committee on 4 May 1957. But the UMNO never dropped from its objects the commitment:

> To safeguard and preserve the Constitution of the Federation of Malaya, particularly the provisions relating to the Muslim Religion, Malay language and custom, the dignity and prestige of Their Highnesses the Malay Rulers and the special privileges of the Malays. [38]

What is more, in 1965, the new Constitution of the Alliance Party mentioned as one of its objects the following: '. . . to promote the economic and social well-being of the indigenous people in accordance with the provisions of the Constitution of Malaysia'. [39] But the earlier constitution of the Alliance (1958) had made no mention of the indigenous people and their well-being. This is very significant because if the Malays did not want these privileges in perpetuity there was no need to inscribe it into the Alliance constitution.

The concessions conceded by the MCA caused very widespread dissatisfaction within the Chinese community and among large sections of the MCA rank and file. A three-man delegation consisting of Lau Pak Khuan, Yap Mau Tatt and Tan Kee Gak, representing the powerful Chinese Guilds and Associations, left for England in May 1957 to make representations to the British Government with regard to the new Constitution. Before leaving for England, Tan Kee Gak declared:

> The 1,094 guilds and associations which represent over 2,000,000 Chinese in Malaya has given us a mandate. We are going to carry it out. . . . *We do not expect the MCA to do anything for the Malayan Chinese.* [40]

This was the beginning of the disillusionment of large numbers of Chinese with the MCA. They felt that the MCA, as a member

---

[38] *Undang-Undang Tuboh, op.cit.* pp. 1-2.

[39] *Constitution of the Malaysian Alliance Party* (mimeographed), 16 April 1965, p. 2.

[40] *The Straits Times,* 6 May 1957. Emphasis added.

of the Alliance, was in no position to protect their particular interests.

After Independence was obtained the leaders of the Alliance set themselves the task of formalizing the organization of the Alliance and defining the relationship of the three partners. However, the idea of forming a single non-communal political party in place of the three communal political parties was soon given up. Independence had heightened the fear of the Chinese among the Malays. The 'protecting power', the British, were no more. The Malays themselves had to safeguard and protect their own interests against the non-Malays. Such fears were later to be expressed by the MCA and the MIC also. In the MCA such fears were expressed particularly by the powerful Chinese Guilds and Associations who were desirous of remaining in the MCA but who had doubts that they would be able to accept willingly certain aspects of Alliance policies, in particular those relating to the questions of citizenship and Chinese language and education.[41]

On 3 July 1957, just before the country became independent, the Alliance formed a sub-committee consisting of Tan Siew Sin, Hamid Khan, Ong Yoke Lin, V. T. Sambanthan, V. Manickavasagam, Mohammed Khir Johari and T. H. Tan to draft a new constitution for the Alliance.[42] The purpose was to tighten the organization of the Alliance so as to make the ties among the three member parties stronger. The Alliance spokesman making the announcement said that with the new constitution the Alliance party would be put on a single party basis, instead of the tacit understanding that bound the UMNO, the MCA and the MIC together.

The recommendations of the committee were announced on 13 October 1957.[43] The idea of a single non-communal political party was abandoned and was never to be revived again in the future. The member parties were allowed to retain their independent existence, membership and rules and regulations. *The Straits*

[41] Ibid. 1 November 1957.

[42] It should be noted here that this important committee consisted of two Malays, three Chinese and two Indians and that the Chairman of the committee was a Chinese. This was not to happen again in the future.

[43] Ibid. 14 October 1957.

Times expressed its disappointment in an editorial on 15 October 1957:

> Although the Alliance is to be registered as a political party it is obvious that mere registration is not going to bring important changes immediately in the organization . . . .
>
> It is time now for the Alliance to take the logical step and mix the UMNO-MCA-MIC ingredients to produce a single Alliance Party — a merger in fact instead of a coalition. There would be advantages, not the least in world affairs, for it is a little difficult for Malays to maintain that racialism has disappeared in the country when the ruling party is made up of three communal associations.

At the same time Tunku Abdul Rahman announced the appointment of a new committee with Tan Siew Sin as chairman and Dato (later Tun) Abdul Razak bin Hussein, Mohammed Khir Johari, Rahman bin Talib, Ong Yoke Lin and Yong Pung How as members.[44] The recommendations made by this committee were to form the basis of the new constitution of the Alliance which came into effect on 20 May 1958.

Not much change has taken place in the Alliance set up since its beginnings in the early fifties. It does not exist as an independent political party though under the amendments made in the constitution in 1958 its name was changed from the Alliance Organisation to the Alliance Party and it was formally registered as a political party. The constitution of the Alliance states that 'Alliance Party means the joint UMNO, MCA and MIC political parties and such other parties as may join them after adoption of this constitution'.[45] It does not allow individual membership: the membership clause states that the membership of the party shall be open to the UMNO, the MCA and the MIC and 'such other party or parties of a national character whose membership is confined only to Federation citizens as the three above-named parties shall unanimously decide to admit into the party'.[46] The curious result

[44] Ibid. 14 October 1957.

[45] *Constitution and Rules of the Alliance Party*, 1958, p. 10.

[46] Ibid. pp. 1-2. None of the constitutions of the three member parties makes any mention of the Alliance or the fact of the party's membership of the Alliance. Consequently, a member of any of the three parties cannot be expelled from the party for working against the aims or any provisions of the Alliance Constitution.

is that a person who does not belong to any of the three communities represented in the Alliance through their own exclusive communal organizations cannot join the Alliance as a member. In order to join the Alliance he has to become an associate member of one of the three communal organizations. However, this would not allow him to have a voting right and occupy an office within the party. What is more, a Malay, Chinese or Indian or any other person, who does not want to join one of the three communal organizations, but wishes to join the Alliance, cannot do so. He is compelled to join one of the communal bodies.

The party constitution has established two top bodies of the Alliance, *viz.*, the National Council and the Executive Committee; [47] it does not provide for any other body whether at the national, state or lower levels. This allows a complete central control of the Alliance. The constitution, further, does not list any particular duties or functions to be performed by the National Council. It does, however, enumerate in detail the 'Duties of the Executive Committee':

(a) To consider candidates for the national elections and/or by-elections and submit them for approval of the National Council;

(b) To initiate policies for submission to the National Council . . .;

(c) To deal with financial problems in connection with contesting national elections and/or by-elections;

(d) To recommend disciplinary measures affecting members of the Alliance generally;

(e) To appoint an Alliance chief whip and/or other whips in the Federal Legislative Council or Parliament;

(f) To approve appointment of agents for national elections and/or by-elections;

(g) To disseminate Alliance publicity. . . ;

(h) To nominate National Council members and others to go on electioneering tours of the Federation. [48]

[47] The National Council consists of sixteen representatives each of UMNO and the MCA and six representatives of the MIC. The National Council elects from among its members an Executive Committee consisting of six representatives each of the UMNO and the MCA and three representatives of the MIC.

[48] *Constitution and Rules of the Alliance Party*, pp. 4-5.

All emphasis is on elections; almost all the functions relate to contesting the elections. The important point is that this is as far the three member communal parties, in particular the UMNO, would go in defining the powers of the Alliance. They are chary of delegating any further powers to the Alliance.

The MIC has been passing a resolution regularly urging the Alliance leadership 'to hold an annual or biennial conference of delegates of all the organizations forming the Alliance'.[49] They would not want this conference to pass any formal resolutions or take any definite action. Their whole idea is that the lower level leadership of the three communal bodies should be brought together so that they can know each other better and facilitate the eventual formation of a single party.[50] But this move has found no support from the other two member parties of the Alliance.

It is interesting to note here that towards the end of 1964 and the beginning of 1965 there was considerable talk of a reorganization of the Alliance in Singapore following its complete rout in the Singapore elections of September 1963, and the fast worsening relations between the leadership in the Federation and the leadership of the ruling People's Action Party of Singapore. It was suggested by the UMNO that the Alliance in Singapore should be reorganized on the new basis that the UMNO alone, of the four constituents of the Alliance in Singapore, would be allowed to remain a corporate member of the Alliance.[51] Singapore units of the MCA and the MIC would be disbanded and the Alliance would allow direct individual membership to all non-Malays. The suggestion, though rejected outright by the MCA, gives a good indication of the UMNO view of the Alliance and its basis. The unity and organized strength of the Malays is of the greatest importance to them.

The most serious crisis that the Alliance had to face came in

[49] Resolution approved unanimously at the 17th Annual Delegates' Conference of the Malayan Indian Congress, 30 November and 1 December 1963.

[50] Interview with Athi Nahappan, a senior leader of the MIC, Kuala Lumpur, March 1964.

[51] Interview with Syed Jaafar Albar, Secretary-General of the UMNO, Kuala Lumpur, January 1965. Asked if this could be the future pattern of the Alliance in Malaya, Syed Jaafar promptly replied: 'Why not?'

mid-1959, soon after the completion of the state elections and before the beginning of the parliamentary elections. The importance of the crisis is that it very clearly indicated the relationship of the three parties forming the Alliance and the basis on which the Alliance idea is acceptable to the UMNO.

Before the details of the crisis are discussed it would be worthwhile to have a look at the MCA and its leadership. The MCA was formed in 1949 with the primary object:

> To foster and safeguard the social, political, cultural and economic welfare of the Malayan Chinese by legitimate and constitutional means.[52]

From the time of its formation the Association was led by a group of leaders who were not the real representatives of the Chinese people in Malaya. They did not, by and large, represent their aspirations. These leaders, Tan Cheng Lock, Yong Shook Lin, Khoo Teik Ee, Leong Yew Koh, Henry H. S. Lee etc., were all prosperous businessmen. They were all English-educated and some of them could not speak even one of the Chinese dialects. They had hardly anything in common with the rank and file of the Chinese community. Also, many of them, in particular those at the middle and higher levels, were in politics not because of any political convictions and aims but because they found that their business interests would be better served through politics.

The MCA, during its twenty-year existence, has seen only three Presidents: Tan Cheng Lock (1949-58), Lim Chong Eu (1958-9) and Tan Siew Sin (the son of Tan Cheng Lock) since 1961. During Tan Cheng Lock's nine-year tenure, UMNO leaders came to have faith in him. It was partly because of the nature of his leadership of the MCA that there was no serious crisis in the Alliance. However, soon after independence, Tan Cheng Lock's way of protecting the position of the Chinese came under serious criticism by certain sections of the MCA. In early March 1958, it was reported that a group of young leaders were making a bid to depose Tan Cheng Lock and were attempting to reorganize the MCA 'to pro-

---

[52] *Constitution of the Malayan Chinese Association* adopted at the General Committee meeting held on 12 June 1949.

tect more strongly the interests of the Chinese'.[53] It was the feeling of the new group that the older leadership had put major emphasis on cooperation between the MCA and the UMNO. In order to maintain the existence of the Alliance, they had not fought strongly enough for the interests of the Chinese community. To the new emerging leadership, the primary purpose of the existence of the MCA was to protect the rights and interests of the Chinese community. If it could be combined with cooperation with the UMNO they would have it. But they would not have cooperation with the UMNO and maintain the Alliance at the cost of compromising the fundamental interests of the Chinese. The leaders of the new group were: Dr Lim Chong Eu (38-year old Chairman of the important political sub-committee of the MCA), Too Joon Hing (MCA Secretary-General), and Tan Suan Kok (Chairman of the Youth Section). These people were much closer to the rank and file of the Chinese community and had no big business interests. It may also be noted that members of the old guard were represented in the Alliance Government and were the people in whom the leaders of the UMNO had great trust and confidence.

The showdown took place at the annual meeting of the Central General Committee of the MCA on 23 March 1958. The younger group nominated Lim Chong Eu as its candidate for the presidency of the MCA against Tan Cheng Lock and fielded candidates for the other positions. Victory came to the non-ministerial group and Lim Chong Eu was elected President defeating Tan Cheng Lock by eighty-nine votes to sixty-seven. Too Joon Hing defeated Ong Yoke Lin, the Minister of Labour and Social Welfare, for the post of Secretary-General. All other important positions went to the members of the new group. The ministerial group was completely eliminated and the Association's leadership, to UMNO's surprise and concern, passed into the hands of the new and younger group.

Before the change of leadership took place the UMNO made it very clear as to where its sympathies lay. The Secretary-General of the UMNO warned on 21 March 1958, just before the election

[53] *The Straits Times*, 3 March 1958.

took place: 'Alliance unity depends on the type of leaders [of the MCA] who take office. Right leaders are vital to unity.'[54] It was also reported that the Prime Minister, Tunku Abdul Rahman, was personally very concerned over the challenge to the leadership of Tan Cheng Lock.

Soon after the new leadership took over it made known its desire for the existing equal partnership with the UMNO to remain unchanged.[55] The emphasis was on equality in the relationship. The orientation of the new leadership became very clear when on 30 November 1958 Lim Chong Eu declared in Ipoh that the basic desires of the Chinese in Malaya were:

> Firstly, we want equality in this country.
> Secondly, we are for an assurance of our way of life, our language, and our schools.
> Thirdly, we express the hope that we shall find economic advancement and economic equality.[56]

Earlier, on 11 May 1958, the Political, Organisation, Election and Membership (POEM) Standing Sub-Committee of the MCA had decided that

> ... as a partner of the Alliance the MCA Headquarters should have complete authority in the selection of MCA candidates in all Federal, State, municipal and local council elections, though, again as a partner the MCA Headquarters would always try to get agreement from the other two partners in such selections.[57]

At the same time with regard to the proposal by the General Assembly of the UMNO (7-8 June 1958) relating to representation on the Alliance Executive the Central Working Committee of the MCA decided:

> On the UMNO General Assembly proposal that the ratio of representation in the Alliance Executive Committee should be changed from 6 UMNO, 6 MCA, 3 MIC to 6 UMNO, 5 MCA and 3 MIC, the letter to the Alliance Secretary should state that the MCA Central

---

[54] Ibid. 22 March 1958.

[55] Ibid. 7 July 1958.

[56] Ibid. 1 December 1958.

[57] *Minutes of the Central Working Committee Meeting*, 6 July 1958.

Working Committee felt it would be invidious to make such a change in view of the long established principle of equal partnership which had applied to all levels of the Alliance thus far . . . . [58]

And, consequently this change initiated by the UMNO was not effected.

Under the circumstances a showdown with the UMNO was bound to take place sooner or later. This assertion of equality was a clear challenge to the entire basis on which the Alliance had worked thus far and on which alone the Alliance was acceptable to the UMNO. Also, the ministerial group, which had been displaced and which had continued to occupy positions in the Government, was not idling. They were busy making manoeuvres, in which they were at least encouraged by the leaders of the UMNO, to come back to power. And the occasion for the showdown was provided by the parliamentary elections of 1959.

On the night of 9 July 1959, Yong Pung How, the head of the Publicity Section of the MCA, announced:

> The question of Malayan Chinese Association breaking with the United Malays National Organisation and leaving the Alliance is a very, very grave one because of the national issues involved. It is clearly the last thing we want to do. But if the MCA is left in a position within the Alliance in which it can get little support of the people it claims to represent, then the situation is completely different. [59]

The Central Working Committee of the MCA after a meeting on 9 July demanded:

1. That the MCA should be given 40 seats in the Federal elections because in at least 39 constituencies the Chinese voters outnumbered the Malays; and

2. That the Alliance Manifesto must clearly express its intention to review in general the implementation of its educational policy so that the medium of examinations in Chinese schools could be the medium of instruction. [60]

---

[58] Ibid.

[59] *The Malay Mail*, 10 July 1959.

[60] The following record of the meeting of the Central Working Committee of the MCA on 9 July 1959 is taken from the official minutes:

As for the first point in the MCA demand, the real issue was not the fight over the number of seats to be given the MCA. The fear of the MCA leaders was that if the MCA was not given a minimum of one-third of the total number of seats it could result in an amendment of the Constitution of the country by the representatives of

---

The Alliance Manifesto Committee [report of the speech by the President, Lim Chong Eu] was set up six months ago but never met. The first time he saw a draft manifesto or the semblance of one was on 2 July 1959. According to Too Joon Hing [Secretary-General of the MCA], on 8 July the Committee met to discuss the manifesto and UMNO could not agree to accept the Education Clause agreed to by Dato Razak [the Deputy Prime Minister] for inclusion in the Manifesto. . . .

The clause on education as drafted was as follows:

> Until such time as Malay is fully developed and teaching facilities of Malay are adequately provided in all schools, schools may hold examinations for the purpose of promotion in the medium of instruction in the school; and, provided that Malay shall be a compulsory subject, these promotion examinations will be recognized by Government as of equal standard to the National Certificate examinations, and be accepted as a qualification for the purpose of conforming to the new policy.

In his letter to the Tengku he suggested the addition of the words 'and of assessment of scholastic achievement on leaving school' after the words 'for the purpose of promotion'.

Sir Henry Lee said that he had spoken to Dato Razak and he promised that the medium of instruction should be the medium of examinations. But last night when he met Dato Razak he was told that if this clause was included in the Manifesto the UMNO would lose all its votes . . . .

On the question of how many minimum seats we should accept (the question was put by the President) the results were as follows:

Yong Pung How	:	ask for minimum 40; minimum acceptable 36. We must have at least one-third.
Chin See Yin	:	Minimum 40
Gun Cheng Bin	:	Minimum 40
Foo See Moi	:	40 fair, 35 acceptable
Tan Suan Kok	:	Minimum 40
Lee Tee Siang	:	Negotiate 35 to 40
Peh Seng Khoon	:	Minimum 36
Too Joon Hing	:	Minimum 39, ask for 42
Sir Henry Lee	:	Minimum 30
Ng Ek Teong	:	Minimum 36, ask for 40
Wong Foo Nam	:	Minimum 40
Wong Yeow Wye	:	Minimum 40
Chua Song Lim	:	Minimum 35

On the question of education policy the meeting agreed that education policy was even more important than the number of seats. If there was no modification to the present policy MCA candidates could not hope to win any seats at all.

On the question whether nomination to seats should be left to the Alliance or MCA, all members (except Chua Song Lim) were adamant that the choice must be left to the MCA Central Working Committee.

the Malays without the consent of the representatives of the Chinese. In his letter to Tunku Abdul Rahman, which had been the starting point of the crisis, Lim Chong Eu had said:

The fear of Malayans of other racial origins — Chinese, Indians, Eurasians — is simply one of fear of Malay communalism. A fear that this unbridled attitude can not only destroy the kind of progress as Malayans, which the Alliance plans for, but further that it can also lead to constitutional oppression of the minorities.

It has, therefore, been the MCA policy ever since the constitutional talks began to support what we consider to be a fair and equitable constitution, which would ensure the equality of the fundamental rights of our citizens and further to uphold and maintain this constitution . . . .

Nevertheless, it is correct to say that the fear still remains and it is kept alive by the provision of the constitution, which allows amendment to the constitution by a two-third majority.

For then in the parliamentary sense, the danger of communalism can only be the danger of Malay communalism, for only the Malays can obtain the two-thirds majority necessary in Parliament to effect any changes in the constitution.

We have ourselves watched with anxiety and care the swing in the Legislative Council towards a more Malay attitude caused by the pressure of the back-benchers from the East Coast.

But after the Trengannu election results, I think, you will agree with me that it will be hazardous . . . for the Alliance to 'swing' further in that direction and that the only safe way to ensure the destiny of our nation is to hold a firm course towards a Malayan comity.

Under the circumstances, I feel that it is necessary for me to draw your attention to how very important it is for the Alliance Manifesto to clearly express the Alliance determination to uphold and sustain the Federation Constitution as it stands.

. . . consider an allocation of about 40 of the seats to be equitable and just.[61]

The feeling of the leadership of the MCA was that the Constitution which was a fair one and which had come to be accepted by all communities should not be amended for the benefit of any one community. Too Joon Hing, the Secretary-General of the MCA

[61] *The Straits Times,* 10 July 1959. Emphasis added.

and former Assistant Minister of Education, said in a meeting of the Central Working Committee of the MCA on 12 July:

> Regarding seats — in 39 constituencies there was a Chinese majority and asking for only one-third of the total Parliamentary seats was quite a reasonable request. The Constitution could not be changed unless the amendment was passed by a two-thirds majority. . . . Already the PMIP [Pan Malayan Islamic Party] who were victorious in the State elections in the East Coast States were saying they wanted to amend it. To safeguard the Constitution and our position in Malaya we had spent a lot of money, time and energy to get Chinese to become citizens and the result was that the Chinese were in the majority in 39 constituencies and our request for one-third was therefore not excessive.

The Tunku, as the leader of the Alliance, reacted violently. He immediately issued a letter announcing that the Alliance would contest all the 104 seats in the federal elections without the MCA group led by the President of the MCA, Lim Chong Eu. He demanded that the MCA should unconditionally withdraw its two demands.[62] The Tunku called Lim's letter to him an 'ultimatum' and 'a stab in the back'. Later, in a press conference he announced that he was taking over all the functions of the Alliance National Council and would personally undertake the selection of candidates and the allocation of seats. At the press conference the Minister of Education, Mohammad Khir Johari, jokingly called this 'guided democracy'.

On 12 July, Lim Chong Eu met the Tunku when he was offered the following deal. He was told by the Tunku that the MCA would be allowed to continue as a member of the Alliance only if it accepted his terms. The following is a report given by the MCA President to the Central General Committee of his conversation with the Tunku:

> With regard to the allocation of seats it is most likely that we shall be allocated 32 seats. With regard to the nomination of candidates [it] will be made by the Tunku alone, because of the shortness of time, but before finalizing the list I would be consulted and I presume after

[62] Ibid. 11 July 1959.

my consultation it would be presented to the Alliance National Council.

... with regard to this highly publicized clause now on education, this clause will not be included in the manifesto but the Government will implement it by Administrative Directive as soon as possible. [63]

The MCA Central General Committee accepted the Tunku's terms for the return of the MCA into the Alliance by eighty-nine votes to eighty. In a pathetic speech, evincing all the helplessness and frustration of belonging to an immigrant community, Lim Chong Eu told the Central General Committee before the vote:

The question now is no longer a simple question of allocation of seats, of candidates or of conditions in the manifesto and so on. It is only a question of the reiteration of your faith in the Alliance and the leadership of the Alliance. What will happen with regard to the seating and allocation and manifesto and so on, I do not know. But I have every reason to believe that if confidence is restored in the Alliance then what we have gained so far in negotiations can be sustained. This is only my belief.

That, Gentlemen, is the position. I am very sorry that the Central Working Committee cannot give you any clear guidance in this matter. [64]

The final allocation of seats was announced late on 12 July. The UMNO was given seventy seats and the MCA and the MIC were allocated thirty-one and three seats respectively. In accordance with the agreement, the Tunku selected the MCA candidates. But it should be noted that the President of the MCA was not taken into confidence and was not only not consulted but was never shown the list of candidates. In fact, the Executive Secretary of the Alliance, T. H. Tan (belonging to the pre-1958 leadership of the MCA), refused to give him a list of the candidates when the President of the MCA asked for one. Lim Chong Eu had no idea until the time of nomination who were the candidates from the party of which he was the President.

[63] *Minutes of Central General Committee Meeting,* 12 July 1959, p. 17. See also *The Straits Times,* 13 July 1959.

[64] Ibid. p. 8.

The UMNO's insistence on Tunku, as the head of the Alliance, selecting the candidates from the MCA was not without significance. This was the way the UMNO could ensure the selection of MCA candidates acceptable to it and leaving out, as far as possible, the new emergent leadership of the MCA. As part of this, MCA leaders like Tan Siew Sin and Ong Yoke Lin,[65] who did not enjoy the confidence of the MCA rank and file, were given safe Malay majority constituencies. The UMNO fear was that if the new leadership, which was insistent on equality for all the racial groups, was allowed to last through the elections, it would be able to stabilize its position within the MCA. By pushing in a large number of its own candidates in the elections it would assume a firm control over the party.

Many leaders of the MCA felt that the UMNO had taken a 'dictatorial attitude' towards them, and had treated the MCA as a 'satellite' of the UMNO. One of them said: 'The future of the MCA would be bleak. In the 1955 elections we won because we obtained fair terms and consequently the Chinese were solidly behind us.'[66] Completely frustrated, many top-ranking leaders resigned from the party.[67] They chose this course as against that of withdrawing the MCA from the Alliance. The latter was too drastic an action, and would have been used by the UMNO to brand them, belonging to an immigrant community, as being disloyal and anti-national and opposed to cooperation between the Malays and the Chinese.

It resulted, however, in a great deal of dissatisfaction among the Chinese, in particular among the non-English-educated Chinese, who formed a large majority within the Chinese community, and affected the MCA badly in the 1959 federal elections: it was able to win only 19 of the 31 seats alloted to it.

The MCA was able to win only in constituencies with a significant Malay vote where the defection of Chinese voters could be

---

[65] None of them held a leadership position in the MCA. Ong Yoke Lin had earlier been defeated in the election for the Secretary-General of the MCA.

[66] Ibid. p. 18.

[67] The important ones were: Too Joon Hing, Chin See Yin, Quek Kai Dong, Tan Suan Kok, Lawrence H.C. Huang, Yong Pung How, Ng Ek Teong. Dr. Lim Chong Eu did not leave the MCA immediately.

compensated for by the votes of the Malays.[68] This suited the UMNO very well for it made the MCA very much dependent on the UMNO in gaining electoral support and winning elections. This inevitably further weakened the bargaining power of the MCA *vis-à-vis* the UMNO. The UMNO has been quite content with the MCA winning only a part of its allotted seats, enough to give the Alliance a comfortable majority in the Parliament. They fear that, with a large number of representatives in the Parliament and securing solid support of the Chinese community, the MCA was bound to assert itself and claim equality within the Alliance.

It was not long before the old guard was to return and take over the leadership of the MCA. Tan Siew Sin, the son of Tan Cheng Lock, was elected the President of the MCA in 1961 and with him were to return all the leaders with their big business interests. This leadership has allowed the UMNO to control the Alliance. Being dependent on the UMNO for their position in the MCA and lacking a popular base among the Chinese, these leaders are in no position to assert an equal position for the MCA within the Alliance. The 1959 crisis in the Alliance was a very clear evidence of the dominant position of the UMNO and the secondary roles played by the MCA and the MIC in the Alliance. Even the Tunku's biographer has commented that

> . . . the Alliance is really made up of one principal party, the UMNO, with the MCA and the MIC as branches clothed with the intelligentsia and capitalist classes of each community. The MCA is not representative of the two and a half million Chinese in the Federation, neither is the MIC of the six hundred thousand Indians. Neither of them has roots in the villages and small towns. [69]

At the height of the crisis in 1959, Tunku Abdul Rahman had asserted that the MCA fear that the UMNO wanted at least a two-

---

[68] R.K. Vasil, 'The 1964 General Elections in Malaya', *International Studies*, Vol. VII No. 1 (July 1965), pp. 62-63.

[69] Harry Miller, *Prince and Premier: A Biography of Tunku Abdul Rahman Al-haj, First Prime Minister of the Federation of Malaya*, London, Geo G. Harrap & Co., Ltd., 1959, p. 216. Tunku Abdul Rahman, in a Foreword to the book, writes that 'I believe this to be as complete an account of my life as it is possible for another man to write'.

third majority in the Parliament to enable it to amend the Constitution was groundless.[70] He asserted:

> I have always declared that the national Constitution must be upheld and I still maintain that. It is the Constitution which has won freedom for Malaya and it will continue to ensure peace and prosperity for the country.

However, this 'promise' was not kept. Important amendments relating to citizenship and the delimitation of constituencies for the federal elections were made under the Constitution Amendment Act, 1962;[71] and the MCA, under the new leadership, accepted them without protest though they related to matters of vital concern to the non-Malays.

Tunku Abdul Rahman, who has successfully built up an image of the father of the nation (*Bapak Malaysia*) and who is said to be above communal politics, has used his position as the Prime Minister to determine the leadership of the MCA. As Prime Minister the selection of Ministers has been his exclusive privilege. In the selection of his Ministers representing the MCA he does not necessarily have to consult the MCA. He selects trusted men entirely on his own without worrying if they enjoy the confidence of the political party to which they belong.

So far there have been two Ministers of Indian origin and both of them have always held important positions in the MIC leadership. One, V. T. Sambanthan, has been the President of the MIC for more than twelve years, and the other, V. Manickavasagam, has been the Vice-President for the past many years. Both have enjoyed the confidence and support of their party. But the situation has been different in the case of the Ministers from the MCA, many of whom held no important position in the party at the time of their appointment. There is the example of Khaw Kai Boh, who came to Kuala Lumpur from Singapore after leaving the Singapore Police and was straightaway appointed a Minister without Portfolio with cabinet rank. He was later to contest the Secretary-

---

[70] *The Singapore Standard*, 11 July 1959.

[71] See p. 9 above, and *Malayan Constitutional Documents*, op.cit. Part III: 'Citizenship'.

Generalship of the MCA, in which UMNO leaders made a special effort to canvass support for him.[72] He lost to Lee Siok Yew but continued to hold his position in the Cabinet. Several other similar cases can be listed. The complete change in the MCA leadership in 1958 had brought no change whatsoever to the composition of the MCA representatives in the Cabinet. The defeated leaders of the MCA continued to retain their important positions in the Government. And this facilitated their effort to re-establish their position within the party. The general pattern is that a Chinese politician first becomes a leader in the Government and the Alliance and only later emerges as a leader of the MCA. Association with the Government gives him a position where he can distribute favours and gather support for himself within the party. This is effectively used by the Tunku to impose a certain leadership on the MCA. It is significant that this happens only in the case of the MCA and not the MIC, the third partner in the Alliance.

The MIC is jokingly called by many of Indian origin in the country as 'May I Come' (into the Alliance), indicating its weak position in the Alliance. Indians, being scattered all over the country and not forming a majority or a near-majority in any of the constituencies, are in no position to bargain and exert power. The MIC remains in the Alliance as a matter of necessity and under conditions which it cannot determine or influence.

The racial composition of the Ministry further gives a good indication of the relative position of the three partners in the Alliance. The position in late 1963 after the formation of Malaysia and in November 1968 was as follows:

		1963	1968
UMNO:	Ministers with Cabinet rank	10	10
	Assistant Ministers	4	4
MCA:	Ministers with Cabinet rank	4	5
	Assistant Ministers	1	1
MIC:	Ministers with Cabinet rank[73]	2	2

[72] Interview with a top-ranking leader of the MCA, Kuala Lumpur, June 1964.

[73] *Malaysia, Official Year Book, 1963*, Kuala Lumpur, Government Press, 1964, pp. 24-25, and ibid. 1968, pp. 354-5. The figures for 1968 do not include the two Ministers from East Malaysia: the Minister for Sarawak Affairs and the Minister for Sabah Affairs.

The very large number of UMNO representatives gives it a dominant control of the Government.

The two fundamental features of politics under the Alliance — the emphasis on Malay unity and the pre-eminent position of the UMNO in the ruling party — had a serious impact on the non-communal political parties. The result has been that non-communal political parties have assumed more and more the character of essentially non-Malay parties, parties with a predominantly non-Malay leadership and rank and file. This is what happened to the non-communal parties in the mid-fifties, around the time of independence. And once the process started, the parties became caught in a disastrous vicious circle. The lack of support from the Malays turned the parties into essentially non-Malay parties and thus made them even more unacceptable to the Malays who at any rate were chary of joining non-communal political parties. On the other side, the conversion of the Alliance into an instrument of Malay supremacy caused a serious disenchantment with the MCA in the Chinese community. Chinese communal elements who had pinned their hopes of safeguarding the interests of their community through its communal organization, the MCA, have felt frustrated and many of them at different times have left the MCA. They have generally tended to join the existing non-communal parties with the aim to swing them into a communal direction. And in this they were largely successful.

It is this significant conversion of the genuinely non-communal political parties into non-Malay parties and then finally into essentially non-Malay communal organizations that will form the main theme of the following chapters.

II

THE INDEPENDENCE OF MALAYA PARTY AND
THE PARTY NEGARA

THE formation of the non-communal Independence of Malaya Party (IMP) was one of the most significant developments in the post-war political history of Malaya. This was the first major attempt to bring together the people of different racial origins into one non-communal political organization. For the first time it was acknowledged by a prominent Malay that the non-Malay communities too had a legitimate and rightful part to play in the political evolution and development of Malaya. It is significant that the attempt was made by Dato Onn bin Jaafar, the foremost leader of the Malays. He had been the person most responsible for political awakening among them and had formed the United Malays National Organisation. Confronted with the problem of achieving communal harmony, integration of the different communities into one nation, and eventual independence for his country, Dato Onn launched the IMP. The new party was started with a great deal of fanfare and a very definite feeling among its founders that it would soon emerge as the sole representative of the new Malayan (not Malay) nation. But these hopes were belied; the party failed to obtain significant support among either the Malays or the Chinese (initially participation by the Malays was not expected anyway). It was only the Indian community which extended full support for the venture. The lack of support from the Chinese community, whose leaders had pledged full backing to Dato Onn and had played an important part in the formation of the IMP, angered Dato Onn who felt that he had been cheated. He had sacrificed his unique position as the unchallenged leader of the Malay community to establish a non-communal organization which was to promote and safeguard the interests of all the communities on an equal basis. He had launched the venture with the definite assurance from the leaders of the Chinese community and their communal organization, the MCA, of full support, cooperation and participation by them. However, following the formation of the UMNO-MCA Alliance and its success in the crucial municipal elections in Kuala Lumpur (where the Chinese did not support the IMP), most of the Chinese and their leaders gradually dissociated themselves from the IMP. Dato Onn then lost all faith in the Chinese community and the cause of non-communalism, and formed the Party Negara, essentially a Malay communal party, as a successor to the non-communal IMP.

The Independence of Malaya Party

The establishment of the IMP was not a sudden development. The party evolved gradually. Countering charges that the then British High Commissioner in Malaya, Sir Henry Gurney, had anything to do with the establishment of the party, Dato Onn bin Jaafar, the founder, asserted that the IMP was 'a logical move in the logical development of the country'.[1] It was not a desperate move by a disgruntled and dissatisfied politician. It was the attempt of a visionary who was willing to take a great risk for the sake of a principle and for the good of his country. Dato Onn, when he took the decision to establish the IMP, was the supreme and unchallenged leader of the UMNO. He gave it all up for a venture in which he could not have been at all certain he would succeed, but which seemed to him to be for the good of the country.[2]

It seemed to Dato Onn that the IMP was the logical development of the UMNO. But because the leaders of the UMNO and the Malays, fearful of the non-Malays, were not willing to go as

[1] *The Straits Times*, 20 June 1951.

[2] Husein Onn, the son of Dato Onn who was the Secretary-General of the UMNO at the time of the formation of the IMP, told the author (Kuala Lumpur, September 1963):

> Dato Onn was not a real politician. He never bothered about tactics and strategy. If he believed something was good he would do it despite the fact that the people were opposed to it. Otherwise he would not have left the UMNO in 1951. He was gaining no support by speaking against the Malay Sultans but he did it. He did these because he believed in them sincerely.

far as that in their concessions, Dato Onn chose to form a party outside the UMNO.

Onn bin Jaafar and the UMNO

The Malays had remained politically disorganized right up to 1946. However, in 1946, the publication of the White Paper on Malayan Union[3] aroused the Malays who considered this to be an act amounting to a complete annexation of their country, and afforded them the opportunity to get organized politically. A Pan-Malayan Malay Congress was held at Kuala Lumpur from 1 to 4 March 1946. At this Congress forty-one Malay organizations from all over the country were represented and it was unanimously resolved to establish the United Malays National Organisation.[4] The first major organization of the Malays was born out of the very wide-spread Malay opposition to the Malayan Union plan. The Congress, in the first and the most important resolution, urged His Majesty's Government 'to withdraw the aforesaid proposal immediately and restore the status quo with no change whatsoever for the present'.[5] The Congress did not say anything about the dependent status of the country. Even the UMNO Charter did not make any mention of independence. The Charter vested in the UMNO the following powers:

(a)   To promote by all manner of lawful means the common objects of its members and to exercise any act in such other matter or matters as may be delegated to it by any one or more members;

(b)   To represent its members or each of them in the promotion of such objects and any other matter or matters; and

(c)   To arbitrate in any difference arising between its members.[6]

Being a conglomeration of varied organizations of Malays, the Congress did not find it possible and probably also did not consider it necessary to define the aims of the UMNO. The common

[3] See James de Vere Allen, *The Malayan Union*, New Haven, 1967.

[4] *Hidup Melayu - A Brief Review of Activities of the Malay National Movement*, Malay League of Perak, Ipoh (undated), p. 4.

[5] Ibid. p. 12.

[6] Ibid. p. 16.

ground was there in the opposition to the Malayan Union plan. The slogan adopted for the organization was *Hidup Melayu* (Long Live the Malays). It was only later in March 1951 that *Merdeka* (Freedom) was accepted as the slogan of the party.[7]

Confronted with the unprecedented opposition of the Malays, which the policy-makers of His Majesty's Government had not expected, the British Government dropped the Union Plan in favour of a Federation.[8] The UMNO had achieved its victory when the Federation of Malaya Agreement became effective on 1 February 1948. Thus the UMNO had fulfilled the purpose for which it had been established.

And now started a period of rethinking among some of the leaders of the UMNO about the future role of the organization. This was to result in a certain slackening in the activities of the organization. A clear idea of the direction in which the activities of the organization were to be directed had not crystallized. Indicating that the UMNO was at crossroads, a special correspondent of *The Straits Times* wrote on 2 September 1947:

Although there is no mention of it on the agenda of the Congress (to be held at Johore Baharu soon), they will, explicitly or by implication, decide whether UMNO is to emerge as a real political force or whether it has lost its power and coherence and is to fall into virtual eclipse.

Having substantially achieved the purpose for which it was originally formed—rejection of the Malayan Union Plan and establishment of a Constitution in accord with the Malay conception of their basic rights and aspirations—UMNO must now seek a new impetus, direct its energies into new channels, and produce a political programme which allies Malay progress to that of the whole country.

---

[7] *The Straits Times*, 26 March 1951. This change, sponsored by Dato Onn, could not be effected without opposition from a section of the UMNO. See Ishak bin Tadin, 'Dato Onn: 1946-1951', *Journal of Southeast Asian History*, Vol. 1 No. 1 (March 1960), p. 81.

[8] Some have suggested that it was far more the letters to *The Times*, by several former British civil servants in Malaya, arguing that the British had let the Malays down, that caused the Colonial Office to change its mind and to withdraw the Union arrangement.

In fact, the same day that this newspaper story appeared, Dato Onn, opening a meeting of the UMNO General Assembly, himself asserted:

> Though the task of fighting the Malayan Union is nearly complete the Malays must be aware of the fact that it is only the beginning of our struggle. There are many other things that the Malays must do ... The UMNO has been formed not only for the purpose of opposing the Malayan Union, but also to fight against the Malays themselves. We have to find ways and means of how we shall change the habits and way of life of the Malays in order to enable them to realize their duties and responsibilities. [9]

The real origins of the Independence of Malaya Party lie in the period between late 1947, when the Malayan Union plan was already in the process of being scrapped, and the middle of 1949, a period during which Dato Onn bin Jaafar envisaged a new and wider role for the UMNO. Having succeeded in warding off the threat posed by the Malayan Union plan to the Malays' position, Dato Onn started thinking in terms of the larger problems of the society, those of inter-communal harmony, integration of the different communities, and eventual independence for his country.

During the interregnum between the Japanese surrender and the coming of the British Military Administration Dato Onn had seen some of the worst communal trouble in the country in Batu Pahat, Johore, where he was then the District Officer. He had been very deeply hurt by this and he realized the seriousness and the dangerous potential of the problem. As early as 27 April 1948, long before the Communities Liaison Committee [10] was established, Dato Onn was suggesting mixed marriages among the different communities, including the Malays, as a way of integrating the different people and creating a new Malayan nation. [11]

---

[9] *Minutes of the General Assembly of the UMNO*, 2 September 1947, quoted in Ishak bin Tadin, op.cit. p. 70.

[10] The Communities Liaison Committee, supported by the prominent leaders of the various racial groups in Malaya, was established early in 1949 with the aim to seek and promote cooperation among the different communities in Malaya.

[11] *The Straits Times*, 27 April 1948. Dato Onn was the first, and perhaps the last, Malay ever to suggest this.

It was in this frame of mind that Dato Onn began to visualize and conceive of the UMNO as a national organization representing all the different communities in the country rather than as a communal organization of the Malays. It must be emphasized here that it was not a move of expediency by a politician as no immediate political ends seemed reckoned upon. When Dato Onn visualized a national role for the UMNO it was not because he felt that this was the only way independence could be secured from the British,[12] rather it was the idea of a visionary who wanted to bring the different communities together for the future good and happiness of them all.

Earlier, chiefly under the influence of the British Commissioner General in Southeast Asia, Malcolm MacDonald, the Communities Liaison Committee had been established on 10 January 1949, 'to maintain a happy understanding between the communities and to suggest ways and means of strengthening it through the testing days of the present and the future'.[13] The Committee was headed by Dato E. E. C. Thuraisingham, a very close friend of Dato Onn, and included Dato Onn, Dato Tan Cheng Lock, Dato Panglima Bukit Gantang, Dato Zainal Abidin bin Abas (Secretary-General of the UMNO) and many others, all of whom later were to play an important role in the formation of the IMP. However, it must be made clear that this in no way suggests a necessary link between the IMP and the Communities Liaison Committee.

The Chinese community until this time had remained more or less unorganized. But then, on 27 February 1949, the Malayan Chinese Association was inaugurated in Kuala Lumpur.[14] The establishment of this organization with the aim of safe-guarding

[12] Interview with R. Ramani, a close friend of Dato Onn and now Malaysia's Permanent Delegate to the United Nations, Kuala Lumpur, November 1963.

[13] Press Statement by the Communities Liaison Committee, March 1949. It has been claimed by Dato Onn that the important meeting of leaders of different racial groups that took place at his residence in Johore Bahru on 31 December 1948 was convened by him and was not at anybody else's suggestion. This meeting had led to the formation of the Communities Liaison Committee. Many, however, believe that Malcolm MacDonald, the British Commissioner General, had played an important role in its formation. See Ishak bin Tadin, op.cit. p. 71.

[14] See K. J. Ratnam, *Communalism and the Political Process in Malaya*, Kuala Lumpur, University of Malaya Press, 1965, pp. 152-4.

the special interests of the Chinese community clearly indicated to Dato Onn the course Malayan politics was taking. He felt that for politics to assume a definitely communal pattern was bad for the country. The Malays had formed the UMNO to look after their interests and the Chinese and Indians had launched their own organizations, the MCA and the MIC, to protect the interests of their own communities. Dato Onn found this communal basis of politics distasteful and could visualize the dangerous potential of the development. He feared that this would keep the different communities apart and would preclude and hinder the integration of the different peoples into one nation. At the time of the establishment of the MCA Dato Onn had felt that the new party would only serve the interests of the Chinese and create rivalry with the Malays.[15] Dato Onn's fear of the MCA was not ill-founded, for within two years of its formation, the MCA, which was formed as a social organization, was to develop into a strong pressure group of the Chinese. With his planned national role for the UMNO, Dato Onn had hoped that the Chinese loyal to Malaya would join the UMNO; thereby the MCA would be weakened and the UMNO would shed its communal character.

In the context of these developments Dato Onn started seeing himself more and more as a national leader given the task of creating a nation, rather than the leader of the Malay community alone. To attain this, the character and composition of the UMNO had to be altered. He set himself to convert the UMNO into a national organization representing all communities. The first step was to associate non-Malays with the UMNO. The 11th General Assembly of the UMNO, after a very heated debate on 28 May 1949 at Arau (Perlis), approved the new party constitution to make the organization more political and to allow non-Malays to become associate members.[16] This decision, which was approved by a majority of fourteen to eight, was supported by delegates from Perak, Pahang, Penang, Sabak Bernam, Johore, Kedah and the Saberkas.[17] The opposition had come from the delegates of Ke-

[15] *The Straits Times*, 24 February 1950.
[16] Ibid. 30 May 1949.
[17] See Chapter III, Footnote 19, below.

lantan, Perlis, Selangor and Negri Sembilan. Dato Onn, in supporting the change, asserted:

> It is absolutely important for Malays to obtain closer relations with other people in this country. It is time for us to take the view wider than the *kampong* view. Let it not be said that Malays are narrow-minded and suspicious.[18]

Within three months Dato Onn was taking a bigger and a much more significant step. In a ninety-minute Presidential speech at the 12th General Assembly of the UMNO at Butterworth (Penang) on 27 August 1949, he said that the Malays must accept as nationals peoples of other races who were prepared to give their all to the country. He said that a single nationality was essential if 'we are to achieve self-government and independence in Malaya', and that nationality must replace citizenship obtainable under the Constitution. He further suggested: 'We must find ways and means to end feudal rule and replace it with a constitutional form of government.'[19] This was a very significant move. *The Straits Times* asserted in an editorial:

> Malaya crossed a watershed of its social and political history in the little town of Butterworth ... when Dato Onn made his speech to the General Assembly of the UMNO calling for a Malayan nationality instead of federal citizenship, acceptance by the Malay race of Malayan nationals of other races ....
>
> Only three years ago Dato Onn headed the UMNO delegation in the Anglo-Malay Committee which drafted the Constitution of the Federation. At that time the idea of a Malayan nationality had not even entered the heads of the UMNO delegates. They were extremely reluctant to accept even the proposal for a new Federal Citizenship open to non-Malays, hedged about though it was with all kinds of restrictions.[20]

The next significant move of Dato Onn in this direction was his attempt to force the controversial citizenship recommendations of the Communities Liaison Committee upon the UMNO. On 9

[18] *The Malay Mail*, 30 May 1949.

[19] Ibid. 28 August 1949.

[20] *The Straits Times*, 30 August 1949.

May 1950, the Executive Committee of the UMNO, after a long and heated debate, decided to accept these recommendations in principle.[21] However, there was very widespread opposition to the proposals among the Malays who felt that this was an 'attempt to obtain loyalty by granting citizenship, whereas citizenship should be granted only in return for loyalty'.[22]

In spite of definite indications of widespread and vehement opposition to the citizenship proposals, Dato Onn made an attempt to push them through an emergency meeting of the General Assembly of the UMNO which was held at Kuala Lumpur during the second week of June 1950. There was open hostility to the proposals and some of the speakers went to the extent of branding Dato Onn a 'traitor to the Malays and the country'.[23] The opposition was led by a Singapore lawyer, Sardon bin Haji Jubir, President of the Singapore Malay Union (now for many past years a Minister in the Malaysian Cabinet), who had the support of the Kelantan, Perlis, Selangor and Negri Sembilan Divisions of the UMNO (the same Divisions which had opposed Dato Onn at the Arau General Assembly in May 1949). Sardon bin Haji Jubir, speaking against the proposal, said: 'If they are adopted, the Malay race will fade into obscurity as it has done in Singapore.'

Thereupon, to force the issue, Dato Onn resigned as President of the UMNO and at the same time announced the resignation of the entire executive committee. The UMNO General Assembly had not bargained for this. Confronted with this, the opposition reversed its position. The Kedah branch of the UMNO flew the UMNO flag at half mast indicating 'the sense of loss'. On 27 July 4,000 Malays, men, women and children, representing UMNO Divisions from all parts of the country, went in a mile-long procession to Dato Onn's residence in Johore Bahru in a bid to persuade the founder of the UMNO to return to its Presidency.[24] And, on 27 August, a month later, the UMNO General Assembly at its annual session at Kuala Kangsar re-elected Dato Onn as

[21] Ibid. 10 May 1950.
[22] Ibid. 17 May 1950.
[23] Ibid. 11 and 12 June 1950.
[24] Ibid. 28 July 1950.

President by sixty-six votes to three, and at the same time approved the citizenship proposals which it had turned down earlier.[25]

Towards the end of 1950, Dato Onn took the final plunge. On 20 November 1950, he told a correspondent of *The Straits Times* that he believed that the UMNO had progressed sufficiently and had reached the stage when it had to open its doors to non-Malays with equal membership rights and privileges. It had to be turned into a national organization. 'Merely opening the door to associate members is not enough. This must be a national body and non-Malay members should be offered all the rights and privileges of the organization.'[26] He also felt that this change in the character of the organization would necessitate a change in its name and he suggested that it be renamed the United *Malayan* National Organisation. At the same time he had prepared a detailed programme for the Independence of Malaya Party. He stated that if the UMNO accepted his proposals for the necessary changes he would remain within the UMNO and implement his programme for the new party through it.

On 5 June 1951, Dato Onn announced that Malaya could achieve independence in seven years with the establishment of the IMP.[27] Further, he warned that he would form a new party if the UMNO at its General Assembly meeting rejected his suggestion to convert it into the United Malayan National Organisation. Outlining some of the principles (which to most Malays at that time were extremely undesirable and dangerous) for which the new party would work, he said that it would make efforts for the merger of Singapore with the Federation. The party would stand for the elimination of the nine States and Settlements. 'We should not even use the term "State" to denote Johore, or Sclangor, or Perak. The word should be "territory".'

On 6 June, a day after Dato Onn had formulated the principles of the new party, *The Straits Times,* after interviewing a number

[25] Ibid. 28 August 1950.

[26] Ibid. 21 November 1950. There were about 1,000 non-Malay associate members of the UMNO at this time including the then President of the MCA, Dato Tan Cheng Lock.

[27] *The Straits Times*, 6 June 1951.

of prominent leaders of the different communities, reported that a large number of them had declared their support for Dato Onn. [28] On 8 June, a staff correspondent of the newspaper reported: 'No recent political pronouncement has created so much interest in the Federation as Dato Onn bin Jaafar's proposals for the formation of an Independence of Malaya Party.'[29] Also, on 6 June, Dato Onn disclosed that he had received a questionnaire from Dato Tan Cheng Lock, the President of the MCA, on the possibility of forming a non-communal political party. One of the questions posed by Dato Tan was:

> Would it be possible to form a political party in the Federation with membership open to all without distinction of race, class, creed, colour or nationality?[30]

Within a few days of Dato Onn's decision to leave the UMNO and form the IMP there was a spate of letters in *The Straits Times*, all by Malays, emphasizing the dangerous consequences of the course that Dato Onn had chosen. Ahmad bin Haji A. Rahim, President of the Johore Peninsular Malay Union warned:

> ... to force the Malays to share equal rights with foreigners by giving further concessions to them in this country will lead to incidents similar to those in Palestine or India, which neither Malays nor foreigners desire.[31]

A 'Malay' wrote:

> Now it seems the Dato is losing his head! He is becoming over-zealous. He is beginning to forget the people who supported him and placed him where he is now....
> The Malays like the civilized peoples do want independence, at least self-government within the British Commonwealth of Nations, but it is feared that seven years as the target date to achieve that goal is too ambitious. Dato Onn is trying to ask the Malays to run before they can walk.[32]

[28] Ibid. 7 June 1951.

[29] Ibid. 8 June 1951.

[30] Ibid. 7 June 1951. This is only to indicate here that Dato Tan Cheng Lock too at this time was thinking in terms of a non-communal political party.

[31] Ibid. 19 June 1951.

[32] Ibid. 23 June 1951.

A 'Malay Realist' wrote from Penang:

> In comparison with the Chinese and Indians the Malays are merely
> babies just beginning to crawl. Prizes of sweets would still be suffi-
> cient to make them think that Destruction was Protection . . . .
> I wish the Dato would stay his hand for another decade and steer the
> Malays towards economic progress—knowing well that the drive to
> live, if it is steered by the non-Malays, will drive the Malays them-
> selves to only one course, poverty.
> Is the IMP the banding together of lambs, lions and tigers to drive
> out the caretakers? Who then shall replace these powerful caretak-
> ers?[33]

'Kampong Malay' wrote from Kedah:

> Dato Onn has evidently embarked upon a certain folly to throw the
> Malays into confusion and utter helplessness in the face of fierce
> competition for power . . . .
> They will be reduced to the status of the Red Indians striving to live
> in the wastelands of America.[34]

The common ground in this opposition was that Dato Onn was
speeding up the independence of the country and thereby was
attempting to expose the Malays prematurely to the enterprise
and economic power of the Chinese and the Indians.[35]

In spite of definite indications of substantial opposition from
the Malays, Dato Onn went ahead with his plans. Because of the
Malay opposition he had decided to resign from the UMNO on
1 July 1951.[36] He felt that it was futile waiting for the formal decision of the UMNO General Assembly which was scheduled to
meet in August. However, it was reported on 30 June that so important did he consider labour backing for the IMP that he had
decided to formally launch the IMP only after 22 August, when
the Malayan Trades Union Council was scheduled to have its
annual conference.[37] He had been invited to address the conference

[33] Ibid. 30 June 1951.

[34] Ibid. 7 July 1951.

[35] Interview with Husein Onn, Kuala Lumpur, September 1963. Also Dato Zainal
Abidin bin Abas, Kuala Lumpur, August 1963.

[36] *The Straits Times*, 30 June 1951.

[37] Ibid.

and explain the principles of his proposed party. He had some success in wooing the labour unions. P. P. Narayanan, the President of the MTUC, addressing the annual conference, said that while the aim of the trade unions was to strengthen their own movement, they must also support any movement for political advancement.[38] The reference was obviously to the IMP. At the same conference of the MTUC, a proposal for the formation of a labour party was introduced. But the suggestion was withdrawn in view of the impending establishment of the IMP.[39] Later, at the annual conference of the powerful Plantation Workers' Union of South Malaya (P. P. Narayanan was associated with this union), opened by Dato Onn, 130 of the 200 delegates signed supporter forms for the IMP.[40] However, it was clear from the formation of the labour parties in some of the States, in particular the formation of the Selangor Labour Party in December 1951, that labour and its leaders were not all solidly behind Dato Onn in his enterprise.

Thereupon, on 26 August 1951, at the UMNO General Assembly, Dato Onn formally put forward his resignation. This time the UMNO did not request him to remain in the organization and promptly elected Tunku Abdul Rahman, an unknown deputy Public Prosecutor in Kuala Lumpur, as the new President by fifty-seven votes to eleven.[41] But it is important to note here that at the same time, in a very significant gesture, the UMNO reasserted its confidence in Dato Onn and passed the following three resolutions:

a. That this Assembly shows a token of sadness and regret because Dato Onn declined the invitation to stand for re-election to the Presidentship of the UMNO for the 1951-52 tenure of office;

b. As such, this Assembly should make a remembrance that the organization is very grateful for his guidance and advice, for the discharge of his responsibility as President of the organiza-

---

[38] Victor Purcell, *Malaya: Communist or Free*, Palo Alto, Stamford, The University Press, 1954, p. 99.

[39] Saul Rose, *Socialism in Southern Asia*, London, Oxford University Press, 1959, p. 210.

[40] *The Straits Times*, 30 September 1951.

[41] Ibid. 27 August 1951.

tion and for the benefits that the Malays have gained through his sincere, conscientious and hard work;

c.   That this Assembly is confident that the honourable ex-President will continue to work unflinchingly for the safety of the Malay race, country and religion; hence this Assembly prays that the Dato and the party that he intends to inaugurate would be guided and rewarded by God, the Almighty.[42]

Formation of the IMP

On 16 September, the IMP was established amidst a fanfare of trumpets at Kuala Lumpur. 'Today we are making a tryst with destiny', declared R. Ramani, a leading member of the party. 'It was the most impressive formation meeting of any political party in Malaya. One thousand people—representatives of every community—crowded the roof garden of Hotel Majestic and cheered spontaneously when the resolution which brought the party into existence was passed unanimously', said *The Straits Times*.

It is important to note that Dato Tan Cheng Lock, the President of the MCA, presided over the inaugural meeting. The following were elected to serve on the organizing committee:

Dato Onn bin Jaafar, Dato Tan Cheng Lock, R. Ramani, Dato E. E. C. Thuraisingham, Khoo Teik Ee (Treasurer of the MCA), Abdul Aziz bin Ishak, L. C. Hoffman, Yong Shook Lin (Secretary-General of the MCA), P. P. Narayanan (President of the MTUC), Saleha binte Mohammad Ali, F. Arulanandom, and Mohammad Sopiee.

A resolution passed at the meeting declared the following as the major object of the new party:

... the object of the party is to establish a Sovereign Independent State of Malaya aiming at the well-being and advancement of the People based on equality of opportunity and of Political, Social and Economic rights and obligations.

It also committed the party 'to provide and maintain an efficient non-communal national organization in Malaya' and 'to promote

[42] *The UMNO Annual Report for the Year, 1951-2*, p. 9, quoted in Ishak bin Tadin, op.cit. p. 83.

the political, social and economic advancement of the people of Malaya, and more particularly of those who directly depend upon their own exertions, by hand or brain, for the means of life'. Dato Onn, the founder, answering critics, especially Tan Cheng Lock, who had maintained that he should have made an unambiguous declaration that independent Malaya would remain in the Commonwealth, asserted: 'It is tantamount in my view to saying to a person: You are free to do what you like — You can do what you like — but before you can do so I must tie your hands and feet and blindfold your eyes.'[43]

At the time of leaving the UMNO, Dato Onn had not thought, according to his son, Husein Onn, who was the Secretary-General of the UMNO at the time, that he was severing all relations with the UMNO.[44] He had established the movement and therefore he could never think of leaving it altogether. What he had felt was that the UMNO was not ready yet to accept his ideas which were ahead of his time, and therefore, he had to go out of it and establish a new organization with the help of non-communal-minded Chinese, Indians and others and the non-communal elements within the UMNO. The rest in the UMNO, according to his idea, would be left under a moderate and responsible leader who would prepare them for eventual non-communal politics and cooperation with the IMP.

However, the new President of the UMNO, Tunku Abdul Rahman, had different ideas. He forced the issue. On 17 September 1951, a day after the formation of the IMP, he declared that any member of the UMNO who joined the IMP would be expelled from the UMNO.[45] 'We cannot tolerate this ridiculous situation .... We cannot afford to have a split in our ranks. The policies of the IMP and the UMNO are opposed.' He further asserted: 'It is

---

[43] *The Straits Times*, 17 September 1951.

[44] This is based on an interview with Husein Onn, Kuala Lumpur, July 1963. The information was confirmed by Dato Zainal Abidin bin Abas, one of the Malays closest to Dato Onn at that time. Also Silcock and Aziz have reported that Dato Onn 'probably did not intend to break with the organization entirely or take members out of the UMNO into the IMP'. T. H. Silcock and U. A. Aziz, 'Malaya', in William L. Holland, *Asian Nationalism and the West*, New York, The Macmillan Co., 1953, pp. 333-4.

[45] *The Straits Times*, 18 September 1951.

the policy of the IMP to open membership to all persons who are resident in this country. There was no qualification as to their allegiance, loyalty or birthright. Can you form a nation with such flimsy materials?' He said that the UMNO, on the other hand, wanted a proper choice of materials. 'It is not fair for the Malays to throw in their lot with others when others refused to be naturalised, refused to study the language, and refused to adopt the customs of the country.'

Despite these difficulties the IMP made a fair start. Within days of its formation pledges of support started 'pouring into party's temporary headquarters', and according to a party spokesman there was no time to count them.[46] News items appeared in the press indicating the establishment of party branches in many places. The Kuala Lumpur branch, which later turned out to be the only branch to function actively, was established on 27 October 1951. Dato Onn was elected the Chairman securing 186 votes against thirty-three for Abdul Aziz Ishak.[47]

As expected, very few Malays joined the IMP. If many Malays were to go with Dato Onn he would have had his own way within the UMNO and would have converted it into a non-communal organization. He would not have had to establish the IMP. It is certain that Dato Onn had not reckoned on any significant support from the Malays initially.

With the sort of policies and programme for the new party announced by Dato Onn and the serious differences that he had had with the Malay Sultans of the different States while he was the President of the UMNO, the Sultans were bound to look towards the IMP with disfavour. Dato Onn's strained relations with the Malay Sultans coincided with his attempts to change the character of the UMNO and convert it into a national organization representing all the people of Malaya. At the historic Butterworth General Assembly meeting of the UMNO in August 1949, Dato

---

[46] Ibid.

[47] Ibid. 28 October 1951. Aziz Ishak feels that the founder of the party, Dato Onn, should not have contested the chairmanship of a city branch. As a result he soon afterwards resigned from the party. Interview with Aziz Ishak, Kuala Lumpur, July 1963.

Onn, to the discomfiture of the Sultans, had declared: 'Scrap feudal rule, hold elections.'[48] In his Presidential speech he mentioned the following main reasons for the clash with the Sultans:

1. The proposed appointment of a Malay Deputy High Commissioner.
2. The Sultans' view that government servants should be barred from taking active part in politics.[49]

At this time, Dato Onn had been pressing the British to appoint a Malay as the Deputy High Commissioner, as a move to introduce a popular element in the administration. This particularly angered the Sultans, since this meant placing a commoner, a subject of the Sultans, above them. And it was obvious that the only Malay who could be offered the position was Dato Onn.[50] It has been suggested by Husein Onn that the Sultans had been encouraged by some of the senior British officials because they felt that the UMNO was becoming too powerful, and, if not checked, would pose a serious threat to the British position in Malaya.[51] At this time UMNO was a very powerful organization enjoying the support of almost all the Malays. Its leaders had been keenly watching as to what was happening around Malaya, in Indonesia, Burma, India and the Philippines. This frightened the British. Also, at the same time, some in the UMNO were discussing the role of the Sultans and had started thinking in terms of one ruler rather than nine of them. This, according to Husein Onn, was used by the British who told the Sultans that the UMNO was a threat to their position. The Sultans seem to have been taken in by this argument and some of them made it difficult for their officials to participate in politics, which meant participating in the activities of the UMNO. Some even went to the extent of prohibiting State officials from joining the UMNO.

[48] *The Straits Times*, 28 August 1949.

[49] Ibid.

[50] Syed Nasir bin Ismail, one of the most powerful leaders of the UMNO in recent years, told the author (Kuala Lumpur, October 1964) that during those days Dato Onn used to mimic the voice of the then Sultan of Kedah, who led the Sultans' opposition to him, and make fun of him in all public meetings addressed by him in the Malay areas of the East Coast.

[51] Interview with Husein Onn, Kuala Lumpur, July 1963.

This lack of support from the Rulers and the traditional leaders of the Malay community, coupled with the policies adopted by Dato Onn, which seemed to favour the non-Malays, discouraged the Malays from joining the IMP. Husein Onn suggests that if the party had been able to gain the support of the *mentri-mentri besar* (State Chief Ministers) it would not have failed. At that time the *mentri-mentri besar* were appointed by the Sultans and worked during their pleasure, and, therefore, were in no position to go against the wishes of the Sultans. As a result, even those *mentri-mentri besar* who declared their support for the IMP did not really do anything for the new party but only kept up 'a pretence or show of support for the IMP'.[52]

Then, the party participated in an extremely unfavourable test of strength, which proved almost fatal for it. The Kuala Lumpur municipal elections for twelve seats on the partly elected council were scheduled to be held on 16 February 1952. The party went headlong into the elections despite the fact that it had been established only a little while earlier and organizationally was in no position to fight the elections. The party had no ward branches and middle and lower level leadership. Its leaders had no idea of how to organize for elections and it lacked an organizational base.[53]

The party, faced with the elections during the limited time that it had, hurriedly organized itself for the purpose. A very serious consequence was that it was forced to concentrate on activities in Kuala Lumpur, the venue of the elections. The Kuala Lumpur branch, which had Dato Onn as its Chairman, was forced to concentrate its work on organizing for the elections. Instead of first consolidating itself by attracting members, it had to start with wooing voters. The National Council of the party which was scheduled to meet by the end of 1951 could meet only about a year later, in September 1952. Regular office-bearers for the national organization were elected only in September 1952, a year

[52] Interview with Husein Onn, Kuala Lumpur, September 1963.

[53] R. Ramani, a leading member of the party and a friend of the Indian Prime Minister, Jawaharlal Nehru, requested the latter to send a senior Congress Party official who had experience of elections to help the IMP in organizing for the elections. Nehru arranged this, but for some reason the person was not able to come. Interview with R. Ramani, Kuala Lumpur, November 1963.

after the formation of the party. Party activities until then were guided by the Organising Committee formed at the time of the inauguration of the party in September 1951. The Central Organising Committee, it seems, only met twice or thrice. All the members of the Central Organising Committee, with the exception of Dato Tan Cheng Lock, were also members of the Kuala Lumpur branch committee, which met regularly every month and performed the functions of the Central Organising Committee. The result was that the work of organizing and establishing the party outside Kuala Lumpur was, on the whole, not undertaken. By the time the elections in Kuala Lumpur were over, it was too late to do so, as the party suffered a crushing defeat at the hands of the UMNO-MCA, its only rival.

The first meeting of the Kuala Lumpur Branch Committee was held at the Hotel Majestic on 4 November 1951. It was announced by Dato Onn, the Chairman, that until then the branch had 516 members. There were also about 400 names of persons on the supporters' list who were yet to be contacted and enrolled as members.[54] There was not to be much change in the size of the membership of the branch in the future. In May 1952, the branch had a total membership of 1,229, including 115 outstation members registered at Kuala Lumpur.[55]

The very first act of the Branch Committee was to appoint a very large number of sub-committees. Since the elections would involve a 'careful study and careful planning' a special sub-committee was appointed. Dato Onn was appointed chairman of the sub-committee and some of the important members were: Dato E. E. C. Thuraisingham, R. Ramani, Raja Ayoub, J. Brazier, K. L. Devaser, Yong Shook Lin, and Abdul Aziz Ishak.[56]

At the second meeting of the Branch Committee held on 6 December 1951 the party was faced with the problem of members of the IMP organizing elections for communal parties, mainly the MCA. The Committee discussed the question of whe-

---

[54] *Minutes of the Branch Committee Meeting*, IMP, 4 November 1951 (mimeographed).

[55] *Agenda for the Branch Committee Meeting*, IMP, 9 June, 1952.

[56] *Minutes of the Branch Committee Meeting*, 4 November 1951.

ther disciplinary action should be taken against them. It was resolved that since 'communalism was accepted as the greatest
scourge of Malaya and IMP was definitely opposed to it' any
member of the party 'encouraging communal representation on
the municipal council would be expelled from the party'.[57] However, no action was taken against any member. Further,

> Regarding the position of organizations which had promised support
> for the ideals of IMP and were now contesting it, it was decided that
> the Chairman should attempt to see the leaders of such organisations
> and try to explain to them the dangers of communal representation
> in the hope of making them join forces with the IMP. It was agreed
> that the approach should be purely in a personal capacity.[58]

The reference was to the MCA. The Malayan Indian Congress,
the other communal organization, had no desire to put up its own
candidates against those of the IMP. In fact, the President of the
MIC was to contest as an IMP candidate. But the trouble arose in
the case of the MCA, whose top leaders had individually committed
themselves to the IMP idea and had promised all support, but
whose organization had taken no formal decision to support the
IMP and, on the other hand, had indicated its intention to put up
its own candidates in the forthcoming municipal elections in
Kuala Lumpur.

It has been suggested that before the Selangor State MCA decided to contest the Kuala Lumpur elections jointly with the
UMNO, it had made approaches to the IMP leaders for an electoral
arrangement similar to the one that it was to have with the UMNO
soon.[59] However, the IMP leaders 'were very confident that the
party would win the elections hands down' and therefore did not
take the MCA overture seriously. Also, they felt that it was not
proper for a non-communal party to have an understanding with
a communal one. Ong Yoke Lin, at that time a lieutenant of Sir
Henry Lee, the Selangor MCA boss, acted as a go-between. It
seems that Dato Onn had authorized R. Ramani and Dato E. E.
C. Thuraisingham, two of his closest friends and advisers, to hold

[57] Ibid. 6 December 1951.
[58] Ibid.
[59] Interview with R. K. Panikkar (Kuala Lumpur, January 1965) and F. Arulanandom (Ipoh, January 1964).

talks with Sir Henry Lee.[60] However, Dato Thuraisingham chose to negotiate without Ramani. These discussions between Dato Thuraisingham and Sir Henry, which took place before the UMNO-MCA alliance was announced on 8 January 1952, came to nothing. Dato Thuraisingham has been blamed by some of the important leaders of the party for the failure of this very vital attempt.[61] At the next meeting of the Branch Committee which was held on 3 January 1952 the Chairman, Dato Onn, announced that 'the MCA Selangor Branch was not prepared to come in with the IMP for the election'.[62]

Communal feelings seem to have been so deep-rooted among the people that the leadership of the IMP too soon found it difficult to get over it and function in a purely non-communal manner. In the first meeting of the Membership Sub-Committee of the Kuala Lumpur Branch (no membership committee on the national level was ever constituted) on 13 November 1951 the following took place:

> Mr. Tan Tuan Boon suggested that for the purpose of increasing membership, drives should be started among the different communities, and for expediency, the communities should be considered separately. Mr. Chow Yew Fai suggested that if meeting of about fifty Chinese leaders could be called at the Chinese Assembly Hall on Sunday, 25th November 1951, and if Dato Onn addressed the meeting and answered any questions that arose, it would be a great help, as the Dato's presence would be a tremendous encouragement to the leaders, who would then conduct a drive to recruit members themselves . . . .
>
> The problem of drives among Indians and Malays was then considered. The possibility of including Indian and Malay leaders in the meeting of Chinese was ruled out because of language difficulties.[63]

[60] Interviews with Dato Thuraisingham (Kuala Lumpur, July 1963), R. Ramani (Kuala Lumpur, November 1963), and R. K. Panikkar (Kuala Lumpur, January 1965).

[61] Interviews with R. Ramani and R. K. Panikkar.

[62] *Minutes of the Branch Committee Meeting*, 3 January 1952.

[63] *Minutes of the Membership Sub-Committee of the K. L. Branch*, IMP, 13 November 1951.
It may be noted here that Dato Onn was a Malay and did not speak any of the Chinese dialects.

Kuala Lumpur Municipal Elections and the Beginning of the End of the IMP

In the nomination of candidates for the different wards the party could not cut itself loose from the prevailing communal atmosphere. In the predominantly Malay Sentul Ward it fielded two Malays and one Indian as its candidates. In Bungsar Ward which had a large Indian population it set up all three Indian candidates. In the Imbi and Petaling Wards with a very sizeable Chinese majority it nominated four Chinese and two non-Chinese candidates.

The UMNO which had earlier decided not to contest the elections finally decided in favour of contesting. On 3 January 1952, it was announced that the UMNO would field only six candidates — three in the Sentul Ward, two in Bungsar and one in the Imbi Ward, and none in the predominantly Chinese Petaling Ward.[64] At the same time the Selangor State MCA announced that it would put up non-Chinese candidates as well. Then, on 9 January, out of the blue came the joint declaration by the Kuala Lumpur Division of the UMNO and the Selangor State MCA that the two parties would contest the elections jointly.[65] At the same time the names of their candidates were announced — six Chinese from the MCA, five Malays from the UMNO, and one Indian lady, said to be an associate member of the MCA.

The elections were held on 16 February. The UMNO and the MCA were able to capture nine of the twelve seats, three of them going to the UMNO and six to the MCA.[66] The IMP was able to secure only two seats. Both these were in the Bungsar Ward which had a large number of Indian voters. The IMP candidates in the predominantly Chinese Petaling Ward secured the lowest vote among all the IMP candidates. All the six Chinese candidates fielded by the UMNO-MCA were returned while only three of the five Malay candidates were returned. In the case of the IMP all its Malay and Chinese candidates were defeated. Table 2 gives the votes polled by the Malay, Chinese and Indian candidates of the IMP and the UMNO-MCA.

---

[64] *The Straits Times,* 4 January 1952.

[65] Ibid. 9 January 1952.

[66] For the results in full see *The Straits Times,* 17 February 1952.

TABLE 2
1952 KUALA LUMPUR MUNICIPAL ELECTION RESULTS

	Malay		Chinese		Indian	
	No. of candidates	Votes polled	No. of candidates	Votes polled	No. of candidates	Votes polled
IMP	2	1,988	4	1,394	6	3,262
UMNO-MCA	5	5,180	6	4,928	1	232

It is obvious that the IMP found a large part of its support among Indians. It secured a small number of votes in the predominantly Chinese and Malay Wards. On the other hand, the UMNO-MCA secured the bulk of its votes in the predominantly Chinese and Malay areas; it seems to have obtained no support among Indians.

The result was a terrible setback for the IMP. The very poor showing was the result of several factors. As had been indicated earlier the party had no organizational base; ward branches were still in the process of being set up; and the party had hardly acquired a middle or lower level leadership. The others, the UMNO and the MCA, especially the latter, were well organized. More, the atmosphere was strongly communal and the IMP had had no time to influence it in any way. People were communal-minded and voted on a communal basis. It is unfortunate that the non-communal IMP had to contest elections before it had the opportunity to change the communal orientation of the people.[67]

Moreover, most of the IMP candidates were less well-known than their opponents. None of its top leaders contested the elections. On the other hand, the MCA fielded candidates who were well-known and were locally influential. A correspondent of *The Straits Times* covering the elections reported:

Superb organization on the part of the MCA and the UMNO today gave the six weeks old alliance a sweeping victory . . . .

[67] It was for this reason that Dato Onn did not want early elections. He was conscious of the organizational and financial strength of the MCA. He also knew that unless the IMP had time to influence the communal orientation of the voters it would not succeed in securing their support. However, they did not realize the importance of the Kuala Lumpur elections, which had the participation of all the major political parties of the time. Interview with K. L. Devaser, then the President of the MIC and one of the two successful candidates of the IMP, Kuala Lumpur, August 1963.

The merger concentrated their forces on a splendid transport system, proper briefing of voters and a perfect all round organization which worked throughout with a precision surprising in a first election. [68]

The same newspaper wrote in an editorial:

There are several lessons to be learned from Kuala Lumpur's first elections, and the first of them is that organization is the driving rod of political machinery It was to efficient organization that the UMNO-MCA alliance owed its spectacular victory . . . .

The Alliance had at its disposal a large fleet of cars, many of which had come from outside Kuala Lumpur for the occasion, some of them as far afield as Ipoh . . . .

. . . one of the more regrettable conclusions is that by and large it was, however, a communal vote.[69]

The IMP contested the elections essentially on the basis of its non-communal character. Its election posters said: *Vote for Non-Communalism and Progress —Support the Independence of Malaya Party*. It also attempted to emphasize its commitment to popular sovereignty: *Vote IMP — the People's Party: Government of the People of Malaya, by the People of Malaya, for the People of Malaya*. The party manifesto declared *Unity, Freedom, Justice, Equality* as its slogans.

It further attempted to emphasize the political basis of the elections as against the UMNO-MCA view that politics should not be introduced into the municipal elections and affairs.[70] Lashing at the UMNO-MCA view, Dato Onn asserted in a statement:

The very basis of this election is a political fact. Before any one of you could become a voter, one of the qualifications was that you must be a federal citizen, and the question of federal citizenship is purely a political one.

It is absurd and absolute nonsense to appeal for votes in this town under the guise that they are standing for no political bias.[71]

---

[68] *The Straits Times*, 17 February 1952. In Malaya, use of transport by political parties to carry voters to the polling stations is permitted by law.

[69] Ibid. 18 February 1952.

[70] Ibid. 9 January 1952.

[71] Ibid.

On 10 March, soon after the elections, Yong Pung How, the IMP election agent in the predominantly Chinese Petaling Ward, submitted a memorandum on behalf of the Petaling Ward voluntary workers with the object 'to draw attention to the problem of enlisting Chinese support for the party and its aims'. The confidential memorandum said:[72]

We have come to the following main conclusions about the position of the party *vis-à-vis* the bulk of the Chinese community:

(1) The Party has no appeal at all to the majority of the Chinese community.

(2) There is no machinery in the party for establishing contact with the Chinese community as a whole, so that we may not only keep in touch with them but also enlist their support and work through them.

As regards (1) it must be obvious to the Party that the present support the party receives from the Chinese community as a whole is negligible. This fact was clearly demonstrated in the last Municipal Elections in Kuala Lumpur. We as a group which was closely involved throughout the campaign, refuse to believe that it was merely 'blind voting' or superior organization and tactics on the day of the polling which led to our defeat. On the other hand, we are convinced that the Chinese voters did not vote for us because our party had nothing substantial to offer them, and in the absence of any such inducements, Chinese voters as a whole fell on their traditional loyalty to a Chinese organisation, which has after all at least done something for them in the past. It is conceded that the party has objectives, but these objectives have not gone beyond the slogan stage.

As regards (2), the party's Chinese membership consists of —

(a) a handful of Chinese leaders who have a personal following but no organized popular support among the Chinese community;

(b) small and scattered number of active members, whose energies in the service of the party are not coordinated;

---

[72] *Memorandum to the Kuala Lumpur Branch Committee from the former Election Agent, Petaling Ward, Kuala Lumpur.* Yong Pung How is the son of Yong Shook Lin, one of the strongest Chinese supporters of the IMP and the then Secretary-General of the MCA. Yong Pung How later was to play an important role in the MCA.

(c)   a slowly growing group of 'members' who have signed membership forms during membership drives and paid the subscription largely because of the personal influence of various recruiting 'agents'.

These facts alone should make it clear that if we were ever going to incorporate the Chinese in larger numbers into our party, we need some organization whereby we can reach deep into their community, and then maintain a close liaison between the policy-making and executive organs of the party on the one hand and the rank and file of the party on the other. It is realised by us that any such liaison will be on sectional or communal lines, but with the present structure of Chinese society here, we are convinced that it will have to be so.

After thus analysing the situation the Memorandum went ahead to make the following suggestions:

(1)   We suggest, first and foremost, that the party clarify in sufficient detail its policy and programme on the important issues which affect the Chinese community, e.g.

> a. Immigration
> b. Citizenship
> c. National service
> d. Malayanisation of services
> e. Labour policy

It is not sufficient now to fob people off with slogans 'freedom, unity, justice, equality'; most Chinese want to know how far the party is really willing to go in these things.

(2)   We suggest, secondly, the formation of a Chinese Advisory Committee, which would at the beginning merely advise the party on Chinese questions, and might subsequently be given executive powers with regard to the implementing of any Chinese policies which the party might have.

This very important memorandum was discussed by the Kuala Lumpur Branch Committee of the IMP on 11 March 1952 and the committee accepted the suggestion to form a Chinese Advisory Committee 'with powers to advise and implement party policies in so far as they affected the Chinese'.[73] It asked Yong Pung How

---

[73] *Minutes of the Branch Committee Meeting*, Kuala Lumpur, 11 March 1952.

and Tan Tuan Boon to proceed with the organization of the committee. At the next meeting of the Branch on 14 April, after the draft rules of the Chinese Advisory Committee had been presented, the Branch Committee asked the organisers 'to postpone the proposed inaugural General Meeting till the Branch Committee had considered the Draft Rules'.[74] But in a later meeting of the Branch Committee on 19 May the Draft Rules were considered 'and the Branch Committee felt that they would create an organization within the organization. The enthusiasm of the pro-tem committee was appreciated but the Chairman undertook to write to them and explain the dangers of such an organization to the IMP ideals and methods. He undertook to suggest alternative methods for obtaining advice on matters affecting the Chinese members.'[75] It should be noted here that the suggestion to establish a Chinese Advisory Committee was not rejected straightaway.

The matter was to be revived again in the Branch Committee meeting on 11 June when the Chairman, Dato Onn, informed the Committee that he had seen Yong Pung How on re-forming the Chinese Advisory Committee on the lines suggested by Yong Pung How.[76] Yong Pung How, according to Dato Onn, had declined and had suggested the name of Tan Tuan Boon. At the same meeting, Khoo Teik Ee (Treasurer of the MCA) suggested that similar committees should be formed for the other communities. However, on the suggestion of R. K. Panikkar it was decided 'to leave the formation of the other committees aside for a while and concentrate on the formation of the Chinese Advisory Committee and the Chairman undertook to do so'. Thereupon, the matter was dropped. The Chinese Advisory Committee was never constituted. However, it does give an indication of the concern of the IMP leadership at the lack of support from the Chinese community. It was also a sad admission of the fact that a party attempting to use its non-communal character to build up support had little chance of success.

The decision of the UMNO and the MCA to fight the Kuala

[74] Ibid. 14 April 1952.
[75] Ibid. 19 May 1952.
[76] Ibid. 11 June 1952.

Lumpur municipal elections jointly was announced on 8 January 1952. Dato Tan Cheng Lock, then President of the MCA and at the same time an important member of the Central Organising Committee of the IMP, had presided over the inaugural meeting of the IMP, and had not officially said anything with regard to the decision of the Selangor branch of the MCA to join hands with the UMNO for the purpose of the Kuala Lumpur municipal elections. He kept himself away from Kuala Lumpur during the period of the elections and did not take any part in the IMP election campaign. (It may be added that at the same time he did not participate in the MCA election campaign.) There were rumours going round in Kuala Lumpur that Dato Tan was about to resign from the IMP. Dato Tan kept quiet about it. It fell on Khoo Teik Ee to contradict these rumours. On 24 January, speaking at an IMP election rally, Khoo Teik Ee warned the UMNO-MCA speakers against 'trifling' with the name of Dato Tan. He asked them not to exploit Dato Tan's name for organizing support for the UMNO-MCA alliance.[77]

A day after the election results were announced it was reported that Dato Tan had not sent any message on the success of the UMNO-MCA alliance.[78] However, the very next day appeared the message from him congratulating the leaders of the Alliance.[79] In his message Dato Tan said that he was in favour of leaving it to the individual branches of the MCA to decide whether they would cooperate with the IMP or the UMNO or both. Characteristically he added: 'Principles are more important than people. I support the principles of the IMP, UMNO-MCA co-operation and Sino-Malay cooperation.' It was a pathetic attempt to wriggle out of his commitment to the IMP and Dato Onn.

This period of the Kuala Lumpur elections was the beginning of the break between Dato Onn and Dato Tan Cheng Lock. After the decision of the Selangor branch of the MCA to fight the elections jointly with the UMNO was announced, Dato Onn is reported to have approached Dato Tan to issue a statement clarifying

[77] *The Straits Times*, 25 January 1952.
[78] Ibid. 18 February 1952.
[79] Ibid. 19 February 1952.

the position of the central leadership of the MCA on the issue of cooperation with the UMNO.[80] He is also said to have requested Dato Tan to take action against Sir Henry Lee, the President of the Selangor MCA who was chiefly responsible for the arrangement. Dato Tan did none of these things. Sir Henry was too important a person in the MCA to be taken to task by Dato Tan. Also, it is extremely doubtful if Dato Tan, after the significant victory of the Alliance, really wanted to do so. This seems to have infuriated Dato Onn who considered this a case of double-dealing on the part of Dato Tan Cheng Lock.

Further, there was trouble regarding the establishment of the Malacca (the home town of Dato Tan) branch of the IMP. Soon after the formation of the IMP an organizing committee under the chairmanship of Dato Tan Cheng Lock had been organized to form the Malacca branch. But the organizing committee did nothing towards the formation of the branch for quite some time. On 18 January 1952, Tan Siew Sin, son of Dato Tan Cheng Lock and one of the important IMP enthusiasts, wrote to Dato Onn:

> My father informs [me] that Shook Lin [Yong Shook Lin, the Secretary-General of the MCA] is under the impression that we in Malacca are afraid of forming a branch of the IMP just because two lawyers are against it. I can assure you, on behalf of my father and myself, that the opposition of two lawyers is of no importance whatever, as far as my father and I are concerned. If we feel that it should be done, we would not care one DAMN or IOTA for the opposition of *two hundred lawyers* in this country, let alone two. I consider a gross insult to be pictured as afraid of any *twenty people* in this country put together.
>
> The reason why so little progress has been made to date is because we, i.e. the organizing committee, waited for my father to come back before doing anything and, as you may be aware, he has hardly been in Malacca for the last two months. My father has now asked us not to delay any longer and we may therefore have to hold our first meeting without him.[81]

---

[80] Interview with Dato Zainal Abidin bin Abas, August 1963, and R. K. Panikkar, January 1965.

[81] Emphasis in the original.

Yet the inaugural meeting of the Malacca branch was held only on 11 May 1952, four months after the letter by Tan Siew Sin promising an early formation of the branch. Further, on 15 July 1952, it was reported in the press that the Malacca branch might have to close down because it still had no officials.[82] It was only on 10 August 1952, and that too after two previous unsuccessful attempts, that the branch secured the necessary quorum to elect its first set of branch officials.[83] Dato Tan Cheng Lock, who was present at the meeting, declined nomination as chairman of the branch on the ground that his 'hands are full'. He, however, pledged support and both he and his son, Tan Siew Sin, accepted membership of the executive committee of the branch.

Despite this lack of cooperation from the leadership of the Chinese, who were expected to be one of the main sources of support for the party, Dato Onn, it seems, did not give up all hope. He went ahead with the formulation of the policy of the party and attempted to secure a mass base. Some new branches were established during the time. Speaking at the inaugural meeting of the Malacca Branch on 11 May, Dato Onn declared his blueprint for Malaya, the important points of which were:

1. Parliamentary form of government with an executive individually and collectively responsible to the legislature.

2. A monarchical or republican head of state.

3. The constitution should oppose communal policy and should contemplate a secular state with a single common citizenship assured to all, irrespective of religion, colour, creed or sex.[84]

But very soon the crushing defeat of the party in the Kuala Lumpur elections and the realization of the fact that Chinese support had not come, led to rethinking among the leaders regarding the party's attitude to the Chinese and the Malays. At the time of the formation of the party, because of the particular circumstances, no special attempt was made to attract the Malays. The party's programme and the utterances of its leaders contained

---

[82] *The Straits Times*, 15 July 1952.

[83] Ibid. 11 August 1952.

[84] Ibid. 12 May 1952.

nothing which had a special appeal for the Malays. In fact, the party was launched with the definite consciousness of the fact that the Malays were not yet ready to support a non-communal political party and little support, therefore, could be expected from them. The leaders of the party banked on the non-Malay communities, especially the Chinese who were the most numerous non-Malay group. And in order to attract them the party took a position on issues of interest to the non-Malays which had an appeal for them. At the time of its formation the party had committed itself to 'equality of . . . political, social and economic rights and obligations'. However, the Kuala Lumpur elections were an eye-opener to the leadership and were to lead to an agonizing reappraisal of its position *vis-à-vis* the different racial groups.

On 2 July 1952, Dato E. E. C. Thuraisingham, one of the closest advisers of Dato Onn, addressed a personal letter to the latter indicating that during the last few years the Malays had been pushed further down in the economic field and something required to be done immediately to rectify this.[85] He asserted: 'Equality for all communities is an ideal but how can there be real equality when there is so much of inequality in practically all fields of human endeavour'.

He added:

> In new countries like Burma and Ceylon and for many years in Siam the Governments of these countries have insisted that the natives of the land shall be identified with and shall form part and parcel of all commercial and industrial organizations. Certain quotas of natives were, by legislation, to be employed in certain types of businesses and industries run by non-natives.
>
> I propose that suitable legislation could be introduced into the Federal Legislative Council consequent on its acceptance by the Federal Legislative Council, whereby a percentage of employees in non-Malay concerns should be federal citizens, at all levels of employment, and that at least a minimum of 50% of such federal citizens should be Malays. The quota for the first year may well be 10% and thereafter every year could be increased by a further 10% till 50% is reached; thereby in five years we could have secured the entry of

---

[85] Personal letter dated 2 July 1952 to Dato Onn by Dato E.E.C. Thuraisingham.

thousands of Malays and Federal citizens into businesses which are now solely communal.

A more comprehensive registration of businesses is being contemplated for the purpose of yearly registration of all trading and business concerns. On this registration, particulars of compliance with the proposed legislation, can be checked up by the authorities to enforce its implementation.

He further suggested that he would concede the right of *jus soli*, demanded by the Chinese, only if they accepted the above-mentioned proposals. These were very extreme suggestions; even to date nothing of the sort has been done even though the leadership of the Malays would be very happy to implement these measures. However, these suggestions were not put into practice. The only thing that was done was the registration of businesses, which caused a serious flutter among the Chinese. Dato Thuraisingham, as the Member for education, was responsible for it. It alienated large numbers of Chinese from the IMP and created a sort of 'emotional antagonism' towards it.[86] These suggestions by Dato Thuraisingham, however, were the starting point for a changed approach of the party.

By the middle of July 1952, it was becoming increasingly clear to Dato Onn that the experiment in non-communal politics was not working. On 16 July, Dato Onn lashed out at some of the leaders of the IMP, in particular against Dato Tan Cheng Lock. The occasion was provided by the announcement that the members of the Organising Committee of the Malacca Branch of the IMP were thinking of dissolving the branch. Dato Onn said: 'There was no use trying to hide the fact'. Lack of proper leadership had been responsible for the party becoming almost moribund.[87] He further said:

It was impossible to make IMP a strong, non-communal party so long as leaders within the party continued to hold office and lead other communal organizations.

We have to make up our minds on this matter. I have always main-

86 Interview with Dr. Lim Chong Eu, Penang, May 1965.

87 *The Straits Times*, 17 July 1952.

tained that a person, especially a Committee member, cannot bear allegiance to IMP and another communal organization.
I am one of the members of the organizing committee who is not a member of any other communal organization.

Dato Tan Cheng Lock kept quiet again.
The Straits Times writing editorially under the caption 'The Languishing IMP' commented:[88]

> ... Dato Onn himself is far from happy at the way in which the party has, through lack of proper leadership and supervision, been allowed to languish .... Within the short period of a year ... the support which should have come to IMP from the Chinese community has not materialized, but has been channelled to the politically reorganized Malayan Chinese Association; it is not surprising that the branch which has felt the changed circumstances most is that at Malacca, the MCA stronghold.

On 21 July 1952, just before leaving for England, Dato Onn addressed a letter to the members of the Kuala Lumpur Branch Committee asserting that 'there is no doubt whatsoever that there is lack of interest, and there is existent a sense of indifference and apathy'. He asked the Committee to call a special General Meeting of the Branch where the state of the party could be looked into. He further said:

> It has also been put to me that the great divergence of interest in the Branch is having a very detrimental effect on the branch itself and that a line should be made to clarify the position of the leaders of the Branch themselves. It has also been put to me that the Branch as a Branch should put forward proposals that the membership of the IMP should in future be confined only to persons who are federal citizens and that non-federal citizens should be welcomed within the organization as Associate Members.

There is little doubt that Dato Onn was trying to flog a dead horse. The proposal to alter the membership requirements, which was to be effected later, was a clear indication that the founder of the organization had given up all hopes of securing the support of the Chinese community.

[88] Ibid. 19 July 1952.

In an attempt to recover some of the lost ground and in accordance with the wishes of Dato Onn expressed in the above-mentioned letter, the Kuala Lumpur Branch Committee met on 31 August 1952 and decided to recommend to the forthcoming Central National Council meeting a restriction on membership. It suggested that the membership of the party should be restricted to the present members, subjects of the Rulers, federal citizens, and British citizens domiciled in the country.[89] Two amendments to the proposal allowing persons who had lived in Malaya for several years to become members of the party and the creation of an associate membership without voting rights, were rejected. Dato Zainal Abidin bin Haji Abas supporting the restrictions said that these would strengthen the party. If the party permitted people of 'doubtful loyalty' to become members, it was bound to lose the support of others, Malays and federal citizens, whose loyalty to the country was beyond doubt.[90] Dato Onn, as the Chairman of the Kuala Lumpur branch, confirmed the orientation of the party when he told members of the Branch:

> I understand that support in certain quarters has been withheld from IMP due to doubts on IMP's stand on constitutional issues, in particular reference to the position of Their Highnesses the Rulers of the Malay States in the future sovereign and independent State of Malaya. I should like to stress one point: IMP is not a revolutionary party. It seeks to make changes in the constitutional field by evolutionary methods.[91]

The earlier zeal of Dato Onn when he was shouting slogans — *Scrap Feudal Rule* — was gone. He had been let down by the leaders of the Chinese community and now for his political survival he was making a bid to rally Malay support.

The Central National Council of the party met in Kuala Lumpur on 16 September 1952, the anniversary of the formation of the IMP, and made an attempt to attract Malay support. The meeting decided after a heated debate to restrict the membership of the party to five categories of persons — present members of the party,

[89] Ibid. 1 September 1952.
[90] Ibid.
[91] Ibid.

subjects of the Rulers of the Malay States, federal citizens, British subjects born in Malaya, and persons who had lived in Malaya for not less than ten years and were accepted by the Central Executive Committee of the party.

In line with the changing orientation of the party, the Council passed a resolution indicating the new policies and programme. It said that the party shall be guided by the following policies:

1. The establishment of a sovereign and Independent State within the Commonwealth, based on justice, equity, and democracy, and the elimination of communalism and class prejudice so that the advancement and welfare of the people be promoted to provide the greatest good for the greatest number.
2. The recognition of the rights of free enterprise and facilities for and protection of all investments subject to the requirements of national interests and security of the nation.
3. Equality of opportunity and rewards, irrespective of sex, the emancipation of women and free and equal opportunity of physical and mental development for the young.
4. Common citizenship and adult franchise.
5. The best fruits of democracy and those basic freedoms and conditions of life which make life significant and productive . . .
6. Promotion of national peace and security, maintenance of just and honourable relations between nations, respect for international law and treaty obligations.[92]

The programme of the party, among other things, promised independence within nine years. It should be noted that there was a complete absence of any special attempt to attract Chinese support through this programme. Emphasis was put on the fundamental rights of the people and on non-controversial issues, such as adult franchise, free elementary education, improved social security services, subsidy to food producers, establishment of strong defence and security forces, establishment of industries by cooperative efforts, equitable distribution of taxation and minimum living wages for the workers of Malaya. But, in comparison, the resolution moved at the inaugural meeting of the party on 16

[92] *Motions and Resolutions approved by the first meeting of the Central National Council of the IMP* (mimeographed), 16 September 1952.

September 1951 had declared that the object of the party was 'to establish a Sovereign Independent State of Malaya aiming at the well-being and advancement of the People *based on equality of opportunity and of political, social and economic rights and obligations'*, an assertion particularly attractive to the Chinese and Indians who craved for an equal position.[93] It should further be noted that all references to the Rulers of the Malay States and 'reform of the feudal system' to which the party had committed itself earlier, and which were distasteful to the rank and file of the Malay community, were omitted.[94]

Further, in a resolution the Council chose to condemn the running of lotteries by political parties and asked the Government to prohibit such lotteries. According to Dato Onn and other leaders of the party, the MCA had been able through these lotteries to amass large sums of money, part of which it had been using for political work. They felt that this gave the MCA a distinct advantage over other parties in elections. This is what had happened, they thought, in the Kuala Lumpur municipal elections of February 1952. Therefore, they tried to cut at the root of this financial advantage to the MCA.

The last resolution coupled with the Presidential address by Dato Onn at the Central National Council, in which he had been critical of the role of the Chinese in the IMP, provided Tan Siew Sin, the son of Tan Cheng Lock and at that time the head of the publicity section of the MCA, with the chance of withdrawing from the IMP. On 18 September, two days after the meeting of the Council, Tan Siew Sin announced his resignation from the IMP.[95] He had taken serious exception to Dato Onn's criticism of the Chinese. What Dato Onn had said was the following:

> We must face the fact that in Malaya today, particularly in the political field, we have ambitions of different communities.
> We have one community that desires to control the destiny of this country on the ground that they are the sons and daughters of the soil.

[93] Emphasis added.
[94] Eight-Point Programme announced by Dato Onn on 22 June 1951. *The Straits Times*, 23 June 1951.
[95] *The Straits Times*, 19 September 1952.

We have, on the other hand, another community which also desires to control the destiny of this country on the ground of its economic and financial influence.[96]

Tan Siew Sin alleged that this stricture was aimed at the Chinese community. He said:

By passing the resolution on lotteries run by political organizations, the party [IMP] has thrown a direct challenge at the MCA. The resolution is worded so strongly that the party has compelled the MCA to the conclusion that IMP is hostile to the MCA.[97]

Dato Onn apparently feels that MCA is a bar to communal unity. We can only tell him that it is our unshakeable belief that as long as Chinese are discriminated against, the MCA must not only continue to exist—it must also take an active part in politics.[98]

Tan Siew Sin now maintains that his 'first love was the MCA and not the IMP'.[99] He had suddenly come to the realization that the Alliance arrangement was better for the MCA than the IMP. He also asserted that 'Dato Onn was basically suspicious of the Chinese and was distrustful of them', and that Dato Onn was not 'sincere' when he established the IMP; it was purely 'a tactical move'. However, Dato Tan Cheng Lock once again kept quiet in this controversy. He remained formally associated with the IMP for another year.

Towards the end of 1952, when it was fully clear that the IMP had failed, Dato Panglima Bukit Gantang, the Mentri Besar of Perak and a close friend of Dato Onn, wrote to Dato Thuraisingham suggesting that the time had come 'for a few of us to meet in an informal manner but in strict confidence so that we could study the political scene against the Malayan national background'.[100]

[96] Ibid. 18 September 1952.

[97] The resolution on lotteries passed by the Central National Council of the IMP read:

'That this Council condemns the running of lotteries by political organisations the proceeds or part proceeds of which are used for its organisational or political purposes or objectives and is of the opinion that the Government should be asked to prohibit such organisations from running such lotteries'.

[98] The Straits Times, 16 September 1952.

[99] Interview with Tan Siew Sin, Kuala Lumpur, January 1965.

[100] A letter by Dato Panglima Bukit Gantang, 24 December 1952.

He also indicated that the British Commissioner General for Southeast Asia, Malcolm MacDonald, had 'promised to be present at the discussions'. The first of these meetings suggested by Dato Bukit Gantang was held in Ipoh, Perak, on 29 and 30 January 1953 and was attended by the Mentri Besar of Perak (Dato Bukit Gantang), Mentri Besar of Kelantan (Nik Ahmad Kamil), Dato Onn bin Jaafar, Heah Joo Seang, G. Shelley, Yong Shook Lin, Y. C. Kang, Chin Swee Onn and Malcolm MacDonald. The Mentri Besar of Perak asserted that during 1945-8 Malays had great prestige in politics, but their position had deteriorated.[101] The British Commissioner General analysing the contemporary political scene in Malaya said that he was concerned about disunity among the people of the country. The Malays were not united, whereas the Indians and Chinese were united. UMNO had good leaders once. The IMP had leaders but they were lukewarm now. The UMNO-MCA alliance was predominantly Chinese although they claimed to work for communal unity. The main point made by Dato Onn was that the MCA, which was established as a welfare organization, had come under the control of the Chinese Chambers of Commerce and was pursuing politics which reflected the Formosan Government. Towards the end of the discussion the Mentri Besar of Perak suggested the formation of 'a central political body'. The same view was expressed by Malcolm MacDonald who suggested that a central political body was necessary to re-establish cooperation. He gave the analogy of the Round Table Conference regarding the Indian problem. But he added that such an arrangement had the disadvantage that it would have the participation of many officials. He suggested the alternative of an unofficial body called by the political leadership of the country. There could be two or three officials 'like myself in it'. There was the third alternative, according to him, of a new political party. However, he expressed his preference for a central body which later could 'go down to the masses'.

The next meeting of the group was held at the house of Yong

---

101 This information is based on a record of the meeting kept by Dato E. E. C. Thuraisingham.

Shook Lin in Kuala Lumpur on 12 February 1953.[102] The chief issue under discussion was the formation of a central political body. Malcolm MacDonald suggested that they should work through the existing political organizations rather than promote a new political party. P. P. Narayanan, one of the leading trade union leaders present, expressed the view that the IMP should be strengthened. On the other hand, Dato Onn asserted, and this view was supported by Yong Shook Lin, that it was essential to establish a new political party. He held that it was difficult to reconcile the conflicting interests within the framework of the existing political parties. However, a large majority of those present was not keen to establish a new political party and in view of this Dato Onn was in no position to press for the formation of a new political party. The next day, 13 February, the group decided to establish a central body which 'will be created as a result of a conference of leaders which will be convened in the near future'. The central body would have individual members and would have the following aims and objects:

a. National unity and

b. A progressive transfer of power with a view to a complete self-government.[103]

Dato Panglima Bukit Gantang, Yong Shook Lin and Dato E. E. C. Thuraisingham were asked to frame a constitution for the central body. It had been suggested in the meeting that the *mentri-mentri besar* should be requested to play an important role in the central body. It was perhaps felt that they would be successful in securing significant Malay support. As a result the meeting decided that Dato Panglima Bukit Gantang 'should submit a memorandum on the best means of approaching the *mentri-mentri besar* of the Malay States for their support and sympathy'. It was also thought that the proposal of Dato Panglima Bukit Gantang that he should form a political organization in Perak 'on the lines discussed at this

---

[102] Notes on meeting held in the house of Yong Shook Lin, No. 211, Circular Road, Kuala Lumpur, 12 February 1953.

[103] Ibid.

meeting was reasonable and should be treated as a pilot organization'.[104]

The group met again on 16 March 1953 when it was decided to issue a statement in the name of the *mentri-mentri besar* giving a call for a national conference. The statement was issued on 20 March and said:[105]

> It is the historic task of Malayans of all races in this generation to build a united, self-governing Malayan nation. The leaders of the people have the high responsibility to guide them to their destiny.
>
> Several communal associations, political parties and other organizations subscribe to this patriotic aim. They should be partners, not rivals, in working for the cause. With this in view we, the signatories of this declaration, believe that the time has come when all those leaders who strive sincerely for a united, free and independent Malayan nation should take councel together, to consider how they can best, in cooperation forward their splendid ideal. We therefore propose to call a conference for this purpose on 27 April 1953 at Kuala Lumpur . . . .

The Malayan National Conference was held at the Town Hall in Kuala Lumpur on 27 April 1953 with the following organizations taking part: All Malaya Muslim Association, Ceylon Federation of Malaya, Eurasian Association of Malaya, Federation of Indian Organisations, the IMP, Malayan Indian Association, the MIC, Malayan Pakistani Association, Malayan Sikh Association and the Malayan Sinhalese Association.[106] No organizations of the Malays and the Chinese participated in the deliberations. The UMNO, the MCA, the Pan Malayan Labour Party boycotted the conference. Only some *mentri-mentri besar* and prominent individuals like Yong Shook Lin and representative bodies of minorities other than the Chinese participated. The conference appointed a Working Committee consisting of one representative each of

---

[104] This was later to be established as the National Association of Perak in May 1953. See Chapter VIII.

[105] This statement had been drafted by the British Commissioner General, Malcolm MacDonald, and had been presented to the meeting of 16 March 1953 as Paper No. 3 with the heading—Draft Manifesto by the Rt. Hon. Malcolm MacDonald.

[106] *Report of the Working Committee of the Malayan National Conference*, Kuala Lumpur, August 1953.

the above-mentioned organizations and some others 'to make recommendations and report to the conference within three months from the 27th April 1953, as to the steps that should be taken to build a united self-governing Malayan nation'.[107] The committee duly prepared a long report which was presented to a second National Conference held at Kuala Lumpur on 27 September 1953. The report after making detailed recommendations regarding elections, the composition of the Federal Legislative Council, and the Federal Executive Council, concluded:

> ... the Committee recommends that every effort should be made to close the gaps of dissension and opposition which unfortunately exist between political organizations having fundamentally the same aims and objectives.
>
> It is suggested that all political organisations working in the true interests of the country and sincerely striving to weld the plural society of the country into a United Nation, should be prepared to sink differences of opinion and meet together on an equal and representative basis to devise the ways and means to create the United Nation and to achieve that self-government which is the avowed objective of each and everyone of them.[108]

All these, however, were only to be pathetic attempts by Dato Onn bin Jaafar, the father of Malay nationalism, to re-establish himself as the leader of the mainstream of Malayan nationalism.

The UMNO-MCA alliance labelled these recommendations as 'retrogressive in that they proposed to reduce still further the present inadequate participation by the people in the Government'.[109] To them it was 'a brazen effort to delay, for many years, the establishment of popular government in the Federation of Malaya'. And already being at the forefront of the national movement for independence they showed no interest in the pleadings of the National Conference for unity and cooperation among the different political organizations.

[107] Ibid.

[108] Ibid. p. 17.

[109] Statement of the UMNO-MCA Alliance on the report and recommendations of the Working Committee of the Mentri-Mentri Besar sponsored National Conference, 31 August 1953 (mimeographed).

Earlier, the leadership of the UMNO-MCA alliance, sensing that the National Conference was an attempt by Dato Onn to stage a political comeback, had convened a National Convention of their own at Kuala Lumpur towards the end of August 1953. In a resolution it had demanded elections to the Federal Legislative Council in 1954.

Thus failed the attempt to establish a national coalition of all political organizations in the country. And soon, Dato Onn was to direct his attention to the creation of a new party, the Party Negara.

Dato Onn's relations with Dato Tan Cheng Lock and the MCA were at their worst around this time. In a very hard-hitting speech at the IMP headquarters in Kuala Lumpur Dato Onn lashed at the MCA.[110] He alleged that the MCA and the Chinese Chambers of Commerce had joined hands to carry out a plan to make Malaya the twentieth province of China. He asserted that the MCA had assumed the role formerly played by Chinese Consular representatives. The Chinese Chambers of Commerce had become the 'underground Kuomintang Party' which controlled the MCA. He continued:

> I would remind you of the delegation of the Chinese Chambers of Commerce to General Chiang Kai Shek pleading the allegiance of 98 % of the Chinese in Malaya to him . . . .
> I have noted with some interest that moves and demands on behalf of the Chinese population have invariably been initiated by the Chinese Chambers of Commerce and then endorsed by the MCA. Every step that has been taken by the Government in all sincerity for the progress of this country has been objected to by the Chinese Chambers of Commerce.

The Chinese reaction was indignant. MCA branches passed resolutions condemning Dato Onn. Chinese press and Chinese associations gave vent to their anger in no uncertain terms. Dato Tan Cheng Lock, still associated with the IMP, called a protest meeting on 24 May. His son, Tan Siew Sin, who had left the IMP sometime back, went farther and moved a motion of censure in

[110] *The Malay Mail*, 26 March 1953.

the Federal Legislative Council against Dato Onn on 7 May 1953. The motion was defeated (nine in favour, forty against and twenty abstaining). After the motion Dato Tan Cheng Lock called off the protest meeting.[111] Angered by the charges that he was communal and was causing racial disharmony Dato Onn gave vent to his pent up feelings which 'held a packed Federal Legislative Council spellbound for nearly half an hour'.[112] He said:

> It is essential to me that I should go back to a period of my life in order to disprove — as I will disprove — this monstrous allegation against me . . .
> Years ago — 30 years ago . . . in my home state I endeavoured in every possible way to create communal understanding and unity between people who lived in Johore Baharu.
> I endeavoured to persuade the Malays who had exclusively the Malay Club to open its doors to members of other communities . . .
> Later in my life, as I grew older, I took part in Johore State Council. My first motion as a junior member in my maiden speech was to plead with the Johore Government to create a scholarship open to Malays and non-Malays. And also, I was successful.
> I also in Johore State Council pleaded with the Johore Government to approve *padi* land for Chinese even against the wishes of the Malays themselves.
> Is that the desire of a man who wishes to create inter-racial discord?

Referring to his attempts to open membership of the UMNO to non-Malays, he said:

> Unfortunately the time was not ripe, the Malay mind had not been sufficiently tuned that there must be amity and unity in this land and my proposition was rejected until eventually I was forced to leave that organization; to forego the pleasure of being the leader of the Malays, the leader of the organization which I myself had created.
> I had to forego that pleasure because I was convinced in my own mind that there was no other course in this country . . . .
> Having left the UMNO, the present President of the MCA and I agreed to form a non-communal party which would take into its fold members of all races and of all communities. I have kept my part of the bargain.

[111] Ibid. 8 May 1953.
[112] Ibid.

The fatal mistake of the IMP was its decision to contest the Kuala Lumpur municipal elections of February 1952. If it had not blundered into contesting the elections things could have been different for the IMP. The idea of cooperation between the MCA and the UMNO to defeat the IMP would possibly not have taken shape. Also, even if this had been thought of, either it would not have worked or it could not have been extended to the national level. Dato Onn had to leave the UMNO because there was strong opposition to his plan to force the Malays to work with the Chinese and Indians. As late as 30 June 1952, Tunku Abdul Rahman, the new President of the UMNO, had declared in a speech at Serem-ban: 'Malaya is for the Malays and it should not be governed by a mixture of races'. He had further said that Dato Onn by leaving the UMNO and forming the IMP, consisting of peoples of all nationalities, had sold away Malay rights and heritage to other races. [113] With this sort of feeling among the leaders of the UMNO and its rank and file it would have been almost impossible for the MCA and the UMNO to join hands. More, even if an electoral arrangement had been arrived at between the UMNO and the MCA it would not have assumed the significance that it did acquire. With the participation of the IMP, the elections acquired national importance and turned out to be a test of strength among the major political groups in the country. Only two months previously, in the elections for the George Town (Penang) municipal council, in December 1951, the idea of cooperation between the UMNO and the MCA had not yet occurred to the leaders of the two par-ties. The MCA did not even field any candidates. The UMNO which fielded five candidates for the nine seats was able to win only one. In fact, those elections were a great victory for the non-com-munal parties; the local Radical Party had secured six seats and the Labour Party one seat.

The IMP failed to work after the Kuala Lumpur municipal elections because the leadership of the Chinese community did not go with it. Some Chinese leaders like Yong Shook Lin, Khoo Teik Ee and others, who remained loyal to the IMP and worked for it, did not have a strong base among the people of Chinese

[113] *The Straits Times,* 1 July 1952.

origin. Before the Kuala Lumpur elections the leadership of the MCA was not at all certain if the Chinese community would rally round its banner and if the organization could wield political power. There had been no opportunity to test this earlier. The MCA had been established in 1949 primarily as a welfare organization and a large part of its membership had joined the association in order to be able to participate in the very tempting lotteries conducted by it. The leadership of the MCA must have felt that the Association, on its own, could not go very far in protecting the interests of the Chinese community and wielding political power. By this time Dato Onn bin Jaafar, through the UMNO, had emerged as the most powerful political leader in the country. Cooperation with this unchallenged leader of the Malays would not only be beneficial to the Chinese community, but would lead to communal harmony. Moreover, Dato Onn was offering very substantial concessions. As a result they initially went whole-heartedly with Dato Onn and the IMP.

But the Kuala Lumpur elections changed the situation completely. A new and more powerful potential of the MCA became visible. The Chinese community had rallied round the MCA. It could wield political power in its own right. Its six candidates in the predominantly Chinese areas in Kuala Lumpur had all won with large majorities. This opened up altogether new possibilities for the MCA. Cooperation with the UMNO minus Dato Onn was far better than working with him in the IMP. Dato Onn was a tough man, and this was a well-known fact. Cooperation with UMNO meant they could keep their organization, the MCA, intact. More political power could be wielded and greater pressure could be exerted through the organization. Remaining with the IMP would eventually have meant the disbanding of the MCA, and the leadership would not have been able to exert much pressure as unorganized individuals within the IMP.

The Kuala Lumpur elections not only indicated this new potential to the leaders of the MCA, it also affected very seriously the morale of the leaders and workers of the IMP. The party had suffered a crushing defeat in the very first test of strength. Most people who had joined the party with a great deal of idealism became disheartened. Many of them left the party and others ceased to take any active interest. Dato Onn, the founder, had himself started thinking of alternatives.

The Party Negara

In late 1953, soon after the second National Conference, when it had become obvious that it was impossible to establish a national coalition of all political parties in the country because of the refusal of the UMNO and the MCA to cooperate, it was reported in the press that a 'national political party', the Party Negara, would be formed shortly by the Malayan National Conference sponsored by the *mentri-mentri besar*.[114] However, the party could not be launched until the end of February 1954, because of certain differences among its promoters.[115] There was disagreement among the members of the Working Committee of the National Conference on the question of whether the new party should commit itself 'to uphold the position of the Malay Rulers as Constitutional Heads of State'.[116] The first draft of the party's aims had made no mention of it. But because of the insistence of some members of the Working Committee of the National Conference this was finally included in the party's aims.

The new party allowed membership to any person not less than sixteen years of age who was

a. a subject of the Ruler of a Malay State; or
b. a citizen of the Federation of Malaya; or
c. a British subject who has resided in the Federation of Malaya for a period of not less than five years.[117]

The membership qualifications were about the same as those of the IMP which were introduced in September 1952, as part of the new pro-Malay orientation of the party. The new party, however, went a step further when it disallowed membership to the category

[114] Ibid. 1 December 1953.
[115] Ibid. 1 March 1954.
[116] Ibid. 10 January 1954.
[117] *Rules, Party Negara*, February 1954, p. 4.

of persons who had lived in Malaya for at least the past ten years but were not citizens. They had been allowed membership by the IMP. This restriction was to limit severely the entry of non-Malays, especially the Chinese, into the party. However, this did not matter since the new organization hardly looked towards the non-Malays in general and the Chinese in particular for support. The dominant urge was to forge unity among the Malays, the indigenous people. The party 'bears some resemblance to the old UMNO. Its driving force is Malay fear of the Chinese and its main aim a leisurely transfer of power.'[118]

The party, however, called itself 'an all community party',[119] and proclaimed the following as its major aims:[120]

a. To promote national unity.
b. To establish in power a Party Negara Government in the Federation of Malaya.
c. To uphold the position of the Malay Rulers as Constitutional Heads of State.
d. To secure, by constitutional means, the transfer of power and to establish a self-governing United States of Malaya.
e. To promote the political, economic, and social progress of the people.

The party was not able to attract any new support; in fact, a sizeable part of those who had supported Dato Onn and his IMP had serious doubts if Dato Onn and his politics had any future and, therefore, these kept away from the Party Negara. The Malayan Indian Congress, which had formed the most important group within the IMP, did not join Dato Onn's new venture.[121] However, the leadership of the party had a highly exaggerated estimate of the support. In the first issue of *Negara* an editorial jubilantly declared:[122] 'Though only five months old the Party today has

[118] F. G. Carnell, 'Constitutional Reform and Elections in Malaya'. *Pacific Affairs*, vol. XXVII No. 3 (1954) p. 234.

[119] *Negara* (English language organ of the party), No. 1 (August 1954), p. 4.

[120] Ibid. p. 1.

[121] On the other hand the MIC joined the UMNO-MCA alliance in October 1954. Significantly, all MCA leaders who had supported the IMP right up to its end, people like Yong Shook Lin and Khoo Teik Ee, did not join the new party.

[122] Ibid. p. 4.

branches in almost all parts of Malaya — constituting a record in the post-war political history of the country. Never before has any organisation been given so much support by the people in so short a time. In fact, the number of supporters has increased far beyond our early expectations.' By September 1954 the party was able to set up branches in almost all States of the country.[123] But most of these branches, except the ones in Penang, were in the predominantly Malay areas of the country.

The first meeting of the National Council, 'the supreme authority of Party Negara', met in Kuala Lumpur on 15 August 1954, where representatives of thirty-five branches were present.[124] In his address, Dato Onn made an attempt to underline the non-communal character of the new party. He asserted:

> I admit that individuals may form communities; they may create sectional interests; they may establish racial barriers; but it is non-communal institutions or organizations such as Party Negara, which alone can create a nation.[125]

The Council showed its preoccupation with the coming federal council elections when it approved amendments to certain Rules of the Party to enable it to form Divisions of the party in each of the fifty-two Federal constituencies. The National Council further adopted the Party Objectives and Platform 'which flow from the five principles contained in the Rules of the Party'.[126] It com-

---

[123] It had then the following branches:
  Selangor: Kuala Lumpur, Sungei Penchala, Klang and Kepong.
  Negri Sembilan: Seremban, Rembau, Port Dickson and Kuala Pilah.
  Malacca: Alor Gajah, Jasin and Merlimau.
  Johore: Johore Baharu, Bandar Maharani, Segamat and Jurak.
  Penang: George Town, Perak Road, Bayan Lepas, Ayer Itam, Dato Kramat, Kelawei, Sungei Pinang, Bukit Mertajam, Nibong Tebal-Butterworth.
  Kedah: Alor Star.
  Kelantan: Kota Bharu, Budang, Machang, and Tumpat.
  Trengganu: Kuala Trengganu, Dungun, Manir, Marang and Kemaman.
  Pahang: West Pahang.
  Perlis: Chuping and Arau.
  Ibid.

[124] Ibid. September 1954, p. 2.

[125] Ibid.

[126] Ibid. p. 3.

mitted the party to a self-governing United States of Malaya within the Commonwealth of Nations,

> ... in which the special position of Islam shall be recognised as the faith professed by the great majority of the citizens, in which Buddhism, Hinduism and Christianity shall also be recognized as some of the religions existing in the country ....

> ... in which Malay and English shall be recognized as the official languages ....[127]

The party opposed nationalization of any Malayan industry and promised that 'there shall be a preservation and extension of private ownership and enterprise'.

The party's official organ *Negara* in an editorial, 'A Charter for All', declared: 'Another milestone in Malaya's march towards self-government was reached when the Platform and Objectives of Party Negara were approved by the National Council of the Party'.[128] According to it the most significant feature of the party's objectives was its pledge 'to seek adequate representation for minority rights', and it called the document a 'Magna Carta for the freedom of minorities' even though there was no mention of minorities and their rights whatsoever. In fact, the party had taken a pro-Malay position with regard to the two issues of vital interest to the non-Malays: it decided to accord a special position to Islam and to recognize Malay and English as the two official languages of the country. Party Negara had shifted ground significantly. It was only about two years back that Dato Onn had committed himself explicitly to a constitution which would contemplate a secular state in Malaya.[129] Moreover, throughout the short existence of the IMP, its leaders had kept clear of the issue of official language of the country; they had never committed themselves. However, the Party Negara took the position of rejecting the right of the Chinese and the Indians to have Chinese and Tamil recognized as official languages along with Malay and English. The Party's platform had further demanded a 'strictly regulated'

[127] Party Negara, *Objectives and Platform* (mimeographed), 1 August 1954.

[128] *Negara,* September 1954, p. 4.

[129] *The Straits Times,* 12 May 1952.

immigration into the country.[130] In early June 1955, Dato Onn
went farther when he demanded that the Government must restrict immigration of non-Malays by the introduction of a quota
system.[131] He feared that because of the higher birth rates of the
Chinese and the Indians the Malays were doomed to become a
minority community 'in their own country. To the Malay, Malaya
is his only home'.

The fear of the Chinese was also responsible for the party's
desire to seek a much slower transition to independence than that
of the Alliance. In its 'Objectives and Platform' the party did not
stipulate any definite date for the grant of independence. The
Alliance, at this time, however, was promising to secure *merdeka*
within the next four years.

The first elections above the level of city or municipal council
held in the country were the state elections in Johore in early
October 1954.[132] Five Alliance candidates having been returned
unopposed, elections were held for the remaining eleven seats in
the state legislature. Party Negara, the only party to put up candidates against the Alliance, fielded candidates in ten constituencies. Its nominees were eight Malays, one Chinese and one Indian. All Party Negara candidates lost very badly to the Alliance
which captured all the eleven contested seats. The party was to
suffer a similar fate in all the other States where it contested the
elections. Table 3 gives the results in detail.

TABLE 3

1954 JOHORE STATE ELECTION POLL RESULTS

State	Alliance			Party Negara			Independents & Others		
	(1)	(2)	(3)	(1)	(2)	(3)	(1)	(2)	(3)
Johore	78,745	11	11	10,268	10	—	2,525	3	—
Trengannu	54,245	13	13	4,784	10	—	5,087	9	—
Perlis	16,379	9	9	3,472	4	—	4,396	5	—
Penang	47,474	10	10	3,139	3	—	8,165	13	—
Negri Sembilan	8,957	3	3	2,279	1	—	1,166	2	—

(1) Number of votes polled   (2) Seats contested   (3) Seats won

[130] *Objectives and Platform*, op.cit.
[131] *The Straits Times*, 6 July 1955.
[132] Ibid. 11 and 12 October 1954.

The party was not able to secure a single seat in any of the state legislatures. Out of the twenty-eight candidates that it fielded in five different States all except two were Malays. It did not field any candidates in the States of Perak, Selangor, Pahang, Kedah, Malacca and Kelantan. All these States, except Kedah and Kelantan, had very large numbers of non-Malay voters.

In June 1955, it was reported that the party's Central Executive Committee had recommended that it should field only Malay candidates in the elections for the Federal Legislative Council.[133] It further suggested, however, that non-Malays would be recommended by the party for the nominated seats in the Federal Legislative Council.

In the party manifesto for the 1955 elections for the Federal Legislative Council it committed itself to a goal of obtaining independence by 1960.[134] Explaining why the party fixed 1960 as the year of independence the manifesto said:

> ... the date 1960 is not arbitrarily chosen as the nearest rounded number in annual chronology. All parties in the country are committed to the policy of working a new legislature whose alloted span is four years. This takes us to the middle of 1959. If the professions of politicians, within and without the government, are sincere then obviously this interregnum is the necessary and inescapable prelude to full democratic self-government. By the manner in which this period of four years is made to subserve our political purpose, shall we be judged on our fitness to take over full political power.

It promised that if it came to power it would convoke a Constituent Assembly to determine the future constitution of the country. But it hastened to add:

> This does not imply that the position of the Rulers will be short-circuited to their detriment. This Party is aware that an overwhelming majority of the electorate is Malay and to the ordinary Malay peasant the relationship to his Ruler is intimate and strong. It is therefore proposed to take counsel with all concerned and agree upon a political set up which, while recognizing and endorsing that

[133] Ibid. 10 June 1955.
[134] Party Negara, *Election Manifesto, 1955* (mimeographed).

all political power proceeds from the people, will at the same time preserve to the Malay Rulers the functions and privileges of Constitutional Monarchs.

It called for a single nationality in place of the ten separate nationalities. It felt that the existing situation was a 'ludicrous' one: 'For one thing it holds up progress and for another it encourages the sense of separation and division, where our own self-interest demands that there must be more cohesive unity.' On the issue of immigration the party re-asserted its position, in even stronger terms. It asserted that it was 'the Party's objective by suitable legislation to provide a security to the Malays against the risks of becoming a back number in their own country, and also regulate by suitable machinery, such as a quota system, the immigration of nationals of other countries'.

On the question of the national language the party significantly shifted its position. It was only a year back that, at the time of the formation of the party, it had supported both Malay and English as the national languages of the country. It now favoured Malay as the sole national language.

> ... we shall go no forward [*sic*] in promoting the progress of a national language if we divide our loyalty to it with another language however desirable. Much confusion has been caused in the recent past by putting Malay and English on the same footing. The Party therefore proposes that Malay must needs be the only national language of Malaya . . . .

It significantly added:

> But the national language will remain Malay so that in the decades and centuries in the future Malaya as an independent nation will profit by her kinship with Indonesia and other islands of the Eastern Archipelago and not pass into uneasy history as an island of foreign reaction in a sea of Malay culture enriched by Malay tradition and enlivened by the Malay language.

This assertion of kinship with Indonesia is very important for in recent years this has been offered as the solution of the Chinese problem in Malaysia.

In the 1955 elections for the Federal Legislative Council the

Party Negara was the chief rival of the Alliance. It fielded a total of thirty candidates in the fifty-two single-member constituencies. All its candidates, except one (who was a Chinese) were Malays. None was returned; about half of them lost their deposits. The party obtained a total of 79,909 votes, 7.9% of the total.[135] Dato Onn contested the Johore Bahru constituency, his home town, where he was defeated by an Alliance (UMNO) candidate. The result, which is significant, was as follows:[136]

Suleiman bin Dato Abdul Rahman (Alliance)	8,745 votes
Dato Onn bin Jaafar (Party Negara)	2,802 votes

Several other important leaders of the party, people like Dato Nik Ahmad Kamil, lost very badly to the Alliance candidates.

G. Shelley, a non-Malay leader of the party who was also the Vice-Chairman of the Penang Division, felt that it had lost in the 1955 elections because it did not exploit to the full its policy of non-communalism.[137] '. . . We did not stress sufficiently to the electorate that we are a non-communal organization.' However, the feeling of the Malay leadership was very different. They pushed the party into a more pro-Malay position. They had lost all faith in non-communalism and their only hope was to secure the support of the Malays. At the Second Annual National Council meeting of the party, Dato Onn declared that he would never accept a situation where the Malays were controlled by the non-Malays.[138] He threatened, in exactly the same terms as those used by his critics in late 1951 when he was attempting to establish the IMP: 'If the other communities want to control the Malays another "1947 India" will result in this country.' Later, in a speech in Penang, he asserted that he was not anti-Chinese.[139] 'But I will never be a party to making the Malays a back-number, politically, economi-

---

[135] R. K. Vasil, 'The 1964 General Elections in Malaya', *International Studies*, Vol. VII No. 1 (July 1965) p. 60.

[136] Federation of Malaya, *Report on the First Election of Members to the Legislative Council*, Kuala Lumpur, Government Press, 1955, p. 73.

[137] *The Straits Times*, 10 October 1955.

[138] Ibid. 12 December 1955.

[139] Ibid. 10 December 1955.

cally or socially.' Referring to the Labour Party recommendation to the Reid Commission with regard to the Malay Sultans he warned that it was not merely a political or constitutional issue, but a religious one as well. 'The surest way to start racial trouble leading to bloodshed in this country is to tamper with relations between the Malay people and their Rulers.' The Party Negara at this time even thought of merging with the extreme pro-Malay Pan-Malayan Islamic Association (later Pan-Malayan Islamic Party.) [140]

By the time of the 1959 general elections, Party Negara had virtually become a Malay communal party. Dato Onn had adopted an extreme pro-Malay position. In early 1958, he asserted: 'Malays have become aliens in their own land. *Merdeka* means nothing to the Malays as they do not benefit from it.' [141] Waving a copy of the Malayan Constitution he said that it mainly looked after the interests of the non-Malays. At a special delegates' conference of the party he accused the Alliance Party of playing politics with Islam, the religion of the Malays. [142] He stated that the Alliance boast of having made Islam the official religion of the country was empty.

It was as a Malay communal party that the Party Negara contested the 1959 general elections. It fielded seventy-eight candidates in the state elections and nine for the parliamentary elections, all of whom were Malays.

This new role of the party still did not make any significant difference in its electoral support. It was able to secure victories only in the very predominantly Malay State of Trengganu, where four of its candidates for the state legislature and one candidate for Parliament were successful. The solitary successful parliamentary candidate was Dato Onn. The party's seventy-eight candidates for the state elections were able to secure a total of 66,475 votes, 4.2 per cent of the total. [143] In Johore, the home State of Dato Onn and considered to be the party's stronghold, it suffered

---

[140] Ibid. 18 October 1956.
[141] Ibid. 18 March 1958.
[142] Ibid. 24 August 1958.
[143] R. K. Vasil, 'The 1964 General Elections in Malaya', *International Studies*, Vol. VII No. 1 (July 1965).

a crushing defeat. It fielded twenty-one candidates for the state legislature and six for Parliament: all of them were defeated.

Commenting in an editorial, 'End of Negara?', the *Malay Mail* wrote:

> The long series of election defeats, culminating in the disastrous defeat in Johore which Party Negara claimed as its stronghold, must surely have removed the scales from the eyes of the party's leaders.... One of the party's faults appears to have been the emotional appeals which it made a feature in *kampongs* and elsewhere, strongly pro-Malay and using language which many might feel was not best broadcast from a public platform. It seems to have been a deliberate policy stemming from the failure of the strongly inter-racial IMP and the failure of the Party Negara in the 1955 elections.[144]

The party, however, continued to remain in existence, though only in name. It became more and more blatantly communal. The facade of non-communalism was given up. In August 1960, it released its new 'Objectives and Platform' which sought recognition of Islam as the State religion and Melayu as the nationality.[145] It suggested that adequate provision be made 'to enable the Muslims of the Federation to order their lives in accordance with the teachings and requirements of Islam' and that there should be compulsory teaching of the Holy Koran to all Muslim children in the country. It made an extreme demand that the State of Penang be merged with the Malay State of Kedah and the State of Malacca be merged with the Malay States of Johore or Negri Sembilan.

Dato Onn bin Jaafar, father of Malay nationalism and the founder of UMNO, IMP and Party Negara, died in 1962. With him went the reason for the existence of the party. Its chairman, Dato Zainal Abidin bin Abas, left the party in early 1963 to join the newly established United Democratic Party. The party contested the 1964 general elections. Its seventeen candidates in the state elections secured a total of 8,040 votes (0.3 per cent of the total) and its four candidates for Parliament secured 7,310 votes (0.3 per cent of the total).[146] None of the candidates was successful.

---

[144] *The Malay Mail*, 18 June 1959.
[145] 'Objectives and Platform of Party Negara', *Jiwa Negara* (mimeographed).
[146] Vasil, op.cit. pp. 60-61.

The party is still registered with the Registrar of Societies as a political party. However it enjoys little influence. It has a handful of members who keep it existing in memory of Dato Onn bin Jaafar. Thus came to an end a significant attempt at introducing non-communal politics by an important Malay leader.

III

THE LABOUR PARTY

THE Labour Party has been the main ideologically orientated non-communal political party in Malaysia. It was formed as a genuinely non-communal political organization and remained so during the entire pre-Independence period. But with the advent of Independence in 1957, communal pressures and fears manifested themselves more intensely and the party found it increasingly difficult to maintain its non-communal character, appeal and policy orientation. By 1966, the party under its new leaders, the Chinese-educated extremists, came to assume the character of a Chinese communal organization.

Before Independence

The Labour Party of Malaya, which was first started as a group of regional labour parties, was one of the first non-communal political parties to be established in the Federation of Malaya. As early as September 1948[1] the idea of forming a Malayan Labour Party had been toyed with by some leaders of the trade unions of Government employees. However, nothing was done towards the establishment of such a party. The idea was again mooted in October 1950 when some members of the Federal Legislative Council representing labour (these were Government nominees) indicated that they were considering the formation of a Labour Party. On 15 October 1950 the Chairman of the Malayan Trades Union Council, P.P. Narayanan (a Government nominee representing labour in the Federal Legislative Council), announced that the labour group in the Federal Legislative Council had decided to go ahead with the plans to form a Labour Party.[2] However, once

[1] *The Malay Mail*, 6 September 1948.
[2] *The Straits Times*, 16 October 1950.

again no definite action was taken; the pronouncements did not lead to the formation of the party.

The idea of forming a labour party was very nebulous in the minds of these leaders of government employee trade unions. Within the framework of the existing political situation in the country they were not at all clear as to what particular role a labour party would play and what kind of activity it would pursue. Up to 1950 the British had not allowed any representation of the people through elected representatives at any level of administration. Thus, these leaders could not envisage clearly the additional functions of a labour party which were not already being performed by the trade unions.

Therefore, it needed the British announcement of their intention to introduce elections in the municipality of George Town, Penang, to crystallize these ideas. During April and May 1951, the British administration announced the details of the elections and gave the assurance that they would be held in December 1951.[3] This announcement stimulated action. It has, further, been suggested that the British Commissioner in Penang in 1951 played an active role in the formation of the Labour Party and the Radical Party of Penang. Soon after elections for the George Town municipal council were announced, the British Commissioner convened a meeting of the prominent people in Penang and spoke to them about the useful role that political parties could play, and he is said to have encouraged the formation of political parties to contest the elections.[4] A handbill calling on people to join the Penang Labour Party and suggesting why they should join it said among other things:

(1)   The Government itself encourages political parties and the LABOUR PARTY is a properly registered one.

(2)   The Government recognizes the Labour Party . . . .

(3)   Government itself wants people to take more interest in poli-

[3] Federation of Malaya, *Report on the Introduction of Elections in the Municipality of George Town, Penang*, Kuala Lumpur, Government Press, 1951.

[4] Interview with Ooi Thiam Siew, one of the founders of the Penang Labour Party and for several years the Mayor of Penang, Penang, July 1964. Also Sonny Pillay, one of the founders of the Radical Party of Penang, Penang, July 1964.

tics which is after all the running of Government, which in reality is running your own affairs. So you should at once become a member of the LABOUR PARTY, PENANG. The fee is only one dollar a year. Bring your friends and family to join the LABOUR PARTY.

On 8 April 1951, Osman Siru, President of Uniformed Postal Staff Union of Malaya, announced that a group of working people were forming themselves into a Political Discussion Group with the ultimate objective of setting up a political party to contest the municipal elections in George Town. He stated that the idea was to have a group of people to discuss and formulate plans, with a view to getting that group to sponsor the formation of a political party.[5] In pursuance of this Osman Siru and another trade unionist, Yeoh Cheng Kung, jointly convened a meeting on 17 April 1951, which was presided over by Osman Siru. A majority of those present favoured the formation of a political party rather than a discussion group.[6] Osman Siru declared at the meeting that as intelligent citizens of Penang the people present were interested in the forthcoming municipal elections. That indicated the main urge for the formation of the party. Siru also felt that trade unions could protect themselves only by having representatives in the councils.[7] The urge for the formation of the party at this time was neither based on ideological grounds nor for fostering communal harmony.[8]

On 15 May 1951 the Labour Party of Penang was formally inaugurated. The Chairman of the *pro tem* committee, Osman Siru, addressing the inaugural meeting said that among the Chinese, Malays and Indians there were people who were economically poor and politically under-privileged, who were incapable of improving their position because of a dominating monopolistic

[5] *The Straits Echo*, Penang, 9 April 1951.

[6] *Ibid.* 18 April 1951.

[7] This was confirmed by C. Y. Choy, a founder of the Penang Labour Party and a former Labour Party Mayor of Penang, who told this writer that the reason for the formation of the party was mainly to contest the municipal elections of December 1951. Interview with C. Y. Choy, Penang, July 1964. Also interviews with Ooi Thiam Siew, Osman Siru and Rajagopal.

[8] Interview with Ooi Thiam Siew, Penang, July 1964.

economy. 'There cannot be either political or economic emancipation of these under-privileged sections of the community unless there is a political party that plans concerted programmes of
reforms and puts these reforms through the legislative bodies of
the country by properly constituted and established laws.'[9] The
Labour Party aimed at the emancipation of these sections of the
people of all communities not by 'any haphazard or benign' way
but by a planned political economy. The aims, as announced, put
all emphasis on economic questions; no attention was given to
political questions. This was the time when ideas of independence
for Malaya were in the air; when Dato Onn bin Jaafar was working
towards the formation of the Independence of Malaya Party,
committed to secure independence for the country. But the leaders
of the Penang Labour Party chose to keep quiet on the issue of the
end of colonialism in Malaya.

The leaders of the Malayan Trades Union Council had been
contemplating the formation of a labour party for a long time. But
with the formation of the Labour Party of Penang and the announcement at this time of Dato Onn's intention to establish the IMP,
they were caught in an awkward dilemma. On one side, some of
the trade union leaders in Penang, who were associated with the
MTUC, had established a regional labour party over which the
central leadership of the MTUC had no control. On the other side,
Dato Onn announced his intention to establish the IMP soon. In
this situation, P.P. Narayanan, then the President of the MTUC,
convened a meeting of important leaders of the trade union movement on 10 July 1951 to discuss whether those members who
supported the labour party should abandon their aspirations in
support of the IMP. The meeting held in Kuala Lumpur was attended by Dato Onn also and midway through the meeting he was
invited to answer questions.[10] The trade union leaders gathered
at the meeting were very much divided on the issue and they could
not come to an agreement. The issue was again discussed at the
three-day annual conference of the MTUC starting on 24 August
1951 at Kuala Lumpur. And again no decision could be reached.

[9] *The Straits Echo*, 16 May 1951.
[10] *The Straits Times*, 6 August 1951.

The President of the MTUC, P.P. Narayanan, led the group which opposed the formation of a separate labour party and wanted the trade unions to lend their support to the IMP. Narayanan at the time was a member of the Communities Liaison Committee. Narayanan maintains that he opposed the formation of a labour party because he felt that it was very important that all the nationalists in the country remained united and worked together.[11] He believed that the formation of the labour party would create divisions in the national movement as the bulk of organized labour was non-Malay.

Others, who favoured the formation of a labour party, not having been able to secure the support of the MTUC, went on their own and established a labour party in Selangor. These leaders were unhappy about the domination of the IMP by leaders coming from the upper classes — people like Dato Onn, Dato Tan Cheng Lock, Yong Shook Lin, Khoo Teik Ee, — and were unwilling to work with them. They believed, first, that a party with such predominantly upper class leadership would hardly be in a position to look after the interests of the working class; and second, that their own voice would be submerged in the IMP and they would not be able to achieve their goals.[12]

On 23 December 1951, the Labour Party of Selangor was established in Kuala Lumpur. In a statement the party announced that the first of its objects was to strive for the establishment of an independent State of Malaya through constitutional and democratic means.[13] Other objects were to secure an equitable distribution of the fruits of labour by cooperative ownership of the means of production, and the promotion of political, social and economic advancement of the Malayan people.

During this period, similar labour parties, though very much smaller than the ones in Penang and Selangor, were formed in the States of Negri Sembilan, Malacca and Perak.

[11] Interview with P. P. Narayanan, Kuala Lumpur, May 1963.

[12] Interview with Wong Pak Choy, one of the founders of the Selangor Labour Party, Kuala Lumpur, December 1963.

[13] *The Straits Times*, 24 December 1951.

The Leadership

The character of the leadership of the various labour parties is of importance, for these leaders, who in the initial stages were acceptable to the rank and file of the parties, were later to come into conflict with a large part of the new membership. Most of them have now either left the Labour Party or no longer take active part in its activities. Some of those who continue to hold positions in the party today are not trusted by a very large part of the new membership which joined the party after 1956.

One thing common to all of them was their English education.[14] Nearly all of them had been educated in schools with English language as the medium of instruction. The Chinese among them had not been to Chinese-medium schools. This is significant for in later years the Chinese-educated came to constitute a large part of the membership of the Labour Party.

Further, most of them were leaders of 'responsible unions', unions which the British administration had allowed to remain in existence; they were not considered a threat to British rule. Also, a large number of them were government servants. None of them came from 'radical unions' affiliated to the suspect Pan Malayan Federation of Labour. They were also closely associated with the Malayan Trades Union Council, whose formation had been encouraged, if not sponsored, by the British.

This background of the leadership made them suspect in the eyes of the very large present-day Chinese-educated membership of the party. The Chinese-educated believe that the labour parties established in 1951 and 1952 in the different States of the country were encouraged by the British and were meant to be a 'decoration' in the parliamentary democracy which the British had sought to establish in Malaya.[15] They believed that the various labour parties were encouraged by the British to wean people away from the Malayan Communist Party which had been declared illegal

---

[14] Interviews with Ooi Thiam Siew, C. Y. Choy, and Rajagopal, Penang, July 1964.

[15] Interview with Tan Kai Hee, one of the most important leaders of the Chinese-educated of the Labour Party, Kuala Lumpur, July 1964. Since 1965 he has been under detention.

with the start of Emergency in June 1948. They find in it the same pattern as the British sponsorship of the MTUC as a counter to the Pan Malayan Federation of Labour. They allege that the British sponsored the labour parties to attract the working classes, and the Radical Party in Penang to attract people from the professions and the upper classes. They also maintain that the British encouraged the formation of state labour parties rather than an all-Malaya labour party for they were afraid that a single party might eventually become too powerful and threaten their interests.

Membership and Support

The membership of the various parties was very small. The bulk came from ordinary workers (a sizeable portion of them of Indian origin), or the English-educated white-collar workers who were members of the various unions whose leaders had got together to establish the labour parties. In Penang, for example, the party had no mass base. Most of its membership and support came from labour unions in the public services — Municipal and Government Labour Union, Uniformed Postal Staff Union, Clerical and Administrative Staff Union, and the Penang Teachers Union.[16] Support especially came from the unskilled Indian daily-rated workers.[17] A large part of the white-collar workers supported the Radical Party of Penang which achieved a significant success in the December 1951 municipal elections in George Town, Penang.

In Penang, unlike in Selangor where the Selangor Labour Party was formed against the wishes of a section of trade union leaders who had wanted trade unions to support the IMP, many leaders of the Labour Party were sympathetic to the non-communal IMP. At the same time, however, they did not want to fold up their own organization. Therefore, they devised a system of dual membership: the party allowed its members to join the IMP; and most of its members and leaders thus became members of the IMP also. The IMP being more active at the time, many Labour Party mem-

[16] Interviews with C. Y. Choy and Rajagopal, Penang, July 1964, and Osman Siru, Kuala Lumpur, August 1964.

[17] Interview with Ooi Thiam Siew, Penang, July 1964.

bers worked more actively for the former. The Labour Party was
not at all active. Ooi Thiam Siew, one of the leaders of the Labour
Party, was the General Secretary of the Penang Branch of the IMP.

In Selangor, where the membership was even smaller, the character of the party rank and file was no different.[18] However, unlike Penang where Indians accounted for a large part of the membership, in Selangor it was equally divided among Indians and
Chinese. But significantly, in both cases, very little support came
from the Malay community.

The Pan-Malayan Labour Party

Coinciding with the annual conference of the MTUC, representatives of the labour parties of Penang, Selangor, Singapore, Perak
and Malacca and the Saberkas in Kedah[19] met in Kuala Lumpur
on 26 June 1952 to establish a National Council of Malayan Labour
Parties. Seventy-one delegates and observers attended the meeting (the observers came from twenty-one trade unions).[20] At the
meeting P.M. Williams of the Singapore Labour Party said that
the proposed name for the new organization — National Council
of Malayan Labour Parties — gave the impression of a loose organization. He suggested that this could be avoided by naming
the new organization Pan-Malayan Labour Party. The suggestion
was accepted and Mohammad Sopiee and Lee Moke Sang, both
of the Selangor Labour Party, were respectively chosen the chairman and secretary of the Pan-Malayan Labour Party.[21]

The new organization was a very loose one; it was only a confederation of the different labour parties. The constitution did not
provide for direct individual membership. The membership clause
in the constitution stated: 'All labour and socialist organizations,
of democratic composition, which accept the constitution of the

[18] Interviews with Arokiasamy and Wong Pak Choy, Kuala Lumpur, August 1964.

[19] Saberkas, a socialist orientated organization of the Malays, had been formed
towards the end of the Japanese occupation in Kedah. Tunku Abdul Rahman
was the patron of the organization.

[20] Saul Rose, *Socialism in Southern Asia*, London, Oxford University Press, 1959,
p. 211.

[21] *The Straits Times*, 27 June 1952.

party, shall be eligible for membership of the party.' [22] The executive committee consisted of officers of the party elected at its annual meeting, and one member nominated by each of the constituent parties. All decisions required ratification by the executive committees consisting of more than half the member parties, and two-thirds in case of an amendment to the constitution of the national organization.

In a resolution passed at the conference the party declared that the future welfare and security of the country depended on national unity and solidarity. And to 'achieve this, the PMLP believes that the status of citizenship and nationality should be conferred by one central authority and not by the different component parts. Therefore, this meeting of the Party deprecates the present system of State nationalities as a violation of a federal constitution and demands that as soon as possible a single citizenship amounting to nationality be established for Malaya, including Singapore.' [23] The party supported the principle of *jus soli* for the grant of such citizenship. It asserted that 'a Malayan citizenship status be created which shall be available to all persons born in Malaya, and to those who have had a continuous period of ten years' residence in this country and declare to have made this country their permanent home'.

Soon after the formation of the Pan-Malayan Labour Party, on 14 August 1952, the draft of a Policy Statement entitled 'Towards a New Malaya' was issued. The draft began with an indictment of communism in the strongest terms and declared:

The main choice before the country today is between democratic socialism and totalitarian communism . . . .

It is therefore our immediate object to rally the democratic people of this and other countries to oppose this awful tyranny which is threatening to impose itself upon the people. For four years communist terrorism has brought terrible unhappiness to the people of this country, through the violent destruction of life and property. Millions of dollars which could have been spent on the improvement of social services have had to be directed to military purposes for

[22] *Towards a New Malaya*, Pan-Malayan Labour Party Information Bureau, p. 10.
[23] Rose, op.cit. pp. 212-13.

the defence and maintenance of law and order, and the protection of life and property. This drain on the resources of the country must be stopped as urgently as possible, and this can be done by the utter and complete defeat of the communist terrorists.[24]

It further said:

Under present circumstances we place one thing before everything else. Our immediate and foremost task is to restore peace and order in this country.

We must help in the creation, as soon as possible, of conditions in which it will be possible for us to work freely for the establishment of the new society we want for this country.

It is important to note that the document contained no denunciation of British colonialism whatsoever. On the other hand, the statement, under the heading 'Partnership with Britain', said:

The British Government is committed to a policy of preparing this country for self-government. As democratic socialists we seek to create between Malaya and Britain a vital partnership, with the object of making possible a peaceful and rapid transition to genuine democratic self-government in this country . . . .

Of the future relationship between this country and Britain, we can offer no prediction. But of the present we have this to say. Now that Malaya has become the front-line in the world-wide struggle for freedom, it has become abundantly clear that Malaya and Britain are inter-dependent, and are likely to remain so for some time to come. Britain is economically dependent on Malaya. If the partnership between Malaya and Britain is broken, British people would have their standard of life greatly affected. On the other hand, Malaya is at present dependent on Britain militarily.

Through a genuine and equal partnership with Britain and other democratic countries we should be able, through mutual aid on a world-wide scale, to make Britain gradually more and more independent of Malaya economically, and for Malaya gradually to be more and more independent of Britain militarily.

The concern for the standard of living of the people in Britain is interesting. This document is a very clear indication of the orien-

[24] Pan-Malayan Labour Party, *Towards a New Malaya* (mimeographed), 14 August 1952.

tation of many of the leaders of the Pan-Malayan Labour Party in those days and the direction the party was looking to for membership and support.

However, important changes were made to the draft: the anti-communist and pro-British tone of the statement was modified. The final version, which was adopted by the party on 14 September 1952, completely left out the section on 'The Immediate Task' which had contained the denunciation of communism.[25] Also, it changed the section on 'Partnership with Britain', which was recaptioned by the conference as 'Friendship with Britain'. The final version said:

> As democratic socialists we seek to create between Malaya and Britain friendly relations, with the object of making possible a peaceful and rapid transition to genuine democratic self-government in this country. Through this friendship we hope to expand the area of international cooperation between free people ....
>
> It is our belief, however, that for this friendship to be lasting and genuine, it must be one between free peoples.

Mohammad Sopiee (the Chairman), Lee Moke Sang (the Secretary), and C.Y. Choy represented the Pan-Malayan Labour Party at the Asian Socialist Conference held in Rangoon, Burma, from 6 to 15 January 1953.[26] The conference passed a resolution on Malaya which condemned the use of terror whether by the British or the communist insurgents. The resolution was supported by the PMLP delegation. Explaining why the delegation voted in favour of the resolution at Rangoon, the first annual report of the party said:

> Regarding the use of terror, the Malayan delegation supported the resolution because we believed in the principles of British justice. Though British repression, such as collective punishment, could not be bracketed with the inhuman terror of the local Reds, we believed

---

[25] Ibid.

[26] Mohammad Khir Johari (at present the Minister for Commerce & Industry and one of the top-ranking leaders of the UMNO) accompanied the PMLP delegation to Rangoon as an observer. He was then the General Secretary of Saberkas, an affiliate of the PMLP. *The Straits Times,* 2 December 1952.

that any degree of terror was fundamentally wrong. As constitutionalists we preferred the normal process of British justice.[27]

It is obvious that this explanation was for the British authorities rather than the rank and file of the Party. Further, the PMLP delegation supported a move by the Israeli delegation which wanted a fusion of the Asian Socialist Conference and the Socialist International. It was the only Asian party to support the move; all other Asian socialist parties represented at the conference were opposed to the fusion and favoured the formation of a separate Asian organization.[28] The PMLP was not only cut off from progressive elements within Malaya but also the socialist forces in other Asian countries.

It should be noted here that the various pronouncements of the party referred to above did not at all sound like a national programme, the programme of a left-wing socialist party fighting for the independence of the country in the years 1952 and 1953 when almost all the other countries of the region had already attained independence. In all these pronouncements there was no criticism or attack on British colonialism, explicit or implicit. On the other hand, the Policy Statement of the party referred to earlier talked of partnership or friendship with Britain.

At the first Annual Delegates' Conference of the PMLP in July 1953, the first serious attempt was made to consolidate the party organizationally. The affiliate parties, which were very weak and loosely organized, had allowed its members to remain members of other political organizations, especially the IMP. But the first annual conference disapproved of the practice and prohibited all members of its affiliates from continuing their membership in other political organizations.[29] The conference further resolved that the State labour parties should merge into a single organization, with direct individual membership, from 1954.

Then, towards the end of October 1953, the party in a memorandum to the Federal Elections Committee said that it recognized

---

[27] *First Annual Report of the Pan-Malayan Labour Party* (mimeographed), 9 July 1953.

[28] Rose, op.cit. p. 8.

[29] *The Straits Times*, 10 July 1953.

'the need for a gradual transfer of power'. It recommended that a
sovereign independent state of Malaya should be established in
three stages:

Stage I   — 1954-57: Constitution of a Federal Assembly with
              elections by 1954.
Stage II — 1958-60: Formation of a Federal Government by the
              party, or coalition of parties, with a majority of elected
              seats.
Stage III — 1961-64: A fully elected Malayan Assembly with a
              cabinet of 16 Ministers headed by a Prime Minister.[30]

The approach and attitude of the leaders of the PMLP at this
time was a reflection of their background. Many of the top-ranking leaders, such as Mohammad Sopiee (the Chairman) and Lee
Moke Sang (the Secretary), were government servants.[31] Others
were leaders of 'responsible' trade unions which had been encouraged by the British as an alternative to the communist-con-
trolled radical unions. This approach and background of the leadership and the policies formulated by them very much restricted
the chances of securing a large support for the party both as a
national organization working for the independence of the country and as an ideological party fighting for the interests of the
working classes.[32] The membership of the party at this time was
very small. The formation of the central body, the PMLP, had not
resulted in any substantial improvement in its membership. Support from the membership potential of 400,000 was not forthcoming. The party was 'as yet little more than a discussion club

[30] Ibid. 25 October 1953.

[31] Many of these people now hold important positions in the Alliance administration. Mohammad Sopiee was for some time the Director of the Department of
Information in Kuala Lumpur and was recently appointed Malaysian High Commissioner to Ceylon. Lee Moke Sang is the chief Housing Officer in Kuala Lumpur. Osman Siru has been the head of the Tourist Bureau for several years.

[32] However, the first *Annual Report of the Pan-Malayan Labour Party*, 9 July
1953, declared:
    Membership strength of affiliate bodies is showing good signs of increase and
    the potential aggregate membership of the PMLP is more than 400,000 . . . .
    the workers in the estates, in the mines, the factories, the offices-workers
    everywhere are bitterly frustrated by imperial-colonial-feudalist-exploitation
    and they are looking up to the Labour Party to secure for them a fuller, better
    and fairer deal in life.

of social democratic intellectuals deriving scant support from the trade union movement'.[33]

Then about this time, during 1953, a small new group entered the PMLP, in particular in Penang. Some of the prominent persons in this group were: D.S. Ramanathan, Tan Phock Kin, Lee Kok Liang and V. Veerappan. They were very soon to occupy important positions in the party; in fact, they were to lead it for the next several years. Earlier on, they had been associated with the little-known Fabian Society of Penang. The important thing about this group was that their background was quite different from that of the leaders of the PMLP. They were not government servants and none of them was associated with unions of government employees. D.S. Ramanathan was a school teacher and Tan Phock Kin an Australian-trained accountant.

This new group, with its different background, was less susceptible to British influence and felt free to criticize the British and generally take a more fearless and independent stand on issues facing the country. It was also more radical in its socialist orientation. The party, under their influence, started moving farther in a socialist direction and soon attempts were made to consolidate it organizationally.

In early 1954, the party announced its new draft rules which aimed at a centralized organization in place of the loosely organized PMLP. The new leadership further committed the party to 'common ownership of the means of production, distribution and exchange'.[34] Yap Chong Kuen, the Secretary of the Selangor Labour Party, described the new rules as being based on a communist model. He was particularly opposed to the provision relating to 'common ownership' and threatened to move a resolution rejecting the draft rules at a Working Committee meeting of the Selangor Labour Party.[35] Mohammad Sopiee, the Chairman of the PMLP, rejected the allegation and pointed out that the 'com-

[33] F. G. Carnell, 'Communalism and Communism in Malaya', *Pacific Affairs*, Vol. XXVI No. 2 (June 1953), p. 108.

[34] *The Straits Times*, 21 February 1954.

[35] Ibid. 23 February 1954.

mon ownership' provision had been borrowed word for word from the British Labour Party's constitution.[36]

The Labour Party of Malaya

At its second Annual Conference,[37] held in Penang at the beginning of June 1954, the party was renamed the Labour Party of Malaya and a new constitution was approved.[38] Lee Mok Sang, was elected the Chairman and Tan Phock Kin, belonging to the new group, was elected the General Secretary. This was the beginning of a significant change in the character of the party.

The conference passed a number of resolutions. It demanded that the citizenship laws of the country be revised to provide a Malayan nationality for all persons born in Malaya and Singapore and those who were ordinarily resident in these territories for five out of the preceding fifteen years.[39] It further called upon the Government to adopt a non-communal policy in making appointments to the civil service. They felt that the discriminatory treatment of the Government in appointments tended to divide the people instead of uniting them.

The new constitution approved by the conference provided for two types of membership, affiliated members and individual members. Affiliated members were to be trade unions, peasants' organizations, socialist bodies, and cooperative societies 'permitted by law within the Federation of Malaya'. Individual members were to be 'persons of not less than 16 years of age, provided they are not members of political parties or organisations ancillary or subsidiary thereto declared by National Conference or by the

[36] Ibid. 24 February 1954.

[37] The conference was attended by the representatives of the Penang, Selangor, Singapore and Perak Labour Parties.

[38] The actual transformation of the PMLP into the Labour Party of Malaya took place several months later in March 1955 when the party was accorded registration by the Government. A circular letter dated 16 March 1955 signed by Tan Phock Kin, the General Secretary, called upon all branches of the PMLP to 'dissolve your branch and reconstitute as the branch of the Labour Party of Malaya'.

[39] *Proceedings of the Second Annual Delegates' Conference of the PMLP* (mimeographed), Penang, 5 and 6 June 1954.

National Executive Committee in pursuance of Conference decisions to be ineligible for affiliation to the party'.[40] Hitherto, the PMLP had been a loose confederation of independent labour parties, formed in various States and Settlements, with their own set of rules over which the central organization could not exercise any control. But the new constitution provided for Divisions in place of the State and Settlement organizations. These were to be controlled by a Divisional Conference. At the national level the constitution provided for a National Conference, 'the supreme ruling authority of the Party.' There was provision for a National Executive Committee, consisting of a President, one Vice-President, General Secretary, Treasurer, 'one representative from each State and Settlement Division and an equal number of members as those nominated from State and Settlement Divisions to be elected by the National Conference from Conference delegates'. The National Executive Committee was to 'be the administrative authority in carrying out the decisions of the National Conference and in the interpretation of the Constitution'.

In keeping with its changing orientation, towards the end of March 1955, the party for the first time protested against bringing Australian and New Zealand troops to Malaya to fight the Malayan Communist Party.[41]

Then came the 1955 state and federal elections, for which the party had demanded in 1954. In early May 1955, the party issued a ten-point manifesto which, among other things, pledged:

1. Immediate self-government.
2. The union of the Federation of Malaya and Singapore and the creation of a common Malayan nation . . . .
3. The investigation of the workings of the Emergency Regulations and banishment laws with a view to repeal or revision in conformity with the basic concepts of democratic justice.
4. The complete and rapid Malayanisation of the public service by replacement of expatriates.
5. A planned economy directed towards meeting the needs of the

[40] *Constitution of the Labour Party of Malaya* (mimeographed).
[41] *The Straits Times*, 28 March 1955

Malayan people . . . . The Labour Party will strive to prevent the further exploitation of labour for private profit by ensuring public ownership and control of monopolies and inefficient industries.

6. To free the peasants from their heavy burden of debt to unscrupulous landlords and moneylenders by state assistance on the following lines: granting of lands to peasants, establishment of an agricultural producers' cooperative, opening of agricultural banks, formation of collective farming on a voluntary basis.[42]

It should be quite clear that the party had moved significantly from its earlier position. It was willing to commit itself to a measure of public ownership of the means of production and collective farming and condemned the dreaded Emergency Regulations. It was only in late 1953 that the PMLP had announced its three stage transition to complete independence by 1964.

The manifesto argued that the extremely stringent Emergency Regulations would force the country into the arms of the communists. It asserted:

The power of Communism in this country is a real one and we must not minimize the attraction it has for the embittered, the desperate, and the dispossessed. Though the Labour Party regards the activities of Communism as dangerous to the growth of democratic institutions, we feel that we cannot defend a democratic way of life if under the colonial regime we are deprived of the very institutions we are called upon to defend. The best defence against Communism is an immediate and direct stake in democracy. A people cannot be expected to defend a way of life of which they have no direct experience. [43]

However, the party did very badly in the elections. It fielded a total of four candidates for the fifty-two elected seats in the Federal Legislative Council. Two of the candidates contested in

[42] Ibid. 10 May 1955.

[43] Quoted in Rose, op.cit. p. 218. The Chairman of the Penang Division of the party, D. S. Ramanathan, was more explicit in his denunciation. He asserted that Malaya was faced with two 'isms' — colonialism and communism. He said that the Labour Party was aware of the danger of the 'ruthless communist tyranny establishing itself in Malaya. But as democrats and nationalists, we believe that communism can best be fought by a free and independent country.' *The Straits Times,* 24 June 1955.

Penang and one each in Selangor and Perak. None of them was returned; the total number of votes polled by all of them were 4,786, a very insignificant number. In the earlier state elections the party had not fielded any candidate.

The party's support at this time was concentrated mainly in the States of Penang, Selangor and Perak. Also, the bulk of the support came from Indians and English-educated Chinese white-collar workers. The following delegates were present at the important Extra-Ordinary Conference held at Ipoh (Perak) on 7 May 1955 to discuss the party election manifesto:

Chairman: John Emmanuel.
General Secretary: Tan Phock Kin.
Penang Division Delegates: D.S. Ramanathan, Osman Siru, Cheah Thean Ewe, C. Y. Choy, N. Patkunam, V. Veerappan, Tan Tek Lim, Ooi Thiam Siew.
Perak Division: K. R. R. Choudhry, Arasratnam, John Emmanuel, Abdul Karim.
Selangor Division: Lawrence Huang, Tan Tuan Boon, V. David, Zaidi.[44]

The other Divisions of the party only sent a small number of observers. It is important to note here that Johore, which in a few years was to be one of the main strongholds of the Chinese-educated, sent no delegates.

Almost all these delegates were either leaders of trade unions of white-collar workers or men from the professions — school teachers and lawyers. The only exception was John Emmanuel who was a leader of a union comprising largely of Indian rubber plantation workers in Perak. It should further be noted that the Perak Division, which in later years was to be completely controlled by young Chinese-educated Chinese, did not send any Chinese-educated delegates; its delegates consisted of three Indians and one Malay. The same was largely true of Selangor and

---

[44] Labour Party of Malaya, *Proceedings of the Extra-Ordinary Conference held in Ipoh 7 May 1955* (mimeographed). The Second Annual Delegates' Conference was attended by delegates of Labour Parties of Penang, Singapore, Perak and Selangor, *Proceedings of the Second Annual Delegates' Conference of the PMLP,* 5-6 June 1954 (mimeographed).

Penang. The important point is that with this leadership the party could hardly expect to have a mass base.

The lack of any mass support had earlier been reflected in the local council elections. In the Kuala Lumpur municipal elections of December 1952, when the party had a local electoral alliance with the IMP, it fielded two candidates, both of whom lost to the UMNO-MCA Alliance.[45] In George Town, Penang, it fielded three candidates, only one of whom was successful.[46] In December 1954, the party fielded candidates in the muncipal elections in the cities of Kuala Lumpur, Seremban, Klang and Penang; only one of these was successful in Seremban where he defeated an Alliance candidate.[47] The party's candidates in Kuala Lumpur and George Town did very badly.

The utter rout suffered by the party in the 1955 general elections led the leadership to make a reappraisal of the party's organization and working. The party, led by the Penang group which was at the time the dominant group, decided not to contest any elections for one year,[48] and during the period to concentrate on establishing a mass base. Also, at the same time, ideologically the party moved further to the left in an attempt to attract larger support among the working classes, particularly those of Chinese origin.

At the party's Annual Delegates' Conference held on 1 and 2 October 1955, a few months after the elections, a resolution passed by the delegates called the offer of amnesty by the Government to the communists 'more of an ultimatum'.

It said:

> For a Government to dictate peace, it must be in a position to end the Emergency quickly. Since the Government is not able to do so, it should accept the offer to negotiate so that all possibilities of ending

---

[45] *The Malay Mail*, 7 December 1952.

[46] Ibid.

[47] *The Straits Times*, 5 December 1954.

[48] During this period elections were held for the municipal council of George Town. But the Labour Party did not put up any candidates. A leader of the party in Penang who was opposed to this decision, Rajagopal, ignored the party directive, contested the elections, and was therefore expelled. Interview with Rajagopal, Penang, July 1964.

the Emergency can be explored and the resources of the country turned to better use.[49]

The delegates were divided on the issue of multi-lingualism in the Councils. A resolution by the Executive Committee calling on the Government to permit the use of Chinese and Tamil languages in all councils drew conflicting views. And as a compromise it was decided to refer the matter to the Divisions for discussion.[50] A Selangor delegate was very critical of the party for not having accepted the resolution. He said that it was evident from their treatment of the resolution that the English-educated leaders were out of touch with the rank and file.[51]

At this conference the party came under the complete control of the Penang group; D.S. Ramanathan of Penang was elected the Chairman and Tan Phock Kin, also of Penang, was re-elected General Secretary. And the party moved further towards a 'progressive' posture. In its memorandum to the Alliance Merdeka (Independence) Mission at the beginning of January 1956 it said that there was no place for the nine constitutional heads of States if Malaya was to be a nation.[52] The only satisfactory solution, it suggested, lay in acknowledging the sovereignty of the people, rather than that of the Sultans. It summarized its position thus:

> What we are concerned with most is whether Malaya is going to be a true democracy with equal rights and opportunities for all its citizens or whether it is going to be an oligarchic state with local feudalists and capitalists replacing colonial exploiters.

This changing orientation of the party, its swing to a 'progressive' and anti-colonial posture, started attracting some new members and supporters from about the end of 1955. These new entrants were generally young Chinese-educated ordinary workers. Possibly some of the new members were communists instructed to

---

[49] *The Straits Times*, 3 October 1955.

[50] The text of the resolution was: 'This Conference resolves that since Malaya is a polyglot country containing various races, the use of the Chinese and Tamil languages should also be permitted in councils at all levels, as the Chinese and Tamil form half the country's population.'

[51] *The Straits Times*, 3 October 1955.

[52] Ibid. 3 January 1956.

infiltrate civil politics after setbacks in the armed struggle to 'liberate' Malaya. Since about 1954 the Selangor State Division already had a group which was Chinese-educated.[53] The leader of this group was Tan Tuan Boon, a court interpreter. Their position was now strengthened with the entry of some Chinese-educated members in some of the southern States like Johore, Malacca and Negri Sembilan. The Selangor group was soon to make an attempt to move the party further to the left and to wrest leadership from the Penang group.

On 15 January 1956, the Selangor Division approved in principle the formation of a Malayan Peace Front which was to agitate for the end of the Emergency possibly by urging the Government to recognize the Malayan Communist Party.[54] The organisers of the Front expected support from the Party Raayat of Ahmad Boestaman which was being launched.

The Chinese-educated group in the Selangor Division was unhappy with a number of leaders who had entrenched themselves in the Kuala Lumpur branch.[55] They found that the Kuala Lumpur branch always enjoyed a special position; many of the top leaders of the party were from the Kuala Lumpur branch which was a branch mainly of English-educated affluent professional men. There was always a contradiction between the aspirations and orientation of the Chinese-educated and the English-educated. Matters came to a head between the two groups during February-March 1956. The Selangor Division, controlled by the Chinese-educated, dissolved the Kuala Lumpur branch and expelled its Chairman, S.S. Nayagam, a leader of the Central Electricity Board Employees Union. The National Executive Council of the party took the side of the Kuala Lumpur branch and declared that the action of the Selangor Division was unconstitutional. On 18

[53] Interview with Tan Kai Hee, one of the most important Chinese-educated leaders of the Labour Party, Kuala Lumpur, July 1964.

[54] *The Malay Mail*, 16 January 1956.

[55] The Kuala Lumpur branch of the Labour Party has always been considered a centre for the English-educated. There are a number of other branches in the city — Pudu, Bungsar, Batu Road, Bukit Bintang, etc. — which have a predominantly non-English-educated membership and leadership. Some of these, especially the Pudu branch, are very radical. These branches function outside the control of the Kuala Lumpur branch.

March 1956, it suspended the Selangor Division and appointed a five-man committee to take over its administration and organization.[56]

The rebel Selangor Division retaliated, after securing some support in the Malacca, Johore and Negri Sembilan Divisions, by convening an extra-ordinary national conference on 22 April 1956, bypassing the national leadership of the party.[57] This conference decided to expel the National Executive Committee of the Party. Later on 5 August, the same group convened the '4th National Delegates' Conference' at the party's headquarters in Kuala Lumpur.[58] The conference was attended by twenty representatives and observers from the Selangor, Negri Sembilan, Malacca and Johore Divisions (Johore and Malacca Divisions sent only five observers). The resolutions approved demanded, among other things:

1. Recognition of the Malayan Communist Party and an end of the Emergency.
2. Acceptance of the principle of *jus soli* and citizenship for all those resident in the country for five years.
3. Withdrawal of all foreign troops in Malaya immediately as their presence maintained the colonial domination of the country.
4. Nationalization of the transport industry.
5. Merger of Singapore with the Federation of Malaya.

The 'conference' also elected a new set of officials. D.S. Ramanathan, one of the leaders of the group against whom the fight was directed, was curiously elected a Vice-Chairman. Other office-bearers elected were: Yong Kong Yim, See Toh Fatt, Low Chee Men, Gan Yong Beng, Gan Boon Puak, Puah Goh Kin, Lim Sin Poh, Thum Kim Kin, and Ku Sin Kuang. Excepting three of these, who were about 35 years old at the time, all the others were very young.[59]

However, very soon they were to be divided among themselves.

[56] *The Straits Times*, 19 March 1956.
[57] Ibid. 23 April 1956.
[58] *Proceedings of the 4th National Delegates' Conference* (mimeographed), Kuala Lumpur, 5 August 1956.
[59] Interview with Tan Kai Hee, Kuala Lumpur, 8 September 1964.

One group led by Tan Tuan Boon maintained that it was better for them to get out of the Labour Party and wage the fight against the English-educated from outside.[60] On the other side, the group led by Gan Yong Beng believed in fighting from within. Initially many of the Chinese-educated went out of the party with Tan Tuan Boon. However, when they found that it was difficult to launch a new party they came back into the Labour Party and joined the group led by Gan Yong Beng.[61]

This was essentially a showdown between the Chinese-educated and the English-educated in the Labour Party. The victory of the English-educated, mainly the Penang group, in maintaining their position stopped for the time being entry of any new groups of Chinese-educated. It was only later in 1958 and 1959 that large numbers of Chinese-educated of working class origin were to enter the party.

In the meantime the visit of the Reid Constitutional Commission set up by the British Government to recommend a constitution for Malaya was announced. The Labour Party initially had opposed the formation of the Commission.[62] It had declared on 2 January 1956: 'The Alliance's desire to pass the buck to an independent commission is understandable but our view is that Malayan problems must be solved by Malayans themselves.'[63] But once the Commission was constituted they did not boycott it and decided to submit a memorandum outlining their proposals for a Constitution of Malaya.

The memorandum, announced on 28 September 1956, said that the Labour Party rejected 'the false premise that Malaya belongs

---

[60] On 21 May 1956, Tan Tuan Boon announced the formation of the new Labour Action Party. However, this only remained an announcement; the party was never formed. *The Straits Times*, 22 May 1956.

[61] Until recently Gan Yong Beng was the Chairman of the Pudu Branch of the Labour Party in Kuala Lumpur.

[62] *The Straits Times*, 3 January 1956.

[63] The Party Raayat, which later was to become a partner of the Labour Party in the Socialist Front, boycotted the Commission and declared in a statement on 15 July 1956: 'The constitution of an independent country should be framed by the people of the country through an elected constituent assembly and not by a commission imported from foreign countries.' *The Malay Mail*, 16 July 1956.

to any one race and believes that if the proposed constitution is to be based upon this pernicious theory, all hopes of creating a Malayan nation will have to be abandoned'.[64] It opposed any attempt by one race 'to dominate other races or to maintain and extend its privileges over the others', and said:

> All Malayan nationals shall enjoy equal rights and share equal responsibilities. The Labour Party does not regard the safeguarding of the special position of the Malays as a provision which will benefit the Malays in the long run, inasmuch as any special treatment usually results in unfitting rather than fitting the recipient for any active and useful role in society.... There seems to be no reason for perpetuating an anomaly which would only preserve the status quo and tend to render the Malays more unfit to make the contributions towards the progress and development of Malaya....

The party demanded the abolition of the system of dual nationality and asserted:

> In a country the size of Malaya with a population of over six million, there are now nine nationalities and one federal citizenship. We consider this set up to be something unique in constitution-making as to be unparalleled anywhere else in the world.

With regard to the language problem the memorandum recommended Malay as the national language and English as a second language.[65] It asserted that a new Malayan society could not be created unless there were adequate means of communication among the people of different racial origins. It suggested that Malay which was already being used as a *lingua franca* by the people could serve this purpose. Further, it felt that it was of absolute necessity to continue the study and use of English, 'a world language', especially in higher education, if the country was to progress as a modern state. It also, however, pleaded for multi-lingualism; it recommended that 'the English, Chinese and Indian languages be taught in schools and spoken in the councils'. It said that 'every-

---

[64] *Memorandum to the Reid Constitutional Commission*, submitted by the Labour Party of Malaya, Penang, 25 September 1956.

[65] In later years when the party came under the influence of the Chinese-educated it was to oppose vehemently the use of English, the language of the colonial masters.

thing must be done to promote and foster the development of these cultures and languages in the Malayan context. There can be no conflict of cultures when there is harmony in the political sphere. The acquisition of an additional language adds to the breadth and development of human personality.'

The memorandum recommended a unitary type of government and said that the multiplicity of governments was 'wasteful, extravagant and inefficient' and was 'merely a relic of the system of "indirect rule" which dominated the minds of the British colonialists of a generation and more ago'. It further said that if the Commission favoured a federal form of government a 'provision should be made in the constitution for the unification of all the States and Settlements and procedure should be laid down . . . .' It also demanded that Singapore should no longer be 'artificially' separated from the Federation of Malaya, 'and that neither strategic arguments from imperial interests, nor narrow racial arguments from extreme communal elements should be allowed to prevent the unification of the two territories'.[66]

On the extremely touchy issue of the position of the Sultans in Independent Malaya the Memorandum recommended:

The general tendency in Southeast Asia is towards republicanism, but the present leaders of the Alliance, mainly a Party of Privilege, have by subtle and skilful propaganda, led the Malay masses to believe that their interests are identical with those of the Malay Royalty and Ruling Classes. In deference therefore to present Malay feeling on this question, the Labour Party recommends that the present Rulers be made Constitutional Heads of their respective States with restricted powers and privileges to be strictly defined in the Constitution. The Labour Party recommends, however, one important proviso thereto, namely that when the question of a successor to any of the present Rulers comes up for consideration in due course, the

[66] It is interesting to note here that no mention was made with regard to ascertaining the wishes of the people of Singapore before it was merged with the Federation of Malaya. But later, at the time of the formation of Malaysia in 1963, the Labour Party was to oppose the formation of Malaysia in the manner it was being effected by the Alliance Government. Their view was that the people of Singapore had not been given an adequate opportunity to express their views with regard to the merger of Singapore with Malaya.

entire voting population of the State concerned should be given opportunity, by means of a referendum, to express their feelings and views on the matter.

The Memorandum also called for an elected head of State, to be called the President of Malaya.

The party declared its opposition to a religious state and stated that it 'wishes to emphasize that only by the creation of a secular state can religious peace, and consequently, civic harmony, continue to flourish in Malaya'.

The party, throughout its existence thus far, had never found significant support among the Malays. Its small number of Malay leaders, through their personal contacts and influence, had earlier been able to attract a handful of Malays to work for the party. But with the publication of the party's Memorandum to the Reid Constitutional Commission in late September 1956, most of these, including Osman Siru (one of the founders of the Penang Labour Party), left the party.[67] The position taken by the party with regard to some of the issues of communal significance was unacceptable to the Malays.

It was at this time in late 1956, soon after the publication of its Memorandum to the Constitutional Commission, that the first significant breakthrough for the party in its attempts to secure electoral support came. In the municipal council elections of December 1956 in George Town, Penang, all the five candidates of the party were successful; all achieving convincing victories over the Alliance candidates.[68] This was a result of the substantial disenchantment among the Chinese with the MCA and its role in protecting their interests. They had come to feel that the leadership of the MCA, in order to maintain the Alliance in existence, had not strongly pursued their interests.[69] Also, the Labour Party's efforts during the last year or two to strengthen its organization

---

[67] Interview with D. S. Ramanathan, the Chairman of the Labour Party in 1956, Penang, August, 1964.

[68] *The Straits Times*, 3 December 1956.

[69] Similar feelings among the Chinese in Perak enabled the People's Progressive Party to score its first crucial electoral victory in a by-election in Ipoh in November 1957. See p. 232 below.

and its ideological swing to the left had contributed to the electoral success.

This gave the party for the first time control over the George Town Municipal Council, which it retained until 1966. This was significant, for first, it strengthened the position of the Penang group in the leadership of the party, and second, it gave the party an opportunity to establish a popular base in Penang through its control of the Municipal Council.[70]

It is important to underline here that thus far the Labour Party had never subjected its principles, programme and ideology to the compulsions of a plural society. It stuck to its principles, rightly or wrongly, and did not make any significant compromises purely to please one community or another. It never did give up, on the whole, its position on any issues only because of the consideration that this could alienate one community or the other. It never attempted to establish a communal appeal. For example, an official report of the proceedings of the extra-ordinary conference of the Labour Party held at Ipoh on 7 May 1955 to discuss the party manifesto for the 1955 Federal Legislative Council elections states:

> Comrade Karim [a member of the National Executive Committee from Perak] expressed the view that references to the Rulers may antagonise the Malays and this may deprive the party of substantial Malay support. However, the Conference agreed with the sentiments expressed by Comrade Siru that this need not necessarily be so and that the Party should be guided by principles.[71]

And no changes were made in the draft of the manifesto submitted by the Penang Division.

However, prospects of independence changed the situation significantly. Approaching independence sharpened communal antipathies; fear and distrust among the different racial groups increased. The protecting British were to be no more. Consequently, the party gradually embarked on a new course which eventually led to a weakening of its non-communal character and

---

[70] Similarly, in the case of the People's Progressive Party, a substantial part of its popular support in and around Ipoh has come through its control of the Ipoh Municipal Council.

[71] *Proceedings of the Extra-Ordinary Conference* (mimeographed), Labour Party of Malaya, Ipoh, 7 May 1955.

it found itself, to a significant degree, championing the cause of the non-Malays, especially the Chinese. And the conversion of the ruling Alliance Party into an instrument of Malay supremacy and the MCA and the MIC losing their position of equality with the UMNO in the Alliance contributed substantially to this change. The process was further strengthened by the party's link up with the Party Raayat in the Socialist Front.

After Independence

The Labour Party's decision in mid-1957, at the time of independence, to join hands with the newly-established Party Raayat to form a united front was a recognition of the realities of the communal situation in the country and an admission of its own inability to get over it. It was an admission of the party's failure to attract significant support among the Malays. Therefore, the decision to link the party with the then almost exclusively Malay Party Raayat and establish an Alliance-like ideologically-orientated Front. In the pre-independence period it was merely the attraction of the idea of democratic socialism which had brought many Chinese and Indians together into the Labour Party. In their ideological commitment, support of the Malay community or lack of it was of no real consequence. It did not matter if the Malays could not be attracted to democratic socialist ideals. Also, during the pre-independence period, at least until 1955, elections were restricted only to the town and municipal levels, where a sizeable proportion of the electorate was non-Malay. The party had succeeded in capturing control of the Municipal Council of George Town in late 1956 when it had little support among the Malays. But independence changed the situation drastically. The party could now capture political power and endeavour to establish socialism in the country which it could not have attempted when Malaya was ruled by the British. This change made it imperative for the Labour Party to organize support within the Malay community. Without some support among them, representing the largest racial group in the country, it could never hope to capture political power.

Talks for the formation of the united front had begun as early as September 1956. But negotiations dragged on and it was only the approaching transfer of power which stimulated the parties to action. About a month before independence, in late July 1957, it was announced that the two parties had agreed to form a united front.[72] According to an official spokesman the immediate objective of the front was to contest the 1959 general elections in which it hoped to defeat the Alliance. Nevertheless, the consequences of the alliance of these two disparate groups went far beyond the 1959 general elections.

From this time on until January 1966, when the Socialist Front ceased to exist, the Labour Party functioned as a member of the Front along with the predominantly Malay Party Raayat. This has been of great significance. There was soon to emerge an understanding that the Party Raayat would concentrate on extending its influence within the Malay community and the Labour Party would restrict its activities to gathering more support among the non-Malays.[73] The result was that the Labour Party gave up all ideas of attracting Malays, which would have strengthened its non-communal character. Its policy orientation and activities, gradually over the years, became geared to building a mass base among the non-Malays, especially the Chinese. The culmination of this process was the break-up of the Socialist Front in early 1966 when the Party Raayat refused to cooperate with the Labour Party which was by then very largely Chinese. And the Labour Party, not having to bother about maintaining the existence of the Socialist Front, was pushed further to a pro-Chinese position during late 1966 and early 1967.

It was at this time, soon after independence, that Chinese-educated Chinese of working class origin in towns and New Villages began to join the Labour Party for the first time in significant numbers in the States of Selangor, Penang, Negri Sembilan and

---

[72] *The Malay Mail*, 29 July 1957.

[73] Presidential Address by D. S. Ramanathan at the 6th Annual National Conference, Seremban, 17-18 October 1959 (mimeographed), p. 2. D. S. Ramanathan had said that when the two parties were linked together in 1957 the idea was 'that while the Labour Party concentrated on the workers in the towns and cities, the Party Raayat would concentrate on the peasants and agricultural workers in the rural areas'.

Malacca. As we shall see later, they were to join the party in much
larger numbers during 1958 and early 1959, and again after July
1959 following the crisis in the Alliance, especially in Johore,
Selangor and Penang. They had both strong left-wing sympathies
and a Chinese chauvinist position on communal issues. But their
small number within the party did not allow them to make a significant impact on the policy and programme of the Labour Party.
The party maintained its strongly non-communist orientation and
its moderate English-educated leadership. D.S. Ramanathan and
Tan Phock Kin, both of Penang, continued to hold the key positions of Chairman and General Secretary respectively during 1957
and 1958. And the Executive Council was almost entirely comprised of English-educated moderates. At the 5th Annual Conference in August 1957, D.S. Ramanathan stressed that the Labour
Party was opposed to communism.[74] He asserted:

> We detest their methods of regimentation and their total disregard
> for human personality. We also cannot agree with their doctrine
> that the ends justify the means because, as social democrats, we feel
> that the ends are contained in the means.

Later, in October 1957, denying the charge by Tunku Abdul Rahman, the Prime Minister, that the Labour Party was 'openly in
sympathy' with the communists, Ramanathan asserted that his
party was as much opposed to communism as the UMNO.[75] And
explaining the party's demand for the recognition of the Malayan
Communist Party, he added:

> It is true that we have asked for legal recognition of the Communist
> Party, but it is with the important proviso that the Communists lay
> down their arms and agree to abide by the laws of the country and
> work only for constitutional change.
>   We feel this would be a better way to keep them in check than
> by letting them enter the stream of Malayan society and infiltrate
> other parties.[76]

[74] *The Straits Times*, 25 August 1957.

[75] Ibid. 19 October 1957

[76] At the Annual Conference of the party in August 1958 a resolution to congra-

This attitude of the Labour Party towards communism and the Malayan Communist Party was to change significantly starting from 1959 with the entry of large numbers of radical Chinese-educated.

On 30 April 1958, the Registrar of Trade Unions of the Federation of Malaya cancelled the certificate of registration of the powerful and almost entirely Chinese National Union of Factory and General Workers. This made the union an illegal body. In the Legislative Council, the Minister of Defence, Dato Abdul Razak bin Hussein, maintained that the political aims of the Malayan Communist Party and the banned union were identical.[77] He quoted from a directive from the Secretary-General of the union, V. David,[78] to its branch officers which asked them to

> ... point out to the rank and file members that through militant trade unions only the emancipation of the working class could take place. Tell the workers to be prepared for a working class revolution. A working class revolution could only bring a change in the political, economical, and social life of the toiling masses.

The union had very extensive support among the Chinese working classes. Trade unions not suspected by the Government and mostly members of the British-sponsored Malayan Trades Union Congress had not been able to attract the Chinese worker; these unions were generally participated in and led by Indians. Once the Union of Factory and General Workers was disbanded most of its leaders and members sought to join the two member parties of the Socialist Front, the Labour Party and the Party Raayat. They first attempted to enter the more radical and smaller Party Raayat. They were suspicious of the English-educated

---

tulate President Sukarno and the people of Indonesia for the successful extermination of the pro-Western rebel government in Sumatra was defeated. Ibid. 25 August 1958. But later, under the influence of the Chinese-educated radicals the party was to assume a pro-Sukarno and pro-Indonesian position from the time of the Indonesian confrontation against Malaysia.

[77] Federation of Malaya, *Legislative Council Debates*, 1 May 1958, p. 4722.

[78] V. David was soon to be arrested. But curiously he was released within a few months, which was extremely uncharacteristic of the Malayan Government in the light of recent experience. Later David was to emerge as one of the senior leaders of the Labour Party.

moderate leadership of the Labour Party and further believed that in the larger party they would have difficulty in asserting their viewpoint. Party Raayat attracted them more: first, it was a small party and they could more easily take it over, and second, ideologically it was closer to their position than the Labour Party. However, soon after they started joining the Party Raayat its Malay leadership refused to take too many of them into the party.[79] The view of the Party Raayat leadership was that a large number of Chinese in the party would change its racial balance. As a result most of them joined the Labour Party during 1958 and early 1959.[80] Tan Kai Hee, who himself had joined the Labour Party in 1958 after the dissolution of the National Union of Factory and General Workers, states that during 1958-9 more than a thousand members and most of the leaders of the Union joined the Labour Party in the States of Selangor, Johore (a very large number), Negri Sembilan and Perak. Only about 200 of them under the leadership of Thong Yee joined the Party Raayat in Perak and another small group in Johore under the leadership of C.C. Yong.

With independence, the communist propaganda of waging a war of liberation against British colonialism lost much of its effectiveness. By 1958, there was a very considerable decline in the fortunes of the Malayan Communist Party. For all practical purposes the Emergency was over. The communists knew they were beaten. They were not able to organize anything beyond stray incidents. The general elections scheduled for 1959 forced them further to try to enter the existing legal political organizations and capture power through them. In late June 1958, a Malayan Communist Party document dated 1 June 1958 was captured by the Government which said:

Concerning next year's federal general elections:
Our attitude is to support the general elections, but our basic principle is:

[79] Interview with Tan Kai Hee, one of the important leaders of the National Union of Factory and General Workers and later a top-ranking leader of the Chinese-educated in the Labour Party. Kuala Lumpur, July 1964.

[80] Ibid.

1. To bring about the downfall of the Alliance in the general elections for the victory of the political parties of the Socialist Front, such as Party Raayat, the Labour Party, the People's Socialist Youth League ....[81]

In pursuance of this policy many Malayan Communist Party workers left the underground and swelled the ranks of the Labour Party during 1958-9.[82] They also brought with them their sympathisers and supporters who now could openly work with them.

Furthermore, as we have already noted, the crisis in the Alliance in mid-1959, just before the parliamentary elections, had created very widespread dissatisfaction in the Chinese community and many who had traditionally supported the MCA, the communal organization of their community, were disillusioned with its role and left it. In Perak, they now supported the People's Progressive Party and some MCA dissidents (notable among them being Too Joon Hing, the former Secretary-General of the MCA), who contested the elections as independents, were later to help establish the United Democratic Party. In Negri Sembilan they supported the MCA dissidents like Chin See Yin and Quek Kai Dong, who contested the elections as independents and later were to sponsor the formation of the United Democratic Party. But, as can be seen later, the People's Progressive Party had no organizational base outside Perak, in the other non-Malay majority States of Selangor, Johore, Malacca and Penang and, therefore, was not in a position to attract the dissatisfied Chinese in these States. Also, in these States there was no prominent MCA dissident who could organize them. In Penang, the former President of the MCA, Dr. Lim Chong Eu was not inclined to build up a new political base on the basis of these dissidents. As a result, these Chinese had no choice; they had to move into the ranks of the Labour Party which already had become a party with a predominantly Chinese membership. It was under these circumstances that a very sizeable number of the former supporters of the MCA joined the Labour

---

[81] *The Straits Budget*, 3 July 1958, quoted in G. P. Means, 'Malayan Government and Politics in Transition', unpublished Ph. D. thesis submitted to the University of Washington, 1960, pp. 376-7.

[82] Interviews with D. S. Ramanathan and V. Veerappan, Penang, August 1964.

Party in Johore, Selangor and Penang.[83] Their number was larger than the Chinese-educated who had entered the Labour Party following the disbanding of the National Union of Factory and General Workers and in pursuance of the Malayan Communist Party strategy. The result was that the Labour Party increased very substantially its membership and the number of branches in the States of Selangor, Johore and Penang during late 1959 and 1960.

TABLE 4

GROWTH OF THE LABOUR PARTY OF MALAYA, 1958-60

State	Total Number of Branches		
	1958	1959	1960
Johore	15	14	57
Selangor	18	27	54
Penang	18	14	32
Malacca	12	17	31
Perak	9	3	21
Negri Sembilan	10	10	21
Pahang	—	12	19
Kedah	4	3	9
	86	100	244

Source: Labour Party of Malaya, *Annual Report for 1959 and 1960.*

As for the membership of the party a rough idea can be secured from the membership subscription to the different State Divisions for the years 1956, 1959 and 1960.

---

[83] One of the prominent MCA dissidents to join the Labour Party in Johore was Dr. Wee Lee Fong, who later emerged as a senior leader of the Chinese-educated and the party's Secretary-General in 1964.

TABLE 5

MEMBERSHIP SUBSCRIPTION TO THE CENTRAL PARTY BY
DIVISION 1956-60

State	1956	1959	1960
Johore	51.00	225.00	4,946.20
Selangor	101.00	—	2,382.25
Penang	151.00	480.00	1,776.00
Malacca	26.00	150.00	561.60
Perak	51.00	592.80	919.20
Negri Sembilan	76.00	377.60	228.40
Pahang	—	124.40	372.80
Kedah	12.50	320.40	136.80
Malayan $	468.50	2,270.20	11,323.25

Source: Labour Party of Malaya, *Annual Report* for 1956, 1959 and 1960.

The party's annual conferences which used to be attended by about twenty to thirty delegates in the pre-independence period started attracting much larger numbers during this period.[84]

TABLE 6

NUMBER OF DELEGATES AT ANNUAL CONFERENCES* 1959-60

State	1959	1960
Johore	37	103
Selangor	21	55
Penang	31	31
Malacca	12	14
Perak	5	20
Negri Sembilan	9	12
Pahang	1	11
Kedah	4	9
Total	120	255

Source: Labour Party of Malaya, *Annual Report* 1959 and 1960.

Note (*) The representation of the Divisions at the Annual Conference is determined by the numbers of members of the party in the Division.

[84] In both the 1955 and 1956 annual conferences the Johore Division had sent only a small number of observers and no delegates. Addressing the 8th Annual Conference in August 1960, Dr. Wee Lee Fong, the leader of the Johore Division delegation, said

The Johore Division is proud of its record. In the 1958 Conference it had only one delegate. In 1959 it had 37 and today the number has increased to 103. At the moment the Division has 51 branches, and 15 more in the course of being formed (Labour Party of Malaya, *Annual Report*, 1960).

Soon the new entrants were to secure representation in the national leadership of the party. At the 7th Annual National Conference held in October 1959, three important representatives of the Chinese-educated, Tan Kai Hee (Johore), Ng Ann Teck (Selangor) and Chong Chen Wen (Malacca), were for the first time elected to the National Executive Council.[85] Also, V. David, the former Secretary-General of the National Union of Factory and General Workers and closely associated with the Chinese-educated, was elected to the Executive. At the same time, D.S. Ramanathan, the Chairman of the party since October 1955 and one of the most strongly anti-communist leaders, gave way to Ishak bin Haji Mohammad who was unanimously elected the Chairman.[86] Ishak, one of the most prominent radical left-wing Malays from the pre-war period, was a former President of the banned Malay National Party suspected of communist and pro-Indonesian leanings.

Most political parties achieve a measure of ideological clarity with time. In the case of the Labour Party the process has been the reverse. In the early fifties the party had a clearly defined ideological base. But the influx of large numbers of Chinese-educated Chinese, with their communal orientation and extremist ideological commitment, and the party's membership of the Socialist Front made it difficult for the Labour Party to define its ideology and programme clearly. The communally-orientated Chinese, the extreme leftists, and the moderate English-educated leaders all pulled the party in different directions.

It was in this situation that the Labour Party, facing the federal elections of 1959, had to formulate and present its policy. The 6th National Conference, in August 1958, accepted a Policy Statement, *Labour Plans for Malaya,* which made the chief point that with *merdeka* there had been a radical transformation in the political system, but this change was '. . . meaningless if our economic and social structures, which are patterned to suit a colonial system, remain. They are outmoded in many ways because of inherent

[85] Labour Party of Malaya, *Annual Report, 1959.*

[86] Ishak was to remain the Chairman of the party until 1965.

contradictions and also because of the fact that they are at variance with the democratic spirit.'[87]

The Labour Party committed itself to the establishment of a welfare state. With its eyes on the non-Malay communities the party stressed in the statement:

Malaya with a mixture of Chinese, Indian and Malay cultures can be said to be rich in its culture. Yet what do we find? We find an Alliance Government's policy to stifle these cultures by trying to do away with the linguistic advancement of those citizens who would like to further these cultures . . . . The claim of linguistic cultural autonomy deserves due recogintion.[88]

The party, though it would not express it in explicit terms, sought a formal status for the languages of the non-Malay communities. In its plan for education it promised:

. . . six years free and compulsory primary education *in the vernacular* for all children between the ages of six and twelve, with Malay being taught in all the classes. Thereafter, for as many children as suitable, free junior secondary education is planned, *the language of instruction still being the mother tongue*, with special arrangements for the teaching of English and higher Malay, where appropriate.[89]

It also asserted that it would amend the Education Ordinance, based on the *Report of the Education Committee, 1956* (also known as the Razak Report) and adopt an educational policy acceptable to all the communities in the country.

It demanded changes in the citizenship law so as to provide equal citizenship to all the people in the country. It asserted:

The Alliance Government by its relaxation of the conditions to acquire citizenship within one year of the attainment of Malayan independence tries to create the impression that all citizens are equal before the law . . . . There can be no equality before the eyes of the law without equal citizenship — for that is the basis of all other equa-

[87] Labour Party of Malaya, *Labour Plans for Malaya* (mimeographed), 24 August 1958, p. 1.

[88] Ibid. pp. 5-6. Emphasis added. This demand was made several times in the statement.

[89] Ibid. pp. 10-11, Emphasis added.

lities. And the truth is that there are still various classes of citizens which also happen partially to fall within racial distinctions.[90]

Now that the party was linked with the largely Malay Party Raayat in the Socialist Front it did not reject the special position of the Malays as had been specified in its important Memorandum to the Reid Constitutional Commission in September 1956. It also made no mention of the Malay Sultans whose abolition it had sought in 1956. Reiteration of its position on these issues would have created a serious rift with the Party Raayat. In fact, it went a step further when it did not insist on the incorporation of its position on non-Malay languages and cultures and citizenship, which had been outlined in its *Policy Statement* of August 1958, in the *Socialist Front Manifesto* for the 1959 general elections. The party issued no manifesto of its own. The Socialist Front Manifesto made no mention of the citizenship issue and on the question of language its major emphasis was on the rejection of English and the championing of the cause of Malay as the official language. It asserted:

> A common language means unity to the masses. Malay is the language of Malaysia. The English language under the protection of being 'official' is used by the Government and propagated. English is necessary, but the development and the teaching of Malay is of cardinal importance. It is the only way we can develop a Malayan personality . . . . One nation — one language. English as an 'official' language threatens Malay as the national language.
>
> The Alliance Government has betrayed Malay — our national language. There shall be no pretext of preserving the English language in Malaya[91] . . . .

The manifesto did not demand formal recognition for the languages of the non-Malay communities. The radical left-wing Chinese-educated who had entered the party during 1958-9 were keen to preserve the Socialist Front and the link with the ideologically extreme Party Raayat. They believed that in their bid to take over the leadership of the Labour Party from the English-

[90] Ibid. p. 5.

[91] Socialist Front, *The Manifesto of the Malayan People's Socialist Front, 1959.*

educated moderates, links with the Party Raayat would be useful. Therefore, they were quite willing to compromise with regard to matters of interest to the non-Malay communities in order to save the Front.

In the general elections which were held during May through August 1959 the Labour Party made significant gains. It won thirteen seats in the different State Assemblies,[92] and six seats in the Malayan Parliament,[93] where it had failed to secure a single seat in the 1955 elections. It would be useful to note here that in the parliamentary elections only one candidate directly representing the Chinese-educated, Ng Ann Teck, was returned from the Batu Constituency in Kuala Lumpur.[94] Another, V. David, closely associated with the Chinese-educated was elected from the Bungsar constituency in Kuala Lumpur. But the remaining four successful candidates of the Labour Party, Tan Phock Kin, Lim Kean Siew, V. Veerappan and Y.P. Liu, represented the moderate English-educated leadership distrusted by the Chinese-educated. But the Chinese-educated had achieved a greater success in the smaller constituencies for the state legislature; five of their representatives and V. David were returned to the State Assemblies of Johore, Penang, Negri Sembilan and Selangor. The remaining seven seats were to go to the party's moderate leaders — D.S. Ramanathan, Lee Kok Liang, Ooi Thiam Siew, C.Y. Choy, Tan Chong Bee, S. Sathappan, and Gurnam Singh Gill. These were the people who had led the Labour Party before the entry of the Chinese-educated.

It is important to note here that a major part of the support for the party's candidates was not on the basis of its ideological orien-

---

[92] Two in Johore, three in Negri Sembilan, seven in Penang, and one in Selangor.

[93] Three each in Penang and Selangor.

[94] This is of importance for this inability to secure an adequate representation in the legislatures was not to enhance the faith of the Chinese-educated in elections and representative institutions. Many of them, not knowing either English or Malay, were unable to contest the elections. And even those who were able to contest and win the elections, such as Ng Ann Teck, found it impossible to participate in the deliberations of the representative bodies because of their lack of knowledge of Malay or English. They soon came to believe that the system was of advantage to the English-educated leaders and tended to perpetuate their hold on the party.

tation and policies. Several of its candidates in Penang, Negri
Sembilan and Selangor were elected because of their personal
appeal for the voters in the area. In Penang, its successes were
very largely built around the party's control of the city council
during the past three years. The Chinese-educated, all of them,
contested in areas with a very heavy concentration of the Chinese
population and with some Chinese New Villages. Support for
them came mainly because of their ability to quietly campaign on
a communal basis in the Chinese New Villages. Unconcerned with
the party's official policy on these issues they were able to promise
multi-lingualism and promotion of Chinese education.[95] Ng Ann
Teck, who had earlier been defeated in the state elections, won in
the Batu parliamentary constituency purely because of the great
dissatisfaction within the Chinese community following the crisis
in the Alliance, and not because of positive support for his party.[96]

The lack of ability to secure significant representation in the
Parliament and the State Assemblies was not to deter the Chinese-
educated from increasing their control over the Labour Party.
In fact, the successes of the party in the 1959 general elections were
to attract more Chinese-educated. The Labour Party's growing
strength was to make it more attractive to communist sympathisers
and the communally-orientated within the Chinese community.
Soon after the elections, at the 7th Annual National Conference,
the party Chairman, D.S. Ramanathan, was to warn:

> The moderate success we have had so far is bound to bring problems
> in its wake. Communist infiltration is bound to increase and an at-
> tempt made to convert the Labour Party to a stooge organisation.
> Secondly, our ranks are likely to be flooded with political oppor-
> tunists who have not a vestige of socialism in their whole make-up

[95] Interview with Gurnam Singh Gill, Seremban, July 1964. Gurnam Singh, a
leading member of the Labour Party in Negri Sembilan, left the party in July
1964 and stated in a 'Press Release' that after a long-drawn-out struggle 'the
extremists have succeeded in gaining control of the party'. He further said that
'despite some of the pious objects of the Labour Party of Malaya, certain elements have injected a communal spirit in deed and action and are bent on using
the party to give vent to their communist leanings'.

[96] See R. K. Vasil, 'Constituency Studies: Batu', in K. J. Ratnam and R. S. Milne,
The Malayan Parliamentary Election of 1964, Kuala Lumpur, University of
Malaya Press, 1967, pp. 246-9.

but come to us for name, fame and quick success in their personal careers.[97]

And this definitely took place. Following the general elections large numbers of Chinese-educated entered the party, a process that was reflected in the party's membership and branches in the States of Johore, Selangor, Malacca and Penang as we noted earlier. This influx was to strengthen the position of the Chinese-educated within the party. At the Annual Conference in August 1960 at Johore Bahru (Johore State Division had by now emerged as a stronghold of the Chinese-educated) the representatives of the Chinese-educated were able to secure most of the elected positions on the National Executive Council. The following was the vote for the elections:[98]

Leaders of the Chinese-educated and those working closely with them:

Tan Kai Hee (Johore)	247 votes
Ng Ann Teck (Selangor)	234
V. David (Selangor)	239
Wee Lee Fong (Johore)	232
Americk Singh (Selangor)	228
Chong Chen Wen (Malacca)	185
Yet Eng Siang (Negri Sembilan)	148

Not associated with the Chinese-educated:

V. Veerappan (Penang)	223 votes

But Tan Phock Kin, one of the leading moderates in the party, was re-elected the Secretary-General for yet another year. This was the only position which allowed the English-educated moderates any influence over the affairs of the Labour Party.

This conference under the influence of the Chinese-educated adopted resolutions calling on the Government to employ gra-

---

[97] Presidential Address by D. S. Ramanathan at the 7th Annual National Conference of the Labour Party, 17 and 18 October 1959 (mimeographed).

[98] Labour Party of Malaya, *Annual Report, 1960.*

duates of the Nanyang University,[99] to extend the programmes of the Ministry of Rural Development to New Villages, and seek a merger of Singapore with the Federation of Malaya.[100] These were specifically to please the Chinese community which had always believed that it was being discriminated against when the graduates of a Chinese University were not employed by the Government and more important benefits of rural development schemes were restricted only to Malay *kampongs* and not to the New Villages where most of the Chinese peasantry lived.[101] The Chinese community was also opposed to the exclusion of Singapore from the Federation of Malaya. They believed that the sole reason why Singapore had been left out, when the Crown Colonies of Penang and Malacca had been merged into the Federation and thereby had gained independence, was the large Chinese population of Singapore which would have changed the racial balance in favour of the Chinese in the Federation.

After the elections, in February 1960, the Alliance Government appointed a high-powered committee headed by the then Minister of Education, Abdul Rahman bin Talib,[102] to review the implementation of the educational policy introduced by the *Report of the Education Committee, 1956 (Razak Report)* and to make recommendations with regard to its future working.[103] The report of the committee which was submitted in mid-1960, once again brought the issue of education and language to the forefront of

[99] Nanyang University, with Chinese as the medium of instruction, was established in 1954 at Singapore by the Chinese community in the Federation of Malaya and Singapore. The well-known Chinese author and philosopher, Lin Yu Tang, was its first Chancellor. The establishment of the English-medium University of Malaya had geared the Chinese community to action because they felt that the very large number of Chinese students studying in the Chinese medium schools would not be able to enter the University of Malaya and would thus be deprived of facilities for higher education. Later, the University was to become a stronghold of extremist left-wing and Chinese chauvinist elements.

[100] Ibid.

[101] This was finally effected in 1963 after there had been very substantial pressure from the MCA, which had been losing support in the New Villages.

[102] Rahman bin Talib is considered a pro-Malay extremist in the UMNO and is closely associated with such leaders as Syed Jaafar Albar and Syed Nasir bin Ismail.

[103] Federation of Malaya, *Report of the Education Review Committee, 1960, (Rahman Talib Report)*, Kuala Lumpur, Government Press, 1960, p. 1. For details of the earlier *Razak Report* see below pp. 230-1.

communal controversy in the country. As soon as the report and
its recommendations were made public there was an outcry from
parties dependent largely on support of the Chinese and from the
non-political associations of the Chinese community.[104] The
pressure was to be felt in the Labour Party also, which by now had
a very sizeable number of Chinese-educated within its ranks. The
Chinese-educated, led by the Johore Division, took a serious view
of the recommendations and submitted a detailed memorandum
on the subject to the party's Annual National Conference in late
1960. The recommendations of the *Rahman Talib Report* which
agitated the Chinese community were:

1. Secondary schools receiving partial assistance from the Government which failed to make arrangements to conform fully with
   all the statutory requirements as from the beginning of 1962 or
   earlier 'should be regarded as independent schools ineligible for
   any assistance from Government funds as from the beginning of
   1962'.

2. All the 'official, national, public examinations' — the Lower
   Certificate of Education and the Federation of Malaya Certificate
   of Education Examinations — should be held only in the nation's
   two official languages, Malay and English.[105]

The Committee recommended that the Ministry of Education
should cease to organize examinations in Chinese, i.e. the
Junior Middle III Examination, the Chinese Secondary Schools
Promotion Examination and the Chinese Secondary Schools
Leaving Certificate, with effect from 1961.[106] This meant that
all those secondary schools run by the Chinese community where
the medium of instruction was Chinese had to accept of necessity
one of the two official languages as the medium of instruction,
for the recommendations were to make it impossible for students
from these schools to sit in the public examinations recognized

---

[104] A senior leader of the Malay extremists in the UMNO told this writer in early
1964 that Rahman Talib, by his Report, had 'undone the harm done by the
Razak Report of 1956'. In fact, Tun Razak had lost considerable support within
the UMNO because of his *Report*.

[105] Federation of Malaya *Report of the Education Review Committee*, op. cit. pp.
29-31.

[106] Ibid. pp. 32-33.

and conducted by the Government.[107] And if these schools conducted their own examinations they would not have the recognition of the Government and therefore would not enable the students taking them to secure suitable employment. In effect, the recommendations made the learning of languages other than Malay and English useless. These far-reaching recommendations according to the Chinese community were to cut at the very roots of Chinese education and language in Malaya.

The Johore Division of the Labour Party, representing the views of the Chinese-educated, in its Memorandum to the 8th Annual National Conference of the party maintained:

1. The recommendations of the Rahman Talib Report violate the Federal Constitution, Article 152, which guarantees that the use and study of the languages of the other communities will not be prevented. 'The recommendations, on the other hand, limit the development of other language streams to the primary level. Once the secondary schools are reorganized, the University education which is conducted in Chinese will be automatically cut off for lack of students. They also deny the financial support to these schools by withdrawing the grants.'

2. They violate the 1956 Razak Report, Chap. 1, Para. 1, which had promised that the education and culture of the other communities will be preserved and promoted. 'However, the Report of the Review Committee, first and primarily, has violated the spirit of the 1956 Report with regard to education and culture of other communities. They recommend the suppression and elimination of these secondary schools.'

3. They have violated the Alliance elections manifesto of 1955 which had promised to protect 'the legitimate position of the other languages' and had allowed the non-Malay communities

[107] On the other hand, the earlier *Razak Report* had said with regard to the medium of instruction:

We consider that there should be some flexibility in our secondary school system ... For example, *we can see no reason for altering the practice in Chinese Secondary Schools of using Kuo Yu as a general medium* provided that these Chinese schools fall into line with the conditions mentioned in the previous paragraphs.

Federation of Malaya, *Report of the Education Committee, 1956*, op.cit. p. 12. Emphasis added.

the right to safeguard their own language, literature and culture. 'The Report, on the other hand, has deprived the citizens of their fundamental right to preserve their own languages and cultures. They do not encourage, but curb and even limit its development.'[108]

The Memorandum suggested that the right of the various communities to promote and preserve their language, literature and culture be respected, Chinese middle schools should not be reorganized (only the time alloted for the teaching of the national language, Malay, be increased in these schools), the medium of all public examinations be the medium of instruction, and in pursuance of the provisions of the Constitution official status of English must be abolished in 1967.[109] The concern of the Chinese-educated was not without reason for the recommendations were a serious threat to the existence and growth of Chinese education.

The 8th Annual Conference of the party referred the Johore Memorandum to the National Executive Council for consideration which appointed a sub-committee under the chairmanship of V. Veerappan 'to study the document and make recommendations'.[110] The committee consisted of the following: Ishak bin Haji Mohammad, Tan Phock Kin, Wee Lee Fong, Lim Kean Siew, Tan Kai Hee and Chong Chen Wen. The committee after several meetings prepared its recommendations, 'Our Education Policy',[111] which after the approval of the Labour Party's National Executive Council were submitted to the Socialist Front as the basis for discussion of the Front's stand on education. The report, at the very outset, conceding the point made by the Johore Memorandum, said that 'as education is undoubtedly the most sensitive and controversial subject ... any attempt to formulate an educational system must of necessity be directly related to the existing social systems as well as the needs of the various communities'. It maintained that the major objects of their approach were to:

---

[108] Labour Party of Malaya, Johore Division, *Memorandum on the Education Review Report*, submitted to the 8th National Conference (mimeographed).

[109] Ibid. p. 5.

[110] Labour Party of Malaya, *Annual Report, 1960*.

[111] Labour Party of Malaya, *Our Educational Policy, 1961*. Typewritten original signed by the Chairman and other members of the committee.

1. Develop a Malayan consciousness and outlook 'to assist in the formation of a United Citizen Body, that is a Malayan Nation'.
2. Preserve and sustain the growth of the language and culture of all communities with equality and impartiality.

The first objective could be achieved by

1. The use of a Common Content Syllabus and books with a Malayan background and character.
2. The propagation of a common language — in this case Malay — as national language. This should be taught as a compulsory subject in all schools, so that all pupils will be equipped with a common medium of communication.
3. The gradual establishment of Regional Schools with Malay, Chinese and Tamil and English streams under the same roof and a nomenclature which should smack of no racial difference.

With regard to the second objective it asserted that they were convinced that

1. Every child should be free to join any language stream of his parent's choice.
2. Every effort should be made to promote the study of the various cultures of the people of this country and their contribution to this country with the object of evolving a common Malayan culture.
3. All conforming schools should be assisted. [Conforming schools meant those which 'use the home language as the main medium of instruction, but which follow the accepted regulations as to age, common syllabus and the compulsory teaching of the national language'].
4. Equal opportunity for training of teachers of all accepted media should be made available.
5. Equal opportunity for selection to Government and other Public Service by the introduction of Special Public Service Examination apart from the School Leaving Certificate and this examination shall be in the national language and open to pupils of all schools or by utilising the result of a standardised examination. . . .

Further, it suggested three different sets of schools at both the primary and secondary levels:

Regional Primary Schools (with Malay, Chinese and Tamil streams) and *National Comprehensive Secondary Schools* (with national language as the main medium of instruction and with facilities for pursuing a study of the language and literature of the student) — fully assisted by the Government.

Partially Assisted *Conforming Primary* and *Secondary Schools* — conforming only with regard to age regulations, common syllabus and the compulsory teaching of the national language.

Independent Primary and *Secondary Schools* — complying with regulations on courses of study, health and other essential Ministry of Education requirements, ineligible for any governmental assistance.

These recommendations closely followed the fundamentals of the educational policy put forward by the Johore Memorandum. The only significant difference was that these were more systematic and emphasized more strongly the importance of a national system of education.

These views, which were largely very fair, were placed before the Socialist Front but the Front failed to take any action and the issue remained unresolved between the Labour Party and the Party Raayat. In fact, earlier, after the Chinese-educated had launched their opposition to the *Rahman Talib Report,* in the middle of September 1960, Ahmad Boestamam, the Chairman of the Party Raayat, resigned his position as the Chairman of the Socialist Front 'because of differences of opinion with the Labour Party over the *Rahman Talib Report'*.[112] As shall be seen later, a compromise was reached within a few days and Boestamam reoccupied the position of the Chairman of the Front. But it is interesting to note that the Labour Party in its statement, *Our Educational Policy, 1961,* went beyond the compromise and more or less re-asserted the position taken by the Chinese-educated in their Memorandum. The compromise was only a patching up. The Chinese-educated continued to adhere to their position even though it was completely unacceptable to the Party Raayat. The only difference was that in view of the necessity to maintain the Front they were less vocal in their assertion of their approach

[112] *The Straits Times,* 19 September 1960.

to Chinese language and education. The compromise was only a compromise of convenience among the leaders of the two member parties of the Front. It was never accepted by the rank and file.

This was the period of the increasing control of the Chinese-educated over the Labour Party. At the 9th Annual National Conference at Kuala Lumpur on 28 and 29 August 1961, the last of the moderate English-educated leaders occupying a position of influence was not re-elected. Lim Kean Siew, who had by now built up close relations with the Chinese-educated, defeated Tan Phock Kin by 218 votes to 105 for the position of Secretary-General which the latter had occupied uninterrupted since 1954 when the Labour Party had emerged out of the Pan-Malayan Labour Party.[113] The radical Ishak bin Haji Mohammad continued to occupy the position of Chairman. The National Executive Council, completely controlled by the Chinese-educated, comprised the following: Tan Kai Hee, Wee Lee Fong, Ng Ann Teck, V. David, Lam Chok Tong, Yet Yeong Seong, D.S. Ramanathan, Yeoh Ho Huat, Americk Singh and Chong Chen Wen.[114]

The leadership of the party since its inception can be divided into three main categories:

1. The English-educated liberals who had led the party since 1954 when it emerged from the Pan-Malayan Labour Party: D.S. Ramanathan, V. Veerappan, Tan Phock Kin, Lee Kok Liang, N. Patkunam, Tan Chee Khoon, Gurnam Singh Gill, etc.

2. English-educated leaders who, witnessing the rapidly increasing influence of the Chinese-educated, were willing to work closely with them in order to secure positions of influence within the party: Lim Kean Siew, Ooi Thiam Siew, C.Y. Choy, Americk Singh.

3. Leaders of the Chinese-educated: Tan Kai Hee, Wee Lee Fong, Ng Ann Teck, Dr. Rajakumar, V. David, etc.

With the election of Lim Kean Siew as the Secretary-General in mid-1961 the position of the English-educated moderates was completely eclipsed and the party passed into the hands of the

[113] Labour Party of Malaya, *Annual Report, 1961-62*.

[114] These are listed in the order of the votes secured by them.

Chinese-educated who controlled it through leaders like Lim Kean Siew. This was the beginning of the party's rapid movement towards an ideologically extreme position which culminated in 1966 when it assumed a blatantly pro-communist (pro-Peking) and Chinese chauvinist character. However, the moderate English-educated leaders were tolerated and allowed to remain in the party, for they gave it respectability and made it more difficult for the Government to take drastic action against it.

Before proceeding further it would be worthwhile to see what the Chinese-educated stand for and how they differ from the English-educated moderates. The two groups come from very different backgrounds. Almost all of the Chinese-educated are of working class origin from the little towns and New Villages in the country. They are all educated in Chinese-medium schools, centres with a long tradition of Chinese nationalism. They are not all well-educated; most of them can afford only a few years of schooling, perhaps up to the primary level. Basically most of them, except their small number of ideologically articulate leaders, are Chinese chauvinists. Ideological extremism is only incidental. Their basic commitment is to the great fatherland China and its great culture, heritage and language. Most of them talk in cliches and one is not certain if they understand all that they are saying or whether they are only parroting what they have been told by their leaders. Most of them have never been to China and have little or no contacts with the fatherland. Consequently they do not have any first-hand information about what has been happening there. They only have a highly glamorized picture of China and what the great revolution has done to China.

This writer was taken to a very strong New Village branch of the Labour Party in Selangor by Tan Kai Hee, one of the foremost leaders of the Chinese-educated. The meeting at the branch was attended by about forty members, all Chinese in the age-group of about 17 or 18 to about 30 (a small number of girls were also present). I was allowed to put a few questions (this was not arranged in advance) to the ordinary members and the following were their answers:[115]

---

[115] The visit took place during January 1964.

What do you understand by socialism which represents the political creed of your party?

We want to destroy this Government and this system. We want to demolish imperialism, colonialism and capitalism and set up a new society where the State would control the entire economic life of the society. We would have a real government of the people. The workers would secure the full fruits of their labour. The capitalists would not be able to take over the surplus value.

Do you think the present electoral system and the system of government in Malaya is a good or suitable one?

The present system of government supports exploitation of workers and therefore there is dissatisfaction with it. If it was a real democracy there would have been no dissatisfaction.

What in your view is wrong with the educational policy of the Alliance Government?

1. The Government encourages the English language and we are opposed to it.
2. The Government gives greater facilities for English-medium schools. They are doing very little for schools with other languages as the medium of instruction.
3. We are not satisfied with the text-books. Even in the Chinese schools they are in English.
4. No jobs are available to those who secure education in Chinese-medium schools.
5. The medium of examination is English even for Chinese-medium schools. We believe that the medium of instruction should be the medium of examinations.

The Chinese-educated do not at all like the English-educated leaders. They consider them less radical than themselves.[116] The Chinese-educated have all been converted to a belief in complete state control while the English-educated moderates have shown a very cautious approach to nationalization of the means of production. They have put more emphasis on a welfare state as their goal.

The English-educated, who are cosmopolitan in outlook, are genuinely non-communal and have shown little inclination to

[116] Interview with Tan Kai Hee, Kuala Lumpur, September 1964.

exploit communal issues for purposes of gaining support. Their position on communal issues has always been fair and forth-right. But the position of the Chinese-educated is very different. They have always been committed to an extreme position on these issues. But for tactical reasons they have not always openly asserted it. It has been only during recent years, after the break up of the Front, that they have openly espoused it. But at the same time it must be noted that a few of the top-ranking leaders of the Chinese-educated, especially Tan Kai Hee, who are ideologically very articulate, are conscious of the limitations and dangers of this extremist approach and have always attempted to moderate the extreme views of the rank and file of the Chinese-educated.

Finally, the relationship between the two groups, in the words of Tan Kai Hee, is that of *Orang kuasa dengan orang dikuasa,* that of the leaders and the led, those with authority and those subjected to authority.

The growing influence of the Chinese-educated was reflected in the significant successes that the party achieved in the local council elections in the New Villages for the first time during 1959 and 1960. The major successes were in Johore and Selangor, the two strongholds of the Chinese-educated. In the 1961 local council elections the Socialist Front candidates secured as much as 27.6% of the total vote. Most of these votes were secured by the Labour Party, in particular the Chinese-educated in the New Villages and urban centres. Even the votes polled by the Party Raayat were largely for its Chinese-educated candidates in the New Villages. The Front was to maintain this position right through. In fact, the influence of the Socialist Front, as well as that of the People's Progressive Party and the United Democratic Party, was growing so rapidly in the New Villages and urban centres that in late 1964 the Alliance Government suspended all local council elections for an indefinite period.

The ascendancy of the Chinese-educated in the Labour Party coincided with the break between the Chinese-educated (the pro-communist group) and the English-educated moderates (the non-communists led by Lee Kuan Yew) in the People's Action Party of Singapore and the formation of the ideologically extreme and Chinese chauvinist Barisan Sosialis in Singapore in September 1961. As soon as the Barisan Sosialis was formed, the Labour Party, now controlled by the Chinese-educated, established strong links with it through leaders like Lim Kean Siew, Tan Kai Hee, Wee Lee Fong, Dr. Rajakumar, etc. and possibly through the underground Malayan Communist Party. The links grew very rapidly and on the issue of Malaysia and 'Indonesian confrontation' the Labour Party soon came to echo *in toto* the views of the Barisan Sosialis. And, by 1964, after Malaysia had been established, the Labour Party, for all practical purposes, had become an adjunct of the Barisan Sosialis.

On 27 May 1961, in an address to the Foreign Correspondents' Association of Southeast Asia in Singapore, Tunku Abdul Rahman, the Prime Minister of Malaya, expressed the desire that Malaya 'should have an understanding with Britain and the peoples of the territories of Singapore, North Borneo (Sabah), Brunei and Sarawak' and that a plan should be devised 'whereby these territories can be brought closer together in political and economic cooperation'. There was an immediate favourable reaction from the leaders of these territories and Britain.

The first response of the Labour Party to Malaysia was favourable. The 9th Annual National Conference of the party held on 26 and 27 August 1961 adopted a resolution agreeing 'in principle with the idea of Malaysia'.[117] But soon, under the influence of the Barisan Sosialis of Singapore, its position changed. It began to echo the pro-communist attitude of the Singapore organization. At the same time, it joined the Barisan Sosialis in their fight against the People's Action Party of Singapore. The next Annual Conference of the Labour Party in August 1962 adopted the following resolution on Malaysia:

This Conference condemns the Federation [of Malaya] Government for complicity with the British Government in trying to bring about the Malaysian Federation against the wishes of the people and to introduce neo-colonialism into these territories.[118]

[117] Labour Party of Malaya, *Annual Report*, 1961-62.
[118] Ibid. 1962-63.

It was only two years earlier, in August 1960, that the party's 8th Annual National Conference had adopted the resolution:

> In view of the geographical, historical, cultural and economic affinity between Singapore and the Federation, every effort must be made to assist Singapore to merge with this country so that it may enjoy the fruits of complete *merdeka*.[119]

This resolution had made no mention that the merger should be effected only after the wishes of the people of Singapore had been ascertained.

At the beginning, following the Barisan Sosialis line, the Labour Party was not opposed to Malaysia as such, but its opposition was to the way it was being brought into existence and the basis on which it was to be constituted. The 'principal reasons' for its objection were:

1. It is a modern concept that no democratic state can exist unless all its citizens have equal political rights. Without such equality there can be no healthy modern state. At the moment, we are divided into citizens of many varieties, Singapore, Federation and Bornean.

2. Our representation in Parliament which makes all national laws does not truly give equality of representation, weightage is given to Malaya at the expense of the Singapore and Borneo people.

3. Immigration into the Bornean territories to relieve Singapore and Malayan population pressure is prohibited so that there can never be any proper distribution of population to relieve any state of over-pressure of unemployment.

4. Special rights have been so extended to cover so many people in all the territories so as to make it meaningless.[120]

This was the position in late 1963. The next step, again in pursuance of the Barisan Sosialis line, was the adoption of a position by the Labour Party almost identical with that of the Indonesian Government, the Indonesian Communist Party, and People's Republic of China. The Annual Report of the Selangor Division

[119] Ibid. 1960.
[120] Ibid. 1962-63.

(a stronghold of the Chinese-educated) for the year 1963-4, presented on 21 June 1964, said:

> The British colonialists and their stooges in Singapore, Sabah, Sarawak and Malaya had implemented the Malaysia plan for the sake of maintaining their control on the three territories of North Borneo and to prolong the economic, political and military domination of our country. Malaysia has been established for the protection of the interests of the feudalist, bureaucratic compradors and for the suppression of the anti-colonialist forces more effectively in this area. It has created the tense situation in Southeast Asia and strengthened the foreign military bases in the territories. Malaysia was formed on the 16th September 1963 disregarding the strong opposition from the people of the five territories and ignoring the protest from Indonesia and the Philippines and the progressive countries of the world.

The Penang Division of the party at its annual conference on 19 July 1964 adopted the following resolution:

> This Conference warns the Government that the North Bornean States have been put into Malaysia deliberately to bring about discontent in and hostility with Indonesia, which is bound to be afraid of the expansionist designs of the West through Malaysia, thus giving an excuse to foreign powers to enlarge military bases in Malaysia and to apply pressure on Malaysia by putting it under the economic, financial and military dependence of such foreign powers and calls upon the Government to end this hostility and the excuse afforded to foreign powers *by giving the North Bornean States their self-rule and independent action* rather than risk war amongst ourselves in Southeast Asia and thereby playing into the hands of foreign powers through the old imperialist policy of 'divide and rule'.[121]

During 1962 and 1963 (until the time of the formation of the new federation in September 1963) the Labour Party and the Socialist Front in their opposition to Malaysia were supported by the entire opposition in the country: the People's Progressive Party, the United Democratic Party and the Malay extremist Pan-Malayan Islamic Party and the Party Negara. Joint action was possible because they all agreed that the new federation was being

---

[121] Labour Party of Malaya, Penang Division, *Annual Report*, 1963. Emphasis added.

constituted by the Alliance Government without the free consent of the peoples of the territories concerned and that political capital could be made out of it. The People's Progressive Party and the United Democratic Party, like the Labour Party, were also opposed to the unequal treatment being given to the different territories.

These formed a joint opposition group in the Parliament under the chairmanship of Abdul Aziz Ishak who had just left the UMNO. The group convened several public meetings to express their common opposition to Malaysia. On 26 April 1963, they all signed a joint memorandum to U Thant, the Secretary-General of the United Nations, drawing the attention of the Security Council to 'the very arbitrary manner in which the Alliance Government is attempting to impose the formation of Malaysia' and that it was a grave threat to the peace not only of Asia but of the entire world.[122] But very soon the People's Progressive Party and the United Democratic Party, both like the Labour Party dependent very largely on the Chinese community for support, realized that intensified 'Indonesian confrontation' had changed the situation and now opposition to Malaysia had come to imply a pro-Indonesian posture. Therefore, both the People's Progressive Party and the United Democratic Party, as soon as the Malaysian Federation was inaugurated in September 1963, dropped their opposition to Malaysia and asserted that now that it was a *fait accompli*, opposition to it was meaningless. They had their eyes on the forthcoming elections in the country in which they knew that a strongly anti-Malaysia position (which had come to mean a pro-Indonesian stand) would make it difficult for them to secure the support of the Chinese community, since the Alliance Party would make Malaysia the key issue in the elections.[123] Therefore, both the parties did not stress their opposition to Malaysia in their election campaign. But the Labour Party, following the Barisan Sosialis line and disregarding the advice of some of its moderate leaders, strengthened its anti-Malaysia posture. In fact it made Malaysia

[122] Memorandum to U Thant, Secretary General of the United Nations, by the Conjoined Opposition Group (mimeographed), 26 April 1963.

[123] See R. K. Vasil, 'The 1964 General Elections in Malaya', *International Studies*, Vol. VII No. 1 (July 1965), pp. 39-45.

the key election issue even though its leaders were conscious that this would not help the party in the elections.

Expecting the elections in early 1964, the Labour Party organized a political course (*Kursus Politik*) for its key workers in January 1964 at Morib in Selangor. The course was conducted by Tan Kai Hee and was attended by about 150 party workers, almost all Chinese-educated. Addressing the group with regard to 'Our Economic Policy', Tan Phock Kin stated that 'our plans must be aimed towards:

(a) eliminating poverty.
(b) increasing productivity.
(c) stabilizing the price of our primary products.
(d) devising measures for controlling population growth'.[124]

His plan for eradicating poverty meant:

(i) a more equitable distribution of our National Income through a more equitable tax structure.
(ii) A full employment policy which will bring about the maximum utilization of our man power resources.
(iii) A comprehensive social security scheme.

With regard to the ownership of the means of production Tan maintained that it was only a means to an end. If an industry became monopolistic or exploitative of labour or the consumer it must be nationalized. Every industry ought to be considered on its merits. But all public utilities must be nationalized: many of them though were already state-owned in Malaysia. He felt that only with regard to road transport was there a strong case for nationalization.

This programme was hardly of any attraction to the Chinese-educated who were all committed to a complete state control of the economy. This should be indicative of the gap between the

[124] Speech by Tan Phock Kin at the Speakers' Training Course of the Labour Party, 16-19 January 1964 (mimeographed).

English-educated moderates and the Chinese-educated with regard to the ideological orientation of the Labour Party.[125]

On the final day of the course, Wee Lee Fong, the Secretary-General of the party and one of the key leaders of the Chinese-educated, spoke on Chinese education.[126] Being a major address it would be useful to quote extensively from it to give a clear idea of the attitude of the Chinese-educated with regard to Chinese education:

> They [the British Rulers] started 'enslaved people' education policy to paralyze the thoughts of the people, so as to destroy 'national consciousness' and train 'slaves' faithful to the British Empire. At the same time they attempted to destroy 'national education' (especially Chinese education) . . . The 1952 education ordinance, the *Barnes Education Report*, the *Fenn-Wu Education Report*, the *Razak Education Report* were all of the same sort. Their aims were to make education policy agreeable to the interest of the rulers and to serve the coloniser's interest. If one insists on saying that they were not the same, then the difference is only in the way of expressing the meaning; the real intention of all of them is the same.
>
> National education has the function of enlightening the mind of the people, to enable them to understand the changes and developments of all kinds of events . . . If a nation is suffering from oppression

---

[125] None of the Chinese-educated, however, challenged the views of Tan Phock Kin. During the question time only two extremely unimportant questions were asked by the very articulate cadres of the party attending the course. After the talk, Tan Phock Kin told this writer that what he had said represented 'the considered view of the Executive of the party'. But he immediately added that 'he was not at all certain if this would be acceptable to the rank and file of the party'.

[126] Since most of the people attending the course were Chinese-educated the entire proceedings were in the Chinese language. But during the first three days, when the course was attended by four or five Malays, every word spoken was translated into the Malay language.

On the final day, Wee Lee Fong arrived with six top-ranking leaders of the Barisan Sosialis of Singapore (including Dr. Lee Siew Choh). The last day's proceedings were completely dominated by the Barisan Sosialis leaders who spoke for several hours in Chinese and not a word was translated into Malay. The same day in the afternoon Wee Lee Fong spoke about Chinese education and again no translation was provided.

This writer was told by a top-ranking English-educated leader that the Barisan Sosialis leaders had not been officially invited. They had been brought by Wee Lee Fong on his own without the approval of the party.

and exploitation then the function of national education during this period may be to unite the nation and overthrow the oppressor. Since national education plays such an important role and function it is of course against the interest of the British colonialists. This applies especially to Chinese education; this is because Chinese civilization has a history of five thousand years. After this long period of struggle and development it has now become one of the most superior cultures in the world .... Therefore, Chinese education is a nuisance in the eyes of the British colonisers ....

But the British colonialists and their lackeys would not give up, on the contrary, they become more malicious. On the 31st of August 1957, we obtained the socalled 'independence', in fact it was only transferring power from the British colonisers to their agents — the Alliance — to govern on their behalf and ended their direct control that lasted for over a century. This also signified that from this time on, instead of openly suppressing Chinese education, they switched over to the present policy of controlling it from behind the scenes. Of course the appearance of this 'puppet' government did not basically change the history in its real sense. Today our people face the same crisis as under the old British colonialists. Britain is still our most vicious enemy and the main object of our struggle. Today Chinese education is still in the same position as before and there is always the danger of its being destroyed.

Immediately after the Alliance Government came to power it declared that the Government would not recognize the degrees of the Nanyang University and then the *Rahman Talib Report on Education* was published. These contained ample evidence to show that the Alliance policy was only to serve the British colonialists and to be the 'executioner' of Chinese education.[127]

With regard to the *Rahman Talib Education Report* and the attitude of the MCA towards it, he added:

When the *Talib Report on Education* was published the Chinese community was shocked. Everyone talked about it. The report brazenly revealed its intention of destroying education of the other communities.

[127] Wee Lee Fong, *Regarding the Problems of Chinese Education*. Translated from the original in Chinese by Mr. Kiriloff, Australian National University, Canberra.

Here we must talk about the attitude of the MCA. This association always claimed that their organization was the biggest one among the Chinese, that they represented the Chinese and looked after their interests. When all the people attacked the *Talib Report on Education,* this was no doubt good opportunity for the MCA to show their sincerity. But surprisingly, they kept quiet and even supported without reservation the passing of the Bill — *Talib Report* — in the Parliament . . . Therefore, the MCA in fact cannot fight for the rights of the Chinese, but it is selling out their interests.

. . . In fact, Chinese education is facing destruction and this is the result of their work. And yet the MCA attempts to claim that it supports the interests of the Chinese . . . The leaders of the MCA are only interested in making 'an official career'. High positions and good pay have made them forget everything; they have sold out Chinese education just to curry favour from their bosses.

This was the material which was given to the Chinese-educated to use during the election campaign to explain the Labour Party's view with regard to Chinese education.

In the 1964 general elections, the Labour Party was routed. It was able to secure seven seats in the different State Assemblies (two in Malacca, three in Selangor, and two in Penang) and only two seats in Parliament.

The failure of the party was entirely due to its stand on Malaysia and 'Indonesian confrontation'. In a *Post-mortem of the Elections in Penang,* Ooi Thiam Siew, Chairman of the Penang Division of the Socialist Front and a leader of the Labour Party, had this to say:

The Alliance fought on the issue that our party is anti-Malaysia and pro-Sukarno . . . although we kept on refuting the allegation of being pro-Sukarno, we could not convince quite a good section of the electorate. The consensus of opinion is that while we appeared to be strong critics of whatever wrongs the Alliance did, we refrained from criticizing whatever wrongs the Indonesian Government has done. This gave the impression that, notwithstanding our utterances of not being pro-Sukarno, such lack of criticism of what appeared to be wrong in the minds of the people, indicated a pro-Sukarno tendency.

This is the main factor for the loss of a great number of votes to our party.[128]

Indicating that the domination of the party by the Chinese-educated had adversely affected in the elections, he added:

(i) We are too restrictive in our membership in that we have restricted supporters of our party who may not be ideologically sound. If we are to consider ourselves as a party for mass support then we should throw it open to them.

(ii) Our active members who are usually in their twenties seem to think that their views are the views of the people, without realizing that the views of the older people and/or women may not coincide with theirs. Hence at committee level our party should not under any circumstances be dominated by youth alone.

(iii) It is time that our party try to encourage elders and women, both young and old, to participate in the activities of our party. They should be encouraged to attend party meetings by giving them as much voice to say what they think for the good of the party and not, for lack of numbers, drive them away from the activities within the party.

(iv) There should be no suspicion between the English-educated and the Chinese-educated, or between those who work with their hands and those who work with their brains.

It is this suspicion of domination by one section of the other and of their real interest that prevents our party from recruiting people of high intellect to lead our party.

However, the Chinese-educated thought very differently about the electoral reverses. *The Annual Report of the Selangor Division of the Labour Party for 1964,* had the following to say:

In the recent State and General elections, we lost some seats. But this did not mean that the people had accepted Malaysia. This fact only

---

[128] This mimeographed document dated 28 April 1964 was circulated among the leaders of the party soon after the elections. Ooi Thiam Siew, who had associated himself with the Chinese-educated in the hope of maintaining his position within the party, after the elections was disillusioned. He was not re-elected to the Penang State Assembly. In 1967, he eventually left the Labour Party and as an independent was elected the Mayor of the George Town Municipal Council with the support of the Alliance.

further proved that the democratic system praised by the Alliance was deceptive. Their intention was to conceal their reactionary nature. The election was full of deception, falsehood, oppression and corruption.

We must point out that although Malaysia was an established fact, and although our party suffered some setbacks in the election, our party stand is still unchanged. Our struggle is still anti-colonial and anti-Alliance. Our struggle is still against the British colonialist and United States Imperialists and their stooges — the Alliance clique. *As a socialist our main task is to educate the masses and organise the masses. Only when the masses have been organized and educated they will be able to replace the reactionary government once and for all, and to eradicate injustices and to build a new socialist society.*

There is one more point we must make clear and that is to distinguish a party from good or bad does not depend on election results but on whether it is for the people or on the side of reactionaries. We must oppose all forms of exploitation and oppression, whether they fight for the interest of the majority people or the minority. Historical experience had proved that those who are against the law of historical development and want exploitation of others will be wiped out.[129]

As has already been noted, the Chinese-educated do not attach very great importance to elections. To them the most important function of the party is to educate the masses for the eventual and inevitable victory of socialism. Electoral defeats are of no great consequence. On 19 July 1964, soon after the general elections, Lim Kean Siew, the Chairman of the Penang Division of the Labour Party, addressing the Divisional Annual Conference said:

Comrades, we must not turn our backs from the fear of unpopularity and danger . . . We cannot give up our principles in time of difficulty. If we fail, let us go down with our flags flying. Let us not have opportunism as our guide. Malaysia is not to our benefit . . . And the solution is simple. All we need do is to give up our ideas of aggrandisement and expansion. We can give to the Bornean territories their self-rule and allow them self-determination.[130]

---

[129] Emphasis added. The Selangor Division has been one of the main strongholds of the Chinese-educated.

[130] Labour Party of Malaya, Penang Division, *Annual Report, 1963.*

Malaysia and 'Indonesian confrontation' had created an un-bridgeable gap between the English-educated and the Chinese-educated sections in the Labour Party. Following the electoral defeats and even before that, many of the moderates who had led the party for more than a decade either became inactive or left the Labour Party. Others strongly urged the party to change its orien-tation, accept Malaysia 'as a *fait accompli*' and start afresh. The key men who pursued this approach were: Tan Chee Khoon (newly-elected Labour Member of Parliament), Tan Phock Kin, V. Vee-rappan and Ooi Thiam Siew. In the original draft for his first speech in the Parliament (21 May 1964) Tan Chee Khoon said: 'Let me state categorically that the Socialist Front accepts Malaysia as a *fait accompli*.' However, the night before the speech was delivered in Parliament, it was vetted by the Pre-Council Group of the Front at Tan Chee Khoon's house in Kuala Lumpur and it was changed to say: '*Now that Malaysia has been pushed through* let me state quite categorically that our party is pledged to finding a peaceful and constitutional solution to the problems that have been creat-ed.'[131]

It was obvious that the moderates were fighting a losing battle. First, they had no mass base in the party; their group consisted only of a handful of English-educated leaders. A very large part of the party's membership by now consisted of the Chinese-educated. Second, the Chinese-educated, who up to this time had tolerated the moderate leadership to give the party respectability and to save it from repressive action by the strongly anti-com-munist Alliance Government, had by now come to find that this approach had not taken them anywhere. They had no more use for these moderates. Here again they were reflecting the view of the Barisan Sosialis which was finding it impossible to compete against the non-communist People's Action Party in Singapore through constitutional and peaceful means. The Labour Party had already lost very badly in the elections. The Alliance had

---

131 Emphasis added. Tan Chee Khoon, at this meeting, was told to make further changes in the text of his speech and asked to toe the party line. Tan Chee Khoon refused to do so and there was a lot of shouting and thumping of the table at the meeting.

already started inflicting severe repression on the party's Chinese-educated sections. Finally, some of the more reasonable leaders of the Chinese-educated, people like Tan Kai Hee, had been detained by the Government and were not in a position to guide the Chinese-educated. Under the circumstances the leadership of the Chinese-educated passed into the hands of the more extremist middle-level leadership, which is manipulated much more effectively by the Barisan Sosialis. As a result of these circumstances, the approach of the Chinese-educated towards the English-educated moderate leadership changed radically. They were no more inclined to keep up a facade of respectability and a moderate position on ideological and communal issues. They were willing to come out into the open and wage the struggle as they saw it. This led to the exit of most of the moderate English-educated leaders of the Labour Party. Tan Phock Kin, V. Veerappan, Ooi Thiam Siew, and several others quietly severed their connexions with the party. But the very religious Tan Chee Khoon, with a missionary zeal, continued the lone struggle to give the party a moderate orientation. However, as expected, his attempts have been completely fruitless. The party has passed completely into the hands of the Chinese-educated who finally have committed it to an extreme position both on ideological and communal issues.

In late 1966, with the impending complete switch-over to Malay as the official language of the country as provided in the Constitution, the language controversy was once again revived. The Labour Party, now under the full control of the Chinese-educated, drastically changed its official position on the national language issue. The party now said in a statement:

The National Executive Council of the Labour Party of Malaya after lengthy study and deliberations on the language and education policies decided to strive for the Chinese and Tamil languages to make [sic] official languages.

The National Executive Council of the Labour Party of Malaya is strongly against the reactionary policies of the British colonialists plotting with the Alliance Government in implementing its enslaving colonial education policies and attempting to destroy the Chinese language. We avow to struggle for equal treatment of education of all languages and to safeguard Chinese education and we will combine our struggle with the struggle of all registered Chinese Associations and Guilds, School Boards, Teachers' Union and Students' Union for equal treatment of education of all languages and to safeguard the Chinese education. We call on all members and supporters to launch a series of struggles to have the Chinese and Tamil languages made official languages.[132]

When the Language Bill, making Malay the sole official language, was introduced in the Malaysian Parliament in September 1967, Tan Chee Khoon supported it although he had been told by his party to oppose it. He was thereupon asked by the party 'to explain' his conduct and the reason why he should not be expelled.[133]

At the same time the Labour Party moved to the extreme left. In a lengthy resolution adopted at the 13th National Conference in Penang in August 1967, the party outlined its view of the international and domestic situation and the tasks of the party. With regard to the international situation the resolution said:

In the great struggle of the current international situation, the international forces are distinctly divided into two antagonistic camps. The world counter-revolutionary and aggressive forces headed by US imperialism and Russian revisionism and other reactionaries of various countries serving these aggressive forces are encountering the vigorous retaliation of the anti-imperialist and anti-colonialist forces in Asia, Africa, Latin America and the progressive forces headed by the revolutionary people of China . . . In this struggle there is no middle road. We must resolutely and unreservedly plunge into the great struggle against US imperialism and Russian revisionism.
    . . . At present, US imperialists and Russian revisionists are piecing together an anti-communist, anti-people, anti-revolution and anti-China 'holy alliance' so as to accelerate the formation of an encirclement against China. They are bribing and abetting the reactionaries in various places to carry out a series of anti-Chinese activities. The wave of inhuman and barbarous anti-Chinese reverses currently

---

[132] Labour Party of Malaya, *Statement on Language Policy*, undated. It was issued at the time of the by-election at Kampong Bahru in Kuala Lumpur during December 1966.

[133] Tan Chee Khoon in a personal communication to the writer, 4 December 1967.

taking place in India, Burma, Indonesia and Hong Kong are the requirements to suit the scheming of US imperialists and Russian
revisionists. We strongly condemn these racialist, counter-revolutionary and unpardonable crimes.

The Great Proletarian Cultural Revolution taking place now in
China has shaken the whole world and has sounded the final death-
knell of the US imperialists and Russian revisionists . . . . The Great
Proletarian Cultural Revolution have smashed the hope of the US
imperialists and Russian revisionists that a counter-revolution re-
storing capitalism will happen in the second or third generation of
the Chinese revolutionary people . . . it has wiped off the black clouds
spread by Russian revisionists in the anti-US revolutionary movements . . . . Together with the people of the world, we warmly give
a most distinguished comment to the Great Proletarian Cultural
Revolution taking place in China.[134]

With regard to 'The Tasks of the Party in the Current Struggle',
it said:

This Conference holds that 'Malaysia' and 'Republic of Singapore'
are the product of neo-colonialism whose aim is entirely to divert
the attention of the struggle of the revolutionary people in Malaya
and to wreck the concept of an united Malaya so as to perpetuate the
ruling life of the Rahman-Leekuanyew puppet regime and the British
and US imperialists. Therefore, our party must strive resolutely,
thoroughly and uncompromisingly to overthrow 'Malaysia' and
'Republic of Singapore' . . .

As the Rahman-Leekuanyew puppet regime is the most reactionary class enemy in our country at present i.e. they are the most loyal
running dog and important instrument of US imperialist forces,
Russian revisionists, the bureaucratic comprador capitalist class and
feudalistic aristocrats in our country who are protecting 'Malaysia'
and 'Republic of Singapore' and wrecking the Malayan nationalist
movements, this Conference holds that the immediate task in the
national, democratic revolution of our country is to overthrow the
British and US imperialism and Rahman-Leekuanyew puppet re-
gimes . . .

. . . Regarding the question of the form of struggle, this Conference
holds that: the Rahman-Leekuanyew regime supported by British

[134] Labour Party of Malaya, *The Resolution of the 13th National Delegates' Conference.*

and US imperialists and Russian modern revisionists are nothing but a fascist violent ruling organ. 'Parliamentary Democracy' is only a false face cover used to cover up their shame. Therefore, our party must break the old bondage of 'legalism' and we must shatter the superstition of 'parliamentary path'. We must resolutely take the line of mass struggle and we must adopt the policy and tactic of mass struggle in conjunction with parliamentary struggle while using mass struggle as the main form of struggle.

    ... the party must repudiate the thought of the 'parliamentary maniacs' and right opportunism that dominated the party for a long time....

Thus, the Labour Party of Malaya, which had been formed during the early fifties and had operated until the time of independence in 1957 as a moderate left-wing and a genuinely non-communal political party, over the years, beginning from 1958-9, was converted into an essentially Chinese communal and pro-Communist (pro-Peking) party as a result of the left-wing take over of the party and the unique compulsions existent in a plural society such as West Malaysia.

Constitution and Organization

Until the important changes introduced in the *Constitution of the Labour Party of Malaya* at its 10th Annual National Conference in August 1962, the party had three classes of members, (i) Affiliated Members (ii) Ordinary Members (iii) Active Members. The constitution had further provided that only the active members were entitled to become delegates to both the Divisional Conferences and the National Conference. Also, only active members were permitted to hold any official position in the party at the Branch, Divisional or National level. Ordinary members played no important part in the working of the party. They could, however, become active members if they had been members for a period of not less than a year and more important if they were 'considered by the Divisional Liaison Committee and the National Executive Council to be fit and proper persons to be admitted to such membership'.[135] The main purpose of this provision was to

---

[135] *Constitution of the Labour Party of Malaya*, Article III - 4.

stop communist infiltration into the party and to ensure that such entrants were not able to capture important positions in the party. The National Executive Council thus was able to exercise strict control over the active membership of the party and stop undesirable elements from assuming leadership positions.

But once the Chinese-educated came to have substantial influence over the Labour Party, its constitution was amended in August 1962 and the three classes of membership were abolished.[136] The party then only admitted ordinary members and consequently the national organization and leadership lost its control over the membership. Anybody now could quietly join the Labour Party through a branch and the National Executive Council was in no position to stop undesirable elements from entering the party and assuming leadership positions.[137]

The National Conference is 'the supreme ruling authority of the party' and meets in August every two years.[138] The conference is attended by delegates both from the Divisions and Branches.[139]

[136] Labour Party of Malaya, *Annual Report, 1961-62*.

[137] Here it might be useful to have a look at the experience of the People's Action Party of Singapore in this matter.

In 1957, a showdown had taken place between the non-communist and the pro-communist elements within the party. Following the showdown, as soon as the non-communists were able to assume control of the party they amended the party constitution to stop the ordinary members (many among whom were communist sympathisers) from assuming leadership positions. They created a new cadre membership. The following is what Lee Kuan Yew, the leading member of the non-communist section, had to say about it:

After this experience we amended our party constitution to make sure that the party cannot be so easily captured. We instituted two classes of members, ordinary members and cadre members. Ordinary membership is open to all and secret penetration by communists into this group is easy if they send in their people who are not yet well known.

But only those who have proved over a period of time that they are sincerely and honestly with the party can become cadre members. An election of the Central Executive Committee is only by cadre members.

This method of preventing communist penetration and capture is most important. (Lee Kuan Yew, *The Battle for Merger*, Singapore, Government Press, 1962, pp. 26-27).

This was vehemently opposed by the pro-communist elements who later were to form the Barisan Sosialis which came to have very close links with the Labour Party starting from the time of its formation in September 1961.

[138] Before the 1962 amendment the National Conference was held annually.

[139] Both the Divisions and the Branches send one delegate for every two hundred members.

There is no provision for similar Divisional Conferences. The National Conference is a formal affair and little of consequence takes place at these conferences. The chief function performed by the conference is the election of the National Executive Council. Here too the delegates do not exercise a free choice. It is all pre-arranged among a small group of leaders of the Chinese-educated who control the Divisions and Branches.

The National Executive Council consists of 'a Chairman, two Vice-Chairmen, General Secretary, three Assistant Secretaries, Treasurer, twelve Committee members and one representative from each Division'.[140] It is the key body and more or less runs the party. The constitution provides that the Council has

> ... plenary powers to deal with and decide any matter which, in the opinion of at least five members of the National Executive Council, affects the general welfare of the labour movement, provided that no decision of the National Conference shall be abrogated under this rule. The National Executive Council's decision upon such matter shall be binding upon all members of the Party provided that any Division, Branch, or member affected shall have the right to appeal to the next National Conference against such decision.[141]

The constitution also provides for a National Working Committee which 'shall confine its functions to matters delegated to it by the National Executive Council'.[142] In an emergency, the National Working Committee is empowered to take appropriate decisions, but such decisions must be ratified by the National Executive Council. The Working Committee consists of the eight principal national officials of the party and five members elected by the National Executive Council from its membership at its first meeting after the National Conference.

At the Divisional level (corresponding to the States of the Fed-

---

[140] Before the 1962 amendment the National Executive Council used to consist of a Chairman, General Secretary, two Vice-Chairmen, Treasurer, 'one representative from each Division and an equal number of members as those nominated from Divisions to be elected by the National Conference from Conference delegates'.

[141] Article VI-3 (h) of the Constitution.

[142] Article VIII-5

eration) the party is controlled by a Divisional Committee, consisting of a Chairman, two Vice-Chairmen, Secretary, Treasurer, and ten committee members, all elected by the annual Divisional Conference. There is also provision for a Divisional Liaison Committee, consisting of the members of the Divisional Committee and one representative of each branch in the Division, whose sole function is to inform the Divisional Committee 'of opinions in the Branches on issues pertaining to the policy of the Division and other general matters'.[143]

Branches form the basic unit of the organization of the Labour Party. But they do not correspond to any electoral unit. The party has no organization corresponding to the state assembly or parliamentary constituencies. Any New Village where the party has some influence has a branch. But in cities and other smaller urban centres branches have been established fairly arbitrarily. For example, Kuala Lumpur, the national capital, has several branches the locations of which have not been determined by any definite criterion. Theoretically, a branch can be established in any centre where there are at least forty members. But, on the whole, the major factor which has determined the location of branches has been the availability of party workers of the right type and trusted by the divisional leadership. The result is the existence of several branches in close proximity to each other.

Like almost all the other opposition parties in the country, the Labour Party has no front organizations among the youth, students, women, and workers. This is an indication of the extremely limited area of support and influence of the party. As we will see later, a very large part of the membership of the party is derived from Chinese-educated of working class origin in the New Villages and urban centres in the country, and therefore the need for the formation of front organizations of youth, women and workers to attract them to the party has not been felt. They also believe that if they formed such organizations the Government would not allow them to operate freely. Since the domination of the party by the Chinese-educated no attempt has been made to attract members and supporters from other sections

[143] Article X - 1 and 2.

of the society, in whom the Chinese-educated have shown a complete lack of trust.

Membership, Branches and Party Activity

A significant change took place in the character of the party's membership between the pre-independence and post-independence periods. This is of vital importance for this has determined the party's character and policy orientation.

Initially, when the party was formed during the early fifties, the Labour Party's support came from ordinary workers (many of them of Indian origin) and English-educated white-collar workers from unions whose leaders had sponsored the formation of the party. This support was mainly restricted to a small number of urban centres, especially Kuala Lumpur and Penang. Throughout the period up to independence, the party had found little support in the small towns, rural areas and the New Villages. The party had no mass base. A large part of the support was built around the personal influence of its leaders.

But in the post-independence period the situation changed drastically. With the entry of large numbers of Chinese-educated and the declining influence of its traditional English-educated leadership, the type of support it had in its pre-independence era completely disappeared over the years. The membership today is almost entirely Chinese-educated and is found to come from the Chinese New Villages and the urban centres in the country. There are very few Malay members and an insignificant number of Indians. According to an official report of the Selangor Division, the Labour Party's membership in Selangor State in 1964 comprised the following:[144]

Chinese members	1,888
Indian members	65
Malay members	42
	1,995

[144] Selangor Division Committee, Labour Party of Malaya, *A Report by the State Secretary, Tan Kai Hee* (mimeographed, translated from the original in Chinese). The report was the result of a detailed survey conducted by Tan Kai Hee over a period of two months during early 1964. It refers only to subscription-paying members.

Of these, a significant number (462) were women. This situation would be very largely true of the other Divisions of the party.

According to party records its total membership is about 90,000, but only about 15,000 of these are the actual subscription-paying members.[145] It is important to note that this membership is not spread equally over the country. A major part of this is to be found in the three States of Selangor, Penang and Johore. Membership in the States of Perak, Negri Sembilan, Malacca and Pahang is not large, and the party has attracted no members in the States of Perlis, Kelantan, Trengannu and Kedah, which have a very heavy concentration of Malay population.

The party has a total of 250 branches and their distribution by State is as follows:[146]

State	Branches
Johore	55
Selangor	47
Penang	43
Perak	35
Malacca	23
Pahang	23
Negri Sembilan	16
Kedah	8
Perlis	—
Kelantan	—
Trengannu	—

But many of these branches are hardly functioning. For example, in Selangor, the party's forty-seven branches were divided into the following types by Tan Kai Hee in his report to the Divisional Committee referred to earlier:

1.	Active branches	17
2.	Partly-active branches	9
3.	Sleeping branches	5
4.	Branches on the verge of being closed down	7
5.	Branches in the process of being revived	9

[145] Data provided by Tan Kai Hee, in an interview in Kuala Lumpur, July 1964.
[146] Ibid.

Party activity at the Branch level is almost entirely restricted to party members and its known supporters and sympathisers. Branch leaders and cadres have shown little trust in the ordinary people. They are afraid that mass membership and contacts would affect the ideological purity of the party. And also, it would tend to strengthen the position of the moderates. Therefore, no effort has been made to establish contacts with the people at large. A confidential report by the Secretary of the Selangor Division asserted:

> ... our branches have lost contact with the people. This is shocking but that is the truth. Our branches to a very great extent have become fortresses. Fortresses are understandable in so far as it concerns infiltration from undesirable sources, but it becomes ludicrous when these fortresses in their attempt to keep members 'clean' prevent them from mixing freely and effectively with the people and thereby fail to influence them. Our branches have become mere citadels.
>
> It is only during the period of elections that we start actively going out to meet the people and informing them of deficiencies of the governing party and the merits of our views and candidates. This tactic is practised by other parties but with us this is of little use as in the first place the members of the other parties are known to the people through their social and business contacts. [147]

The branches consist of small, close groups, who, by and large, keep to themselves. They look down upon the ordinary masses as people with little courage and slavish in their mentality. Being very young, they too are not accepted by the ordinary people.

The emphasis is not on attracting new members and supporters but on educating the existing membership and creating a solidarity and fellow-feeling among them. The report of the Secretary of the Selangor Division quoted earlier asked the branches of the party to organize their activities along the following lines:

1. Explanation of the constitution particularly of the functions of office-bearers and what socialism stands for.

2. *Language classes:* If there is anyone competent to teach the na-

---

[147] *Secretary's Report,* Selangor Division, Labour Party of Malaya. The report is undated, but it seems to have been prepared around 1961.

tional language then classes should be held once or twice a week. If there are no teachers amongst our own members, then members should be encouraged to enrol for national language classes organised by the Adult Education Association of the Ministry of Education.

3. *Women's section:* Every branch should develop a strong women's section. More than half of the electorate are women and it is important that more and more women should be encouraged to join the party and take an active part in the affairs of the branch. Such activities as

   (a) Language classes
   (b) Sewing classes
   (c) Dressmaking classes
   (d) Film shows
   (e) Political discussions.

4. *General Political Instruction*: in current affairs, e.g.

   (a) The *Rahman Talib Report*
   (b) The Congo
   (c) Assistance to the Malays in commerce
   (d) Rural Development Plan
   (e) Discussion of articles in *Nyala, Petir,* etc.

5. *Films:* The State Division may consider buying a projector and this can be lent out to branches. Films can be hired cheaply . . .

6. *Singing and Dramatic classes:* Branches should try to develop a good singing section to enliven our rallies.

7. *Sports section:* Such games as table tennis, badminton, chess (Chinese and English), draughts should be encouraged. They serve to maintain contacts with members.

8. *Libraries:* The bigger branches should have small libraries . . .

9. Visit to places of interest, e.g. Lever Brothers, factories in Petaling Jaya, Templer Park, etc.

Most of the branches of the party have organized activities on these lines. Some of the larger ones, especially in the New Villages, have set up a Benevolent Fund which provides financial and other assistance to a member's family in case of his death. 'The branches in Northern Perak even have their own music parties to play at funerals in accordance with Chinese tradition.'[148] Many branches have their Volunteer Corps or Work Brigades who help build roads, repair bridges and houses, and other similar work. A few of the branches run their own cooperative stores. The Jinjang New Village branch outside Kuala Lumpur has a large thriving cooperative store.

The major activities at the branch level are political, educational and cultural. Branches run their own self-education courses consisting of eight to ten members. The purpose is '*chuchi kotor*' (literally to wash away dirt), to imbibe socialist ideas and to purge all *bourgeois* tendencies. Emphasis is placed on cultural activities. 'We realize that to develop a healthy culture is one of the ways to enhance the morale of the people and also help the whole anti-colonial cause.'[149]

[148] Labour Party of Malaya, *Annual Report, 1960.*

[149] Labour Party of Malaya, Selangor Division, *Annual Report, 1963-64.*

IV

THE PARTY RAAYAT[1]

THE Party Raayat formed by Ahmad Boestamam has been the foremost radical left-wing organization of the Malays. Not long after its formation, around the time of independence, it joined the Labour Party to form the Malayan People's Socialist Front, the chief aim being to jointly contest the first general elections in the country after independence. Hoping for significant successes in the elections it made a half-hearted effort to modify its policies so as to create an appeal to the non-Malay communities. However, the election results were not very heartening and caused a weakening of the desire on the part of its leadership to strengthen the party's non-communal character and extend its appeal to the non-Malay communities. When the realization that it had little chance of attracting substantial support among the non-Malays dawned, it gradually committed itself more and more to a pro-Malay position, and eventually in late 1965 withdrew itself from the Socialist Front and adopted a Malay communal posture.

In June 1955, Ahmad Boestamam was released after seven years' detention under the Emergency Regulations. In early November, two conditions of his release — that he must stay indoors between 6 p.m. and 6 a.m. and report to the police twice every month — were lifted. Soon afterwards be announced his intention to form a new political party.

[1] The reason why the Party Raayat is not included as a 'party of personage' is that though based largely on the personality of Ahmad Boestamam it has been a Malay left-wing party attempting to attract the Malay peasant and fisherman on the basis of its socialist programme. The National Convention Party, on the other hand, has been referred to as a 'party of personage' for it characterized itself as a socialist body after it joined the Socialist Front as a member. Prior to that it sought Malay support entirely on the basis of Aziz Ishak's personality and all that he had done for the Malay peasant and fisherman during his long tenure as the Alliance Minister for Agriculture.

It is useful at this point to note the background and personality of Ahmad Boestamam, who not only founded the Party Raayat but also dominated it throughout its existence, even during the period of his second long detention between 1962 and 1966. Boestamam, a stormy petrel and one of the most colourful personalities in post-war Malayan politics, has been a front-ranking leader of the Malay left-wing since 1945. In 1945, he was closely associated with the KRIS (*Kesatuan Rakyat Indonesia Semenanjung*, Union of Peninsular Indonesia) which considered the destiny of the Malays to be closely linked to Indonesia, and sought to declare joint independence for Malaya and Indonesia. Later, in late 1945, he was instrumental in the formation of the Malay National Party (MNP) of which he soon became the General Secretary. The MNP, at its first congress at Ipoh in late November 1945, passed a resolution declaring that Malaya was a part of Indonesia. It also accepted the *Merah Puteh* (the Red and White), the Indonesian National Flag. It maintained that the *Merah Puteh* had been the Malay national flag 400 years ago when the Malays had an empire under the leadership of Hang Tuah with headquarters at Malacca.

In February 1946, at Ipoh (capital of Boestamam's home State of Perak), Boestamam formed an extremist wing of the Malay National Party, the *Angkatan Pemuda Insaf* (the Awakened Youth Corps, abbreviated to API — the Fire or the Flame). The major aims of the new organization were:

1.   To unite all awakened youth under one organization.
2.   To strengthen the fighting front of the nation.
3.   To give political, physical and spiritual training to the youth.

'Freedom through Blood' was its motto. *A Political Testament of API*, prepared by Boestamam, saw two roads to independence; through evolution or revolution. API was willing to try both, but had more confidence in the second. It was a party of revolution. Its preparations for independence were two-fold: internal and external. Internal effort meant training the youth for leadership which included development of patriotism and training in gymnastics, drill, sports and warfare. It held many public parades at which drills and military formation were demonstrated. External efforts meant very close links with the World Federation of Democratic Youth. The API had very close contacts with the many youth groups organized in Java and Sumatra during that period to fight against the Dutch. In fact, these youth movements in Indonesia provided the model and inspiration for API.

It was for the authorship of the *Political Testament of API* that Boestamam was tried and first kept in prison from 1948 to 1955.[2]

In November 1955, Boestamam announced that he would soon form a new political party and that 'the former members of the API have responded to the move'.[3] In view of the favourable response from his former comrades in the API, the Party Raayat was launched on 11 November 1955 at the offices of the Labour Party in Kuala Lumpur. It was announced that the new party was opposed to colonialism in any form and sought immediate independence for Malaya. The inaugural conference was attended by thirty-five Malays; no non-Malays were present, but the Secretary-General of the party announced that 'our struggle is based on common sufferings of the people of Malaya. There is no question of race or colour.'[4] Ahmad Boestamam and Abdul Wahab bin Majid were elected interim Chairman and Secretary-General respectively. The conference passed resolutions demanding:[5]

1. Immediate grant of independence.
2. A united political front to achieve independence.
3. Wider political rights.
4. The release of all political detainees.

According to the party's constitution, its basic ideology is *marhaenism*, based on the ideas of Sukarno, former President of Indonesia.[6] It asserts that *marhaen* is different from proletariat.

[2] The information on the Malay National Party and the API was given the author by a prominent left-wing Malay leader who had been actively associated with these organizations. Kuala Lumpur, January 1964.

[3] *The Straits Times,* 10 November 1955.

[4] *The Malay Mail,* 11 November 1955.

[5] Ibid. 12 November 1955

[6] *Marhaenism* was propagated by Sukarno in the late twenties as the ideology of the Partai Nasional Indonesia founded by him in 1927 and which soon emerged as the major Indonesian national organization. *Marhaenism* was promoted as an alternative to communism, as socialism, Indonesian style. Sukarno devised *marhaenism* from the name of an ordinary Sundanese peasant named Marhaen, and therefore *marhaen* came to have the denotation 'the little people'.

According to it, the 'proletariat' refers only to those who sell their labour to others and do not own the means of production. But *marhaen* includes all who are poor, whether they sell their labour or not and whether they own the means of production or not. It refers to all workers, peasants, fishermen, students and small businessmen.[7]

Marhaenism is defined as being based on *sosio-demokrasi* and *sosio-nasionalisizem* and is committed to the following causes:

1. To defend, support and lead workers in the struggle between workers and capitalists . . .
2. To reject dictatorialism in all its forms.
3. To reject racialism, egoism, militarism, heroism (*sic*), adventurism, opportunism and dogmatism.
4. To oppose imperialism because it has exploitive tendencies caused by capitalism. Imperialism, essentially, is the highest stage of capitalism; and imperialism results in colonialism, as has been experienced in Malaya.
5. To oppose liberalism (the idea which has given excessive freedom to capitalists) because it is the basis and source of rampant capitalism.
6. To support all efforts aimed at obtaining independence everywhere and by everyone because only when there is independence that colonialism would disappear.[8]

The party constitution outlined the following as the fundamentals of its economic programme:

1. To promote among the people business and agriculture run on the basis of cooperatives and *gotong rojong* (mutual help).
2. To demand that all sectors of production, which are important and which affect the livelihood of the masses, especially rubber and minerals, be owned by the State.
3. To demand that the distribution of goods which are important for the people, is managed and controlled by the State.
4. To demand that the wealth of the country is used only for the happiness of the people.[9]

[7] *Anggaran Dasar Party Raayat* (mimeographed), Appendix, 'Marhaenism', Party Raayat Headquarters, Kuala Lumpur.

[8] Ibid. translated from the original in Malay by the author.

[9] Ibid.

These ideas were much more radical than those of the Labour Party (with which the Party Raayat was soon to link itself to form the Socialist Front). It sought a much larger role for the State; it favoured nationalization of the means of production and distribution on a large scale. Being a party, at this time, almost entirely supported by the Malays who did not own the rubber estates and tin mines in the country, it had no hesitation in demanding nationalization of the rubber and tin industries. The Labour Party, however, as we have noted earlier, had a much more cautious approach to the issue of nationalization. Until the Labour Party was completely taken over by the extremist Chinese-educated, it favoured only a very limited measure of nationalization. It never suggested nationalization of rubber and tin industries. The only industry it ever committed itself to nationalize was the transport industry, a major part of which was already state-owned. It was conscious of the fact that a significant part of the tin mines and rubber estates were owned by Chinese and any demand for nationalization of these would affect the party adversely in securing the support of this community. The Party Raayat was critical of this approach of the Labour Party and maintained that it had given in to the Chinese vested interests.

Another important object of the Party Raayat, the creation of a 'Malay Homeland', consisting of Malaya, Singapore, Sarawak, North Borneo, and Brunei, enjoying strong links with Indonesia, was a source of discord between the two parties.[10] This object of the party was not often explicitly formulated, but the pro-Indonesian leanings of the leaders of the party were well-known and it was obvious that they considered that the future of Malaya was very closely tied with that of Indonesia. They did not see how Malaya could exist and maintain its independence outside Indonesia.

The Party Raayat appealed only to a very small section of the Malay community; this was essentially a small group of young Malays influenced by the personality of Boestamam and the left-wing pro-Indonesian orientation of the party. Older Malays,

[10] *The Malay Mail*, 21 February 1956.

orthodox and devout Muslims, have traditionally supported the Pan-Malayan Islamic Party which is entrenched in the Malay *kampong* through the religious teachers and appeals to them through its commitment to establishing an Islamic State in Malaya. Malays from the upper and middle classes and from professions have favoured the UMNO. The personal appeal of Boestamam has not proved effective enough to attract these educated Malays. Moreover, many of the Malays belonging to the middle class are to be found in the country's civil service and are therefore in no position to support a party in the opposition. They have strong links with the ruling party, the UMNO.

In the context of the racial situation in the country there are only two bases on which the Malay can be effectively influenced: first, the preservation of the rights of the Malays as the *bumiputra;* and second, their common religion, Islam. The UMNO has effectively appealed to the Malays on the basis of the first one. It has proclaimed itself as the protector and promoter of the Malay rights.[11] The Pan Malayan Islamic Party has attracted Malays on the basis of its commitment to the establishment of an Islamic State in Malaya. It has also maintained that the UMNO, by co-operating with the communal organizations of the Chinese and Indians, the MCA and the MIC, and working together with them in the Alliance, has sold away Malay rights. The problem for the Party Raayat was that it first attempted to influence the Malay through its ideological, left-wing orientation. This soon proved to be very ineffective. Later, when it attempted to supplement its ideological appeal by its emphasis on the Malays' special position, it was too late. In this it had to compete against the more powerful and strongly entrenched UMNO and the PMIP.

The UMNO and the PMIP propaganda directed against the Party Raayat has been that communism and left-wing ideas are anti-religion and anti-Islam and that the Party Raayat was trying to peddle a foreign ideology. This has been the most serious handi-

[11] In a by-election in Kuala Lumpur in late 1966 an Alliance banner displayed prominently said the following in Malay: *Undilah Perikatan Untok Kepentingan Bangsa, Ugama dan Tanah-Ayer* (Vote for the Alliance for the interest of your race, religion and native land). But in Chinese it said 'Vote for Peace, Progress and Prosperity', and in Tamil 'Vote for Peace, Justice and Prosperity'.

cap suffered by the Party Raayat. Addressing the 8th Congress of the party in September 1962 at Kuala Trengganu, Ahmad Boestamam said:

> At the recent annual General Assembly of the UMNO its President Tunku Abdul Rahman condemned us by saying that we used an ideology which came from abroad, which was borrowed from outside. It is true that *marhaenism* did not arise in the land of Malaya. But it is true again that there is not one political ideology in this world, under the skies of this whole wide world, which originated from the land of Malaya. Not Islam, not Conservatism, not Fascism, not Anarchism, not Syndicalism, not Capitalism, not Feudalism, not Socialism, not Communism. None of them.
>
> Nationalism also did not originate in the land of Malaya. Even the patriotism of Hang Tuah, Datuk Bahaman, Datuk Janggut, Mat Kilau, Dol Said, Datuk Maharajalela and others, boasted by the Tunku as nationalism which arose in this land, in fact was stimulated by the patriotism of patriots abroad who lived before them. [12]

Earlier, in late 1961, addressing the annual conference of the party, Boestamam asked: 'Is it true that we are anti-religion?' He said that *marhaenism* 'which was not guided by *Pantjasila* was not *marhaenism*'.[13] And the very first basis of *Pantjasila* was faith in God. Can people who are guided by their faith in God in their life be anti-religion?

Also, with the predominant participation of the Chinese in the Emergency (1948-58), communism and left-wing ideas had become closely identified with the Chinese, and consequently these ideas were considered to be against the interests of the Malays. Party Raayat's attitude towards the Emergency certainly did not win it many friends among the Malays. In fact, it created strong suspicions which were exploited by the UMNO to allege that the Party Raayat's activities were against the interests of the Malays.

The Party Raayat considered the Emergency as a war of independence. In late 1958, the party had asserted:

[12] Party Raayat, *Amanant Ketua Umum Party Raayat Malaya:* 8th Party Raayat Congress, (mimeographed), p. 18. (Translated from the original in Malay by the author.)

[13] Ibid. Party Raayat Congress, 24-25 December 1961, p. 32. (Translated by the author.)

The lie is that the Alliance Party won *Merdeka*. And along with this is the lie that the Alliance won *Merdeka* in a peaceful manner. It is only necessary for the people of Malaya to think of the armed struggle going on in this country to realize whether *Merdeka* came with or without a fight. For nine years millions of dollars were spent and the military machine of Britain was functioning day and night. A modern war was and still is being fought and the British Imperialists rather than face total defeat and be forced to give the country to their enemies preferred to give the country to their collaborators and stooges....[14]

In late 1958, before the 1959 elections, the Party Raayat in a detailed document expressed its policy orientation with modifications so as not to displease the Chinese. With regard to internal policy it demanded an end to the Emergency and annulment of 'all colonial laws which belong to the past and pass laws which answer the spirit of independence'.[15] It demanded the fundamental and democratic rights of the people and called for the reunification of Singapore and the Federation of Malaya. It committed itself to introduce the use of the National Language, Malay, as soon as it was possible and 'as smoothly as possible'. 'As smoothly as possible' was all the assurance that it was willing to give to the non-Malay communities. Nothing was said with regard to the languages of these communities.

With regard to external policy it asserted that Malaya must closely identify itself with the Afro-Asian Group of Nations and pursue 'a dynamic foreign policy of World Peace and World Freedom'. It called for the complete annulment of 'all Pacts and Treaties which are the legacy of colonialism and which subjugate Malaya to any foreign country'.

Its economic programme, now revised so as not to alienate the Chinese, called for nationalization of only '*all foreign-owned* rubber estates, tin mines, transport companies and plantations'.[16] It further demanded a ban on all foreign insurance companies. It also called for state supervision and control of the distribution of

[14] *Party Raayat Policy* (an undated confidential party document), mimeographed, p. 2.
[15] Ibid.
[16] Emphasis added.

essential goods and services. It did not touch on rubber estates, tin mines, and other enterprises owned by Malayan nationals. In fact, Chinese concern regarding nationalization was considered so great that, in late 1962, Boestamam felt it necessary to give an explicit assurance that his party's nationalization programme did not include Chinese-owned rubber estates, tin mines, and other industries whose owners were either Federal citizens or those who qualified for citizenship.[17]

However, its educational policy showed no such concern for the sentiments of the non-Malay communities, who were worried about the future of their languages and educational systems. It called for free compulsory education at the primary and middle levels and state assistance to deserving students. It demanded a takeover of foreign-owned newspapers and a rigorous censorship on all films and propaganda materials of foreign origin. But significantly, it said nothing about the non-Malay languages and Chinese- and Tamil-medium schools. This was the issue which was to plague the relations between it and the Labour Party in the Socialist Front.

In the agricultural sphere it promised to start large-scale collective farming and establish marketing facilities for peasants. It called for an end to sub-division of land and uneconomic holdings.

But none of this helped the party very much in the 1959 general elections. It was not at all successful in extending the area of its support either to the poor Malay peasantry and fishermen or the non-Malay proletariat. And its Malay leadership was in any case not too keen to secure the entry of large numbers of non-Malays into the party. At this time a small number of ideologically extreme Chinese joined the party after the National Union of Factory and General Workers had been declared illegal by the Government in April 1958, but the Party Raayat leadership was not very happy about this, fearing that their entry would affect the racial balance in the party. Therefore, they discouraged other Chinese seeking entry into the Party Raayat from doing so: as a result they joined the Labour Party.

[17] *The Straits Times*, 3 October 1962.

Undeterred by an apparent lack of a mass base and organization, the Party Raayat fielded a large number of candidates in the 1959 general elections. In fact, it fielded more candidates in the state elections than the larger and better organized Labour Party. Lack of a realistic appreciation of their support was to be borne out by the election results which were a great disappointment to the leadership of the party. Only four of its candidates, two each in the parliamentary and state elections, were returned. Ahmad Boestamam and K. Karam Singh (an Indian) were elected in Kuala Lumpur in the parliamentary constituencies of Setapak and Damansara.[18] The successful candidates in the state elections were C.C. Yong (a Chinese) and Nazar Nong, contesting from the Tanjong Petri (Johore Bahru) and Sentul (Kuala Lumpur) constituencies.[19] The important point about the election results was that the party's limited successes were only in the two urban centres of Kuala Lumpur and Johore Bahru. It was routed in the rural areas inhabited by the Malays where it had fielded a large number of candidates. It was obvious that the party's four candidates had succeeded mainly with the support of the Chinese and Indians that the Labour Party, its partner in the Socialist Front, had been able to attract, and not because of the support of the Malay electorate. Later, this inability on the part of the Party Raayat to secure support among the Malays was to create serious strains in the relations between the Party Raayat and the Labour Party.

Soon after the 1959 general elections the party was caught in a serious controversy with the Labour Party on Chinese language and education issues. The crisis had been precipitated by the publication of the *Rahman Talib Report on Education* which had created quite a stir among the Chinese. Sections of the Labour Party rank

---

[18] Both these constituencies had a majority of non-Malay voters. Malays formed only a minority of the total electorate. The racial breakdown of the electorate in the two constituencies was as follows:

Setapak:	Malays	7,482 (33.2%)
	Non-Malays	15,012 (66.8%)
Damansara:	Malays	2,755 (13.9%)
	Non-Malays	17,005 (86.1%)

[19] These two constituencies had a majority of non-Malay voters and were urban seats.

and file were considerably agitated about the recommendations and the threat to the Chinese language and Chinese schools. But the Party Raayat viewed the recommendations as fair and considered them a right step in the direction of creating a united Malayan nation. Party Raayat believed that a united Malayan nation could be created only through the Malay language. Addressing the 6th Congress of the party in 1960, Boestamam said that the 'first step towards achieving the object of creating a single Malayan nation is to spread the use of the Malay language to all citizens of our country until there is none who is not able to speak or write the national language. Only then a truly united Malayan nation will be born.'[20] This had no place for the non-Malay-medium schools. The whole educational system had to be based on the Malay language in order to effectively build a united Malayan nation. But for the transitional period, the leaders of the Party Raayat were willing to allow Chinese and Tamil schools to remain in existence. At the height of the controversy between the Party Raayat and the Labour Party, Ahmad Boestamam fully explained his party's position:

> I have always stated that as long as the position of English is maintained, then the position of Chinese and Tamil education should be on the same level with English. According to the Federal Constitution, the position of English should be reviewed in 1967. If the result of the review is to scrap English in fully-assisted schools, then instruction in Chinese and Tamil should also be ended. If this happens, then I say the three languages should be taught as compulsory subjects in all secondary schools for all time.
>
> My contention is that by 1967 Malay will be so well advanced that it will be possible to have it as the sole medium of instruction. [21]

The party was completely opposed to multi-lingualism for it believed that it would hinder the growth of a united Malayan nation. It further maintained:

> Every citizen who owes undivided loyalty to Malaya irrespective of racial origin must accept it [Malay as the sole official language]. To

---

[20] *Presidential Address by Ahmad Boestamam*, Party Raayat, 6th Congress, Johore Bahru, 1960, typed copy, p. 4.

[21] *The Straits Times*, 17 September 1960.

oppose this means his loyalty to this country is still in doubt and this is bad.[22]

The issue was not resolved to the satisfaction of either the Party Raayat or the Chinese-educated in the Labour Party. The differences were just temporarily patched up for the sake of inter-party harmony in the Socialist Front. The problem was to raise its head again in 1965, when it led to the final disintegration of the Socialist Front.

However, the proposal of Tunku Abdul Rahman with regard to the formation of Malaysia in May 1961 and the Indonesian opposition to the idea, temporarily submerged the differences between the Party Raayat and the Labour Party and the two joined hands to oppose the formation of the new federation. But their opposition was not for identical reasons. The Labour Party, which by now had come under the substantial influence of the Chinese-educated, almost entirely reflected the views of the Singapore-based Barisan Sosialis, whose attitude towards Malaysia was determined by the internal struggle for power in Singapore between the Barisan and the pro-merger and non-communist People's Action Party. Soon the Labour Party saw Malaysia as a racial concept and as a step towards the creation of a *Melayu Raya* formed to protect the Malay communities in Malaya, Indonesia and the Philippines against China and the Chinese in these countries. It vehemently opposed the idea of Maphilindo when it was suggested in 1963 at Manila and was immediately approved by Sukarno, President Macapagal and Tunku Abdul Rahman.

But it was only for the sake of this *Melayu Raya* that the Party Raayat had opposed the formation of Malaysia. Initially it had supported the idea of Malaysia 'as a first step towards the birth of *Melayu Raya*'.[23] But as soon as there were indications that Indonesia would not approve the formation of Malaysia the Party Raayat had to reverse its position because it could not conceive of Malaysia without the blessings of Indonesia and a Malaysia which eventually did not lead to *Melayu Raya* participated by Indonesia. Addressing the 7th Annual Congress of the party,

[22] *Presidential Address by Ahmad Boestamam*, 6th Congress, op.cit. p. 4.
[23] *Amanat Ketua Umum*, 8th Party Raayat Congress, op.cit. p. 13.

Boestamam, its Chairman, said in late December 1961:

> In fact, the idea of Malaysia is not a new one. It is not Tunku Abdul
> Rahman and his Alliance who have put forward the idea for the first
> time. Before there was the Alliance, before there was the UMNO,
> before there was the PAP . . . there existed the idea of Malaysia. Even
> during the earlier period of colonialism there existed the idea of
> Malaysia.
>
> The first legal political organization which was established in this
> country after the colonial power attempted once again to establish
> its foothold was the Kesatuan Melayu Muda under the leadership of
> Ibrahim bin Haji Yaakub . . . And it was this Kesatuan Melayu Muda
> which for the first time put forward the idea of Malaysia. But at that
> time it was named *Melayu Raya* and not Malaysia. And the aims of
> *Melayu Raya* were:
>
> 1. To free all the countries which formed the Malay island group
>   from Western colonialism.
> 2. To unite all these countries thus freed into an independent State
>   to be called *Melayu Raya*. [24]

This was the Party Raayat's conception of Malaysia and it was for
this reason that it did not condemn the idea of Maphilindo when
it was suggested in 1963 even though it was vehemently opposed
by the Labour Party as 'a racial plot'. In fact, the Party Raayat
saw Maphilindo as *Melayu Raya*. To it the most important thing
was cooperation with Indonesia and the idea of the common destiny of the two countries. The Labour Party, on the other hand,
was extremely disturbed with regard to the suggested formation
of Maphilindo. Its fears were well expressed by the *Annual Report
of the Socialist Front, 1962-63*, prepared by a senior leader of the
Labour Party:

> The creation of Malaysia right within the Malaysian region that has
> been moved by the concept of *Melayu Raya* as reflected in the de-
> mand for Maphilindo would put its non-Malay population at a dis-
> advantageous position. The revival of *Melayu Raya* concept can
> easily be turned into a racialist cry.

And this was to create friction between the two parties with regard
to their attitude towards Malaysia.

[24] Ibid. p. 12.

The relations between the Party Raayat and the Labour Party were further strained by the issues of language and education and the attempt by certain sections of the Labour Party to forge a united front of the opposition. It was in this situation that the party contested the 1964 general elections as a member of the Socialist Front. It was full of optimism and fielded a large number of candidates; it put up twenty-seven candidates in the parliamentary elections and seventy-three in the State elections. But the party suffered a crushing defeat when none of its candidates was returned. This seriously strained the relations between the Party Raayat and the Labour Party and raised doubts in the minds of many of the leaders of the former about the usefulness of being a partner in the Socialist Front. There was similar lack of interest in the Front on the part of the Labour Party. Following the elections, as the Labour Party under the Chinese-educated started moving rapidly towards a strongly Chinese chauvinist position, the Party Raayat found it no longer possible to cooperate with it, since cooperation with the Labour Party would make it impossible to secure support among the Malays. Consequently, in late 1965, the Party Raayat took unilateral decision to withdraw itself from the Socialist Front and maintain its separate existence.

Party Organization and Support

The Party Raayat's membership is open to all the people of Malaya who have attained the age of 18 and who agree with its aims and objects. Each application for individual membership has to be approved by the Party Council. The constitution also provides for affiliation of organizations which have similar aims and objects. Their application for affiliation would have to be approved by the Party Council.[25]

The national organization of the party is led by a Party Council (*Dewan Partai*) which consists of the nine members of the Working Committee of the party (*Dewan Harian Partai*) and one representative each from the State Divisions and the affiliated organizations. The Working Committee is elected by the Annual

---

[25] *Anggaran Dasar Party Raayat*, Article 6b.

Congress of the party. From amongst the membership of the
Working Committee the party Congress elects the office-bearers:
Chairman, Vice-Chairman, Secretary-General, Assistant Secretary-General, Treasurer, and a General Assistant to carry out the
day-to-day work of the organization. 'The Supreme power of the
party rests with the Congress. But when the Congress is not in
session the Party Council exercises the supreme authority. And
when the Party Council is not in session the Working Committee
takes over the supreme authority.'[26]

Organization at the state and branch levels follows very closely
the pattern for the national level. With regard to party branches
the constitution only provides that they must have at least twenty-
five members.

Exact figures with regard to the party's membership are not
available. But a fairly good idea of its membership and relative
strength in the different States can be secured from the number of
delegates from the state bodies to the Ninth Congress of the Party
in November 1963. The following is a list of delegates and membership based on the representation:

TABLE 7

PARTY RAAYAT: ESTIMATE OF MEMBERSHIP NUMBERS, 1963

State	Number of representatives	Membership
Trengannu	2	376 - 625
Penang	10	2,376 - 2,626
Perak	9	2,126 - 2,375
Kelantan	3	626 - 875
Negri Sembilan	2	376 - 625
Pahang	4	876 - 1,125
Malacca	4	876 - 1,125
Johore	4	876 - 1,125
Selangor	9	2,126 - 2,375
Kedah	4	876 - 1,125
Singapore	3	826 - 875
Perlis	—	—
	54	12,336 - 14,876

Source: Party Raayat, Peringatan Congress Ke-IX (Minutes of the 9th Congress),
Kuala Lumpur, November 1963.

[26] Ibid. Article 9.

Thus according to party records its membership in 1963 was somewhere between twelve to fifteen thousand. But the important point to note is the heavy concentration of membership in the three States of Penang, Perak and Selangor, which are States where non-Malays form a majority of the population. In the predominantly Malay States of Perlis, Kelantan, Trengannu, Kedah and Pahang the party has not been able to attract a large membership. It is purely a result of the fact that Malays in the predominantly Malay States of the East Coast have not come into as close a contact with the non-Malays and the outside world as in the non-Malay majority States of the West Coast and consequently have remained more traditional and orthodox, and hence less attracted to the radical left-wing orientation of the Party Raayat. These are the areas where the PMIP has found strong roots, whereas in the non-Malay majority States of the West Coast it has never obtained strong support.

The three major bases of the party's appeal have been its left-wing socialist orientation, the personality of its founder Ahmad Boestamam, and the pro-Indonesian position of the party and its leaders. This appeal is effective only in the case of young Malays, mainly in the West Coast States. The party's pro-Indonesian orientation has not been able to attract young Malays in the Malay-majority States of the East Coast where the same appeal has been exploited by the PMIP.

The party's small Chinese-educated Chinese groups joined during 1958-9 not because of any particular appeal, but mainly as a matter of convenience and for tactical reasons. The important point about them is that they have never been integrated into the party; they form an organization within the organization and have never seen issues and problems in the same way as the Malays.

V

THE MALAYAN PEOPLE'S SOCIALIST FRONT

PROSPECTS of independence in mid-1957 changed the political situation in Malaya. The Labour Party and the Party Raayat, which had so far accepted a limited role based on the restricted area of their support, now started seeking greater influence in the country's politics. Introduction of representative government just before independence, whereby political power could be captured through the ballot box, and the resounding victory of the Alliance in the 1955 elections, made it imperative for parties in opposition to form united fronts to face the Alliance colossus which had captured as many as fifty-one of the fifty-two seats in the Federal Legislative Council. Individually they had little chance of competing successfully against the inter-communal Alliance, consisting of the communal organizations of the three major racial groups in Malaya. Also the limited area of support, in terms of communal groups, enjoyed by the Labour Party and the Party Raayat gave them a strong motivation to get together and, like the Alliance, jointly extend the area of their support and influence. The Labour Party, at this time was a small party with its influence restricted almost entirely to the non-Malay communities; its support among the Malays was meagre. Similarly, the Party Raayat was essentially a Malay left-wing party with little support and influence among the non-Malay communities. Thus the strong desire on the part of the two disparate parties to form a united front against the Alliance and pool their complementary areas of influence.

The background and orientation of the leaders of the two parties, the English-educated moderates from the professions of the Labour Party and the extreme left-wing pro-Indonesian Malays of the Party Raayat, were so dissimilar that *The Straits Times* in a leading article called it a 'Disunited Front' and doubted if the Front had any future. It said:

... will anything come of this move to form a socialist front? ...
Not if the left-wing parties remain for the most part instruments for
the propagation of the esoteric and personal philosophies of its individualistic leaders. The socialists in Malaya have thrown up (and
out) more individualistic leaders than the right-wing parties. This
may be due, in great measure, to the fact that they have yet to devise
a political theory that will harmonize with Malayan facts.[1]

In late 1956, talks were begun between the Labour Party and
the newly-formed Party Raayat to establish a united front.[2]
Ahmad Boestamam, the founder of the Party Raayat, said that
the objects of the two parties were 'similar' and it was only logical
that they worked together. But at the same time he added that
there could be serious disagreement on the position of the Malay
Sultans in independent Malaya and the special privileges of the
Malays. In fact, during the negotiations for the formation of the
front which dragged on for several months, there was serious disagreement between the Labour Party and the Party Raayat on
these two very important issues from the point of view of both the
Malay and non-Malay communities. The Party Raayat demanded
the acceptance by the Labour Party of the position of the Sultans
and the special position accorded the Malays in the Constitution
of the Federation of Malaya.[3] The Labour Party, however, only
less than a year back in September 1956, had asserted in its memorandum to the Reid Constitutional Commission: 'All Malayan
nationals shall enjoy equal rights and share equal responsibilities.'[4]
It had opposed any attempt by one race 'to dominate other races
or to maintain and extend its privileges over the others'.[5] With
regard to the future of the Sultans it had clearly expressed its preference for the discontinuation of the system which it considered
outdated.[6] This was absolutely unacceptable to the Party Raayat.
Therefore, the Labour Party, in its keenness to join hands with

[1] 2 July 1957.
[2] *The Straits Times*, 26 September 1956.
[3] Ibid. 25 June 1957.
[4] *Memorandum to the Reid Constitutional Commission submitted by the Labour
Party of Malaya*, 25 September 1956, p. 4.
[5] Ibid. p. 3.
[6] Ibid. p. 6.

the Party Raayat, went back on its position, which had been so clearly formulated in its memorandum to the Reid Commission, and accepted the stand of the Party Raayat on these two controversial issues.

It was only towards the end of July 1957, about one month before the transfer of power, that the two parties finally agreed to launch the Socialist Front.[7] According to an official spokesman of the two parties the immediate objective of the Front was to contest the 1959 General Elections in which it hoped to defeat the Alliance.[8]

The Malayan People's Socialist Front was inaugurated quietly on Independence Day, 31 August 1957, at the headquarters of the Party Raayat in Kuala Lumpur. The meeting resolved that 'to achieve the task of socialist cooperation in Malaya a united front of socialist parties be established'. It also asserted that the organization of the socialist parties 'will be a democratic and willing association of socialist parties which seek to establish a socialist society in Malaya'. An official resolution laid down the following as the objects:

(a) To organise and maintain in Malaya a united front of all democratic socialist political organizations for concerted political action.

(b) To strive for the establishment of a democratic socialist State of Malaya by securing for the peasants and the workers by hand or by brain the full fruits of their industry and the most equitable distribution thereof that may be possible, upon the basis of the common ownership of the means of production, distribution, and exchange, and upon the best obtainable system of popular administration and control of each industry and service.

(c) To secure the fusion of Singapore with the Federation of Malaya.

(d) To cooperate with democratic socialist organizations in other countries, with a view to promoting the objectives of the Front.

(e) Generally to promote the political, social and economic eman-

---

[7] *The Malay Mail*, 29 July 1957.
[8] Ibid.

cipation of the people and more particularly of those who depend directly upon their own exertion by hand or brain for the means of life.[9]

The Front did not start functioning immediately. In view of a ruling by the Registrar of Societies that no activities of the Front could be organized until its constitution had been duly registered it was almost a year before the organization began functioning. It was finally registered on 26 July 1958.

The membership of the Front, according to its constitution, was open 'to all lawful democratic socialist organizations' which operated on a national scale and which accepted the programme and policy of the Front.[10] The main organs of the Front were: (i) The Congress, (ii) The Central Council and (iii) The Secretariat. The Congress, comprising twelve representatives each from the member parties, was the 'supreme organ of the Front'. It elected from its membership a Chairman and a Vice-Chairman of the Front. It considered and approved the budget and 'shall issue such directives and entrust such duties and tasks to the Central Council as shall further the interests of the Front'. The Congress met only annually.

The Central Council consisted of six representatives each from the member parties. The Council elected from its membership two joint secretaries and a treasurer. The Chairman and the Vice-Chairman elected at the Annual General Meeting of the Congress also acted as the Chairman and Vice-Chairman of the Council. The Council met at least four times a year and had the following major functions:

i   The Central Council shall study and review the current political scene and the political issues of the day and issue public statements of its opinion thereon.

ii   The Central Council shall direct and control the activities of State Coordinating Committees.

[9]Malayan People's Socialist Front, *Report for the Period 31st August 1957 to 30th September 1958* (mimeographed), 25 September 1958.

[10] *Constitution of the Malayan People's Socialist Front* (mimeographed), Chapter 3, Articles 1 and 2.

The Secretariat consisting of two Joint Secretaries, in practice one from each of the two member parties, and any other staff considered necessary by the Central Council, executed the decisions of the Congress and the Council. Its major function was to disseminate information among the constituents of the Front.

At the State level the constitution had provided for the formation of State Coordinating Committees which had five representatives of each of the member parties. The state body was headed by a Chairman and had a Vice-Chairman, a Coordinating Secretary and a Coordinating Treasurer.

The organization of the Socialist Front was a very loose one; it was 'only a liaison body'.[11] None of its organs was given any important functions. The most important function performed by the executive body of the Front, the Central Council, had been to 'study and review the current political issues and the political scene of the day and issue public statements of its opinion thereon'. The constitution of the Front closely followed the constitution of the Alliance Party, but with the significant difference that whereas the latter gave substantial powers and specific functions to the Alliance National Council with regard to elections, the Front constitution did not specify at all the role to be played by the Front and its organs in elections. In fact, the two general elections contested by the Front were conducted by the two parties, by and large, separately and not jointly through the Front. Only the candidates of the two parties were fielded in the name of the Front and were allocated the Front symbol. But in the case of the Alliance Party, the situation is very different. The member parties, the UMNO, and MCA and the MIC, operate jointly and the Alliance organization plays an important part in the elections.

The Annual Report of the Front for 1958-9, lamenting about the weakness of its organization and constitution, said

> To work effectively we must have the power to work but this unfortunately was not so with the Socialist Front.

[11] Statement by the Chairman of the Labour Party, Lim Kean Siew, one of the most important enthusiasts of the Socialist Front in the earlier years, *The Straits Times*, 11 January 1966.

We found that the constitution did not give us powers to act. We had only power to meet and decide certain matters whereas for policy matters a unanimous vote was necessary.

Apart from this we could do nothing. We had no power to make anyone do anything. We had no branches, no money, no organisation to carry out our orders. We had to depend entirely upon the Labour Party and the Raayat . . . we found that as long as the Parties would do nothing, we became useless and were only a voice of propaganda.[12]

There was also the serious problem of discipline. The Front had no competence to impose discipline on the member parties or their members.

It would appear that various sections of the Parties at times thought and acted differently and yet they were not called up for questioning by the National Executive due to lack of direction and perhaps a desire to be popular with members. A recent example is the example of certain members of the Congress directly challenging the stand of the Socialist Front over the language issue . . . .[13]

Like the Alliance, the Socialist Front was not allowed to have its own individual membership and branches. This made it difficult for the Front to work effectively:

We only regret that because the Socialist Front has no organisational rights, it could not form new branches in the name of the Socialist Front but had to request new members to join either the Labour Party or Party Raayat.

Thus although the Socialist Front can act in developing support, it is unable to properly organize and direct this support.[14]

Right from the beginning the two member parties of the Front showed little trust in each other. The link-up was essentially a marriage of convenience. Few were impressed by the professions of socialist unity and cooperation for the sake of establishing a socialist society in Malaya. Both the Labour Party and the Party Raayat shared little interest in the creation of a strong and effective organization of the Front. It took a while before the Front even

[12] *Annual Report of Socialist Front, 1958-59.* (mimeographed), p. 4.

[13] Ibid. p. 3.

[14] Ibid. p. 9.

came to acquire its own separate offices. Little official business was transacted. 'There had been no directives or policy decisions apart from the policy stated at the inauguration of the Front.'[15] The Front had no money. The *Annual Report for 1958-59* stated:

> The Front decided that in order to proceed effectively it had to organize a proper office. But there was no money. It was then resolved that the Labour Party of Malaya would contribute $200 a month and the Raayat $50.
>
> But only $140 had been paid by the parties and most of this was spent at the Congress [in July 1958].[16]

The major problem faced by the Socialist Front was how to get over the situation where the constituent parties had mutually exclusive areas of support. The tendency had been to let the Party Raayat work among the Malays and attract their support and the Labour Party woo the Chinese.[17] The situation was well expressed by the organization's *Annual Report for 1958-59:*

> The Labour Party consisting mostly of Chinese members did not understand the Malayan situation as a whole but tended to look upon our problems as Chinese, non-Malay, problems. This is to say they did not understand nor consider Muslim *kampong* problems. The Labour Party leaders had failed to stress on the need of the non-Muslim proletariat to understand the Muslim peasantry.
>
> The Party Raayat, we found, was weak financially. And though many of its leaders had proven themselves to be socialists, many of its followers and smaller officials tended to depend too much on the names of their leaders to win support for the party, and therefore did not themselves seriously try to win support for the party by working in the *kampongs* but depended too much upon speeches and statements of their leaders.
>
> There was a tendency for the Labour Party to ignore the Muslim Malay problem and leave it to the Malays in the Raayat. This was a dangerous trend as the Labour Party though non-communal in concept, was in danger of becoming more and more communal both in its membership and its understanding of the Malayan problems be-

---

[15] Ibid. pp. 4-5.

[16] Ibid. p. 5. The sums mentioned are in Malayan dollars.

[17] Ibid. p. 4.

cause many of its members had not travelled Malaya and could only view our country's problems from their own home town point of view.

The Raayat attempted to enlarge itself on a non-communal basis. It began to take in Chinese non-Muslim members and in one or two cases there was a misunderstanding between the Labour Party and Raayat because of this, e.g. in Province Wellesley and in Salak areas. Since the problem of penetrating the *kampongs* is a much more difficult task, the Raayat began to develop in areas similar to that of the areas covered by Labour Party, i.e. the Chinese suburbs and New Villages.

Since the Federal Elections were coming in 1959, the Secretariat felt that certain political parties, as evidenced by the way they were moving (e.g. the PPP and the PMIP), would exploit the communal issue and use it against us in our fight against communalism and we realized that unless we could move fast and effectively we would have either to capitulate and become communal, or lose all leadership of the people.

Already the PPP and PMIP were threatening to tear the country apart by their dangerous propaganda, and this we found was also beginning to have some effect on the thinking of certain leaders of our party who began to question whether our non-communal stand could stand up against the strong emotional appeal of communalism in the forthcoming struggle and some were therefore inclined towards a certain degree of communalism for the purpose of the electoral campaign.

... As communalism is dangerous, we felt that it had to be countered immediately and we decided to meet it in three ways:

(a)   change the belief that the Labour Party is a Chinese Party by bringing into its Executive a Malay whose task would be to reeducate the thinking of some of our members;
(b)   the laying down of a strong nationalist line in our policy;
(c)   persistent campaign against all communalism outside and inside the Socialist Front.[18]

It was for this reason that in late 1959, at the initiative of the Socialist Front, Ishak bin Haji Mohammad was pursuaded to join the Labour Party where he soon assumed the position of the Chair-

[18] Ibid. pp. 1-3.

man.[19] Later in 1959, after the general election, Lim Kean Siew of the Labour Party was appointed a general adviser to the Party Raayat.[20] But they were not to make any significant changes. The Socialist Front was to face all these problems throughout its existence and eventually they were to cause its disintegration.

It has already been noted that the chief interest of the two parties of the Front was in the general elections of 1959. The over-riding desire of each was to secure a significant number of seats in the national and state legislatures with the help of the other. And therefore, as soon as the Front was recognized by the Registrar of Societies in July 1958, it directed all its attention to the general elections of 1959. The first meeting of the Central Council on 28 August 1958 decided that the member parties should contest the elections in the name of the Socialist Front.[21] At the same time a new symbol to be used in the elections was adopted. But this was not achieved without considerable opposition from the Labour Party. The *Annual Report* of the Front for 1958-9 states:

> ... at the end of 1958 when we insisted on contesting elections under the name of the Front, there was quite a great deal of objection and it is sad to note that in certain areas the Labour Party insisted on using the banner of the Labour Party for a long time in the hope of winning elections which they however lost — such tendency was opportunistic and also showed a failure to understand the basic meaning of the Socialist Front.[22]

The interest in the 1959 general elections was so strong that in May 1958 even before the registration of the Socialist Front,

[19] *The Annual Report of the Socialist Front, 1958-59*, reports:
   As we realized the need in the Labour Party for someone conversant with the *kampong* situation who had been involved in the political history of Malaya, who has the respect of the Malayan people as a whole, and who has not yet involved himself in any other of the present parties, we first directed our efforts towards finding someone to fulfil this historic role, someone who is a tried and a convinced socialist, who has proved himself.
   After months of discussion, questioning and travelling, Ishak bin Haji Mohammad joined the Labour Party and is now Chairman of the Labour Party ... Let us all hope he will prove to be a valuable asset at bringing about unity of the peoples of Malaya.

[20] *The Straits Times*, 9 November 1959.

[21] *Report for the Period 31 August 1957 to 30 September 1958*, op.cit.

[22] *Annual Report of Socialist Front, 1958-59*, pp. 9-10.

Ahmad Boestamam had announced that the Front would field candidates in all the 104 Parliamentary constituencies.[23] (The Labour Party had fielded only four candidates in the 1955 elections and the Party Raayat had not yet then come into existence.)

With elections in mind the Front set itself to the task of defining and presenting its policy and programme, a task which it had hesitated to perform so far in view of the significant differences in the orientations of its two constituent parties. For this purpose each of the two parties was asked to prepare its own separate draft. After considerable deliberation the Labour Party draft was rejected and 'the Party Raayat draft was accepted unanimously as a basis for a Policy Statement'.[24] Based on the Party Raayat draft, the final policy statement was prepared by Ahmad Boestamam and Ishak bin Haji Mohammad and approved by the Central Council on 25 January 1959.[25] It observed that the British rulers had handed over power to a party, the Alliance, which they knew was the most pliable and friendly and which would allow them to continue to maintain their position and power through it. It repeatedly emphasized that integration of the different racial groups had not been attempted since independence and Malay as the common national language had not been promoted. It maintained:

> . . . we cannot even hope to attain a united national outlook unless we develop first of all a genuine national language. Since Malaya is a heterogeneous State developed as a colony with a colonial language system and since the workers were kept divided in separate ethnic groups by the policy of division and rule, we cannot hope to communicate effectively across racial barriers unless we first break through this system . . . Let it now be a policy that all workers be able to communicate with one another by a language common to all workers.[26]

[23] *The Malay Mail*, 14 May 1958.
[24] *Annual Report of the Socialist Front, 1958-59*, pp. 7-8.
[25] A substantially revised version of the Policy Statement was published in May 1963 under the title, *Towards a New Malaya, Policy Statement*. Lim Kean Siew, who performed the revision, was responsible for the publication of the pamphlet on his own initiative. It was never recognized as an official statement of policy.
[26] *Approved Draft Policy Statement of the Malayan People's Socialist Front*, 25 January 1959 (mimeographed), pp. 3-4.

It asserted that the national language, Malay, must be put into use immediately. Citing the example of Indonesia, it asked why, if 85 million people could use the language, a population of less than 7 million could not use it in Malaya. The argument that Malay was still unfit to be used as the national language was false. It called on the Government to immediately launch a national campaign for the education of the masses in the Malay language. With regard to the demand for multi-lingualism, it significantly maintained that Chinese and Tamil should be accepted as official languages as an interim measure. But it added that the demand for multi-lingualism was put forward mainly because: first, people did not understand either of the two official languages, English and Malay; and second, 'the Government in its desire to bring about the National Language has tried to do it at the expense of the Chinese language'.[27] Once the people had learnt Malay there would be no more need for multi-lingualism. At the same time it added that Chinese and other schools should be allowed to develop without government interference. Full assistance should be provided to these schools as long as they 'do not interfere with the national effort'.

With regard to economic policy, the Front did not adopt a radical line. The statement maintained that:

> ... our economy was developed on the basis that it was a colony, a market for the consumer goods of Britain and a source of supply of cheap raw materials such as rubber, tin and coconut oil. The Government was not interested in the development of the country industrially nor did it plan towards ultimate self-sufficiency so that no system of protective tariffs was ever introduced in the country to foster and nurture local trade and industry. Instead, we had Empire preference taxes, which exempted goods made in the British Empire from Malayan import duties, and a system of agency and monopoly houses which moved into the country to gain monopolistic control of Malaya's main industries in the field of our estates, mines and in trade.[28]

The immediate solution the Draft Policy Statement offered was a centrally-planned economy and sound national controls for the

[27] Ibid. p. 9.
[28] Ibid. p. 12.

Malayan commodities. But before central planning could be introduced the national capitalists in the country would be persuaded
'to agree to organize themselves into groups under national control and according to national plans'. Only then the national capitalists would be able to take over from foreign capitalists. It called
for rapid industrialization which, according to it, is 'the ultimate
economic salvation for all under- or undeveloped countries'. The
country's raw materials, rubber, tin, timber, coconut oil, palm
oil, pineapple, etc. should be used to build up industries. It outlined three main stages towards complete 'Socialism':

> First, our national capitalists must be organized and recruited to work
> under our planned system to take over from foreign interests wher-
> ever and whenever possible. We must then absorb these national
> capitalists into our planned socialist economy under the direction of
> a socialist government and establish national enterprises. And we
> should then finally take over direct and complete control of such
> national enterprises.
>
> In that way we should be able to finally bring into the control of
> the government all essential and national enterprises such as mining,
> communications, estates and other national industries and by that
> means we could also gain planned control of the flow and distribution
> of all essential goods. In that way too we would be able to gather all
> means of production directly under government control . . . . [29]

With regard to agriculture and land policy it stated that the
present policy was inadequate and should be abolished. It called
for an end to the 'gruelling taxation by the rapacious landlords and
middlemen' and the fragmentation of holdings caused by the effect
of Islamic law. It further asserted that the fishing industry was an
important industry in the rural areas and it must be emancipated
from the hold of monopolies. A system of cooperative enterprises
in the agricultural sector must be introduced so that the rural
population could 'buy and sell goods without fear of exploitation'.

It demanded the immediate abolition of the Emergency Regulations and other such laws on the statute book. It asked: 'If
such laws are necessary in a democracy, what then is the meaning

[29] Ibid. p. 14.

of democracy?' It further called for the creation of a national army conscious of its role as the defender of the people's freedom and the freedom of the country as a truly sovereign State. Condemning the presence of foreign troops in Malaya it asserted that their presence in times of peace was inconsistent with the concept of national sovereignty and independence. They must be asked to evacuate immediately and to hand over their bases to the Malayan Government.

Singapore was a part of Malaya and there was no basis for their separation. They should be united as soon as possible. Malaya, being an Asian country, 'ought to join the Afro-Asian Group since our interests are closer to theirs'. The fundamental aim of Malayan foreign policy must be world peace and freedom based on the equality of all nations and the country must strive for the independence of subjugated peoples all over the world. And being placed strategically between China, India and Indonesia 'we must be careful of becoming pawns in the world struggle and must not become the tool of oppression or imperialism. We must therefore guard against the temptations of foreign aid which in fact are disguised attempts to subvert Malaya to foreign domination.'[30]

There was considerable opposition to the Policy Statement within the Labour Party, especially on the issue of National Language. The *Annual Report of the Front for 1958-9*, referring to the instances exposing the weakness of the Front organization had the following to say with regard to the language controversy:

When the Socialist Front in its Policy Statement supported Malay as our National Language, this was misunderstood and it came under attack by certain sections of the Labour Party of Malaya which for a long time did not see the difference between 'National' and 'Official' language and confused that issue with the cultural issue, thus becoming agents of chauvinistic forces, the enemy of the Front.

Since this issue is important, since it is logical that Malay is the only language of the peoples of Malaysia, since an attack on this stand would antagonize the Muslim peasants of Malaya who would thus become hostile to us and suspect us of being anti-Malay, anti-national,

[30] Ibid. p. 24.

or of being Chinese chauvinists, and since the reason for the attack might in fact be chauvinistic [it is to be noted that most of the attacks on this policy came from areas which had a predominant Chinese electorate], the Labour Party officials or the National Executive ought to have gone round to explain (1) that public attacks were undesirable, (2) the necessity and the logic of such a stand, (3) the meaning of multi-lingualism etc.... But the Labour Party allowed the misunderstanding to continue unchecked, taking no action against anyone who made public statements to the contrary so that our policy was not taken seriously by the people, and instead of us, it is the Government and the Dewan Bahasa dan Pustaka [Bureau of Languages and Books] which now has the credit for being leaders.[31]

But the Labour Party, dependent very largely on Chinese support, was in no position to carry out these injunctions. Since the leadership of the party consisted at this time mainly of English-educated moderates with no mass base, it had neither the desire nor the capability to force the middle level leadership and the rank and file to give up their pro-Chinese position and accept Malay as the sole national language of Malaya. They knew that if the party was not to suffer the same fate as in the 1955 elections they had to allow the lower level Chinese-educated leadership to campaign in the 1959 general elections on the basis of their pro-Chinese orientation. The crisis in the Alliance in mid-1959, further forced their hands. The mood of the non-Malay communities was such that an essentially pro-Malay position would have brought the party little mass support.

However, this situation was ignored and a shortened version of the Policy Statement was issued as the Manifesto of the Socialist Front for the 1959 parliamentary elections. The Front, though it contested only a limited number of seats, showed a great deal of optimism.

The results, though they did not measure up to the organization's pre-election optimism, meant a significant success. The Front captured eight of the 104 seats in Parliament. In the state elections, it secured sixteen seats. Its share of the total vote was 9.7 and 12.8 per cent for the state and parliamentary elections

---

[31] *Annual Report of Socialist Front, 1958-59*, p. 11.

respectively. The larger vote in the parliamentary elections was entirely a result of the crisis in the Alliance which had caused serious dissatisfaction among the non-Malay communities, especially the Chinese, and had resulted in a sharp decline in the Alliance vote in States with a sizeable non-Malay electorate.

TABLE 8

ALLIANCE AND SOCIALIST FRONT: VOTES POLLED
IN THE STATE AND PARLIAMENTARY ELECTIONS, 1959

State*	Alliance vote (% of total)			Front vote (% of total)		
	State	Parlia- ment	Diffe- rence	State	Parlia- ment	Diffe- rence
Selangor	57.6	44.3	−13.3	17.7	30.4	+12.7
Penang	51.1	44.0	− 7.1	29.4	38.2	+ 8.8
Johore	67.1	65.7	− 1.4	9.8	14.2	+ 4.4
Perak	54.7	49.6	− 4.9	3.9	2.9	− 1.0
Negri Sembilan	55.8	51.9	− 3.9	17.9	10.9	− 7.0
Malacca	67.0	58.9	− 8.1	11.4	11.5	+ 0.1

*States with a large Chinese electorate

It was this vote lost by the Alliance (almost entirely by the MCA) which was collected by the Socialist Front in Selangor and Penang — almost all of it by the Labour Party on the basis of a pro-Chinese election campaign conducted by the Chinese-educated. (It should be noted that the losses of the Alliance in Perak were picked up by the People's Progressive Party, a party based in Perak, and in Negri Sembilan and Malacca by the MCA dissidents who had contested the elections as independent candidates. In these States the Socialist Front was not so well established.)

The most significant features of the elections were first: all the seats captured by the Socialist Front, both in the state and parliamentary elections, were in Penang, Selangor, Johore and Negri Sembilan, States with a large non-Malay electorate; and second, the Party Raayat had not at all been successful. Although the Party had fielded a larger number of candidates than the Labour Party, it was able to secure only two seats each in the state and parliamentary elections. Two of these four candidates were non-

Malays, C.C. Yong, a Chinese returned to the Johore State Assembly, and K. Karam Singh, an Indian, elected to Parliament from Selangor. The other two successful candidates were the party's Chairman, Ahmad Boestamam, and its Secretary, Nazar Nong, elected from the Setapak (parliamentary) and Sentul (state) constituencies in Selangor. A significant point, too, is that all the four successful candidates of the Party Raayat were elected from constituencies with a very large number of Chinese voters, where the Labour Party was able to swing the Chinese vote in favour of the Socialist Front on the basis of its pro-Chinese posture.[32] They were definitely not elected with the support of the Malay vote. All the candidates of the party fielded in the predominantly Malay constituencies were badly defeated.

In the context of the communal situation in the country, the Party Raayat found it impossible to attract Malay support on the basis of its ideological appeal or the personal appeal of its leader, Ahmad Boestamam. And it could not go far with a communal appeal to the Malays in competition with the UMNO and the PMIP, both operating on an exclusive communal basis. Therefore, it had no option except to depend on its ideological appeal. The Labour Party, on the other hand, especially after the crisis in the Alliance in 1959 which had discredited the MCA, could effectively project itself as a champion of the cause of the Chinese community. And this is what it did and made gains in the elections.

The defeat of the Party Raayat candidates was the beginning of the end of the Socialist Front. Both member parties of the Front, the Labour Party and the Party Raayat, were extremely unhappy about the results and each put the blame squarely on the other. The Party Raayat alleged that the Labour Party had lent little support and cooperation to it; the Labour Party maintained that the Party Raayat had failed miserably to secure any support from the Malay community. The Chairman of the Labour Party, D.S. Ramanathan, in his Presidential Address to the 7th Annual Conference

[32] The racial breakdown of the electorate in the Setapak parliamentary constituency was: Malays, 7,482; Chinese, 12,524; Indians and others, 2,488. Sentul state constituency was one of the two constituencies forming the Setapak parliamentary constituency and also had a very large non-Malay electorate.

of the Party at Seremban on 17 October 1959, soon after the elections, said:

> ... the recent elections have clearly shown that the Party Raayat has failed to make, whatever the reasons may be, the kind of impact on the peasants and rural workers that we had hoped they would make. It is significant that, standing under the Socialist Front banner, the only places where Party Raayat members did actually win, were in the urban areas. [33]

Since winning the elections with the help of the other had been the *raison d'être* for the link-up, electoral reverses made the Front unattractive and meaningless. Both the Labour Party and the Party Raayat, therefore, lost interest in the joint organization, the Socialist Front. Both were so disenchanted that the organization of the Front on an effective basis which it had been hoped would be carried out after the elections could not be accomplished. For a period of about two years after the elections there was little activity in the Front. The short *Annual Report of the Front for 1960-61* lists only three activities of the organization during the year.

1. A demonstration of hawkers in Kuala Lumpur organized by V. David to protest against arrests and unreasonable action by the police.

2. An all-party Mass Rally organized by the Socialist Front to protest against 'the murder of Patrice Lumumba, the first Premier of Congo, by the puppets of Colonial Belgium'.

3. A Rally to support the Algerian people's struggle for independence against the French. [34]

No other activity, organizational or political, is mentioned by the *Report*. The *Annual Report of the Front for 1961-62* opens with the statement that the suggestions made in the *Annual Report for 1958-59* 'such as the need for division of labour, for reorganization of the Socialist Front, for more effective dissemination of informa-

---

[33] Presidential Address by D.S. Ramanathan (mimeographed), p. 2. The Statement led to a serious controversy in the Front. It 'brought an immediate retaliation from the Raayat which made two statements in the nature of a challenge' (*Report of Socialist Front, 1958-59*, p. 15). The Raayat called it 'a stab in the back' (*The Straits Times*, 8 November 1959).

[34] *Annual Report of the Socialist Front, 1960-61*.

tion to the Divisions and Branches of our Parties, are still not implemented and that the executive power is still not with the Front'.[35]

The disenchantment of the two parties was also reflected in the several serious crises which arose in the Socialist Front soon after the elections. In fact, the poor showing of the Party Raayat in the elections had prompted certain sections in the Labour Party to suggest in mid-September, about a month after the parliamentary elections, that the two parties should be merged and a new political organization with one constitution, the Socialist Party of Malaya be established.[36] But the Party Raayat was quick to reject the idea. A senior leader of the party said that though the two parties were linked in the Front they were distinctive bodies and there was a wide gap between the two. 'Party Raayat is not 100 per cent the same as the Labour Party. There are a number of things on which we do not see eye to eye.'[37]

Soon after the elections a serious controversy confronted the Socialist Front and for some time threatened its very existence. It was precipitated by the publication of the *Report of the Education Review Committee, 1960 (Rahman Talib Report)* and the Labour Party's reaction to it. The details of the *Report* and the strong opposition to it by the Chinese-educated in the Labour Party have already been discussed. The attitude of the Chinese-educated created a strong reaction in the Party Raayat which felt that the Labour Party had assumed a Chinese chauvinist line on the issue. Matters came to a head when the Segamat branch of the Labour Party, a stronghold of the Chinese-educated in Johore, took Ahmad Boestamam, the Chairman of the Front, to task for his views on education as reported in Chinese newspapers.[38] It promptly sent a telegram to Boestamam: 'We strongly protest your statements regarding the educational affairs of Chinese and Indians in Malaya'. Boestamam immediately retaliated: 'Protest

---

[35] *Annual Report of the Malayan People's Socialist Front, 1961-62* (mimeographed) p. 1.

[36] *The Malay Mail*, 16 September 1959.

[37] Ibid.

[38] *The Straits Times*, 17 September 1960.

accepted. Challenge you to put forward no confidence vote against me'. Explaining the position of the Party Raayat, Boestamam told *The Straits Times:*

> I have always stated that as long as the position of English is maintained, then the position of Chinese and Tamil education should be on the same level with English. According to the Federal Constitution, the position of English should be reviewed in 1967. If the result of the review is to scrap English in fully-assisted schools, then instruction in Chinese and Tamil should also be ended. If this happens, then I say the three languages should be taught as compulsory subjects in all secondary schools for all time.
>
> My contention is that by 1967 Malay will be so well advanced that it will be possible to have it as the sole medium of instruction.[39]

But the Labour Party, in particular the Chinese-educated sections in it, were completely opposed to it. They were insistent that the Chinese people must retain their right to have their own independent system of education i.e. Chinese-medium schools must remain in existence after 1967. To force the issue, Ahmad Boestamam, the President of the Party Raayat, resigned his position as the Chairman of the Socialist Front. The Labour Party, realizing that this would wreck the Front, which at this stage the Chinese-educated did not want, immediately set itself to repair the damage. Following several consultations and a final eight-hour meeting of the Central Council of the Front a 'compromise', in essence representing the view of the Party Raayat, was evolved. The chief points of the agreement were:

1. Government subsidies for Chinese and Tamil schools should continue till 1967 when the issue would be reviewed by the Parliament.[40]

2. Schools which, after 1967, use Malay as the medium of instruction must also teach English, Chinese and Tamil as subjects, 'parti-

---

[39] 17 September 1960. It was only in 1958 when the urge to have a united front, in view of the impending elections, was strong that the Policy Statement of the Socialist Front had said that Chinese and other schools should be allowed to develop without government interference and full assistance should be provided them as long as they 'do not interfere with the national effort'. See above. p. 193.

[40] This had no practical significance because the Alliance Government had already decided that such schools would not be eligible for state assistance after 1961.

cularly the last two as they are the mother tongue of a large number of non-Malays'.

3. The Socialist Front is not opposed to independent schools [schools not eligible for state aid] with their own media of instruction.

4. It reiterates that it regards Malay as the only national language and that it should be widely used in all walks of life.[41]

5. Ahmad Boestamam would reassume his position as the Chairman of the Socialist Front.[42]

But as we shall see later the 'compromise' did not work, for the Chinese-educated in the Labour Party accepted it only as a matter of expediency. It was in their interest at this time to save the Front.

Further friction was created between the Labour Party and the Party Raayat by the local and town council elections in the country in 1960 and 1961. The two parties found it extremely difficult to cooperate and contest the elections jointly under the banner of the Socialist Front. Not only was there trouble with regard to nomination of candidates but there was considerable bickering following the elections. The *Annual Report of the Socialist Front for 1961-62* said:

> ... in Johore, because of the defeats of certain candidates, the Party Raayat blamed the Labour Party for not working hard enough in those wards. Some officials wanted campaigns to be held in the *kampongs* similar in nature to campaigns held in towns. Of course this cannot be, because the circumstances are different. However, the Divisional Headquarters of the Socialist Front attempted to settle the matter, but Party officials refused to attend or convene those meetings, until the National Executive had to intervene.
>
> The National Executive, with the Secretary General and representatives of each Party, met and at first Party Raayat officials boycotted or refused to attend that meeting although they knew that such a meeting was to be held, and insisted on having Boestamam himself

---

[41] The Party Raayat insisted on putting this in to commit the Front once again to this position on the question of official language because certain sections of the Labour Party had started demanding official language status for Chinese and Tamil, though not publicly.

[42] *The Straits Times*, 19 September 1960.

attend although they knew very well that he was in England at that time . . . .

In Malacca, Tan Tuan Boon, who had joined the Party Raayat recently, stood for elections, and the Socialist Front was successful . . . Tan Tuan Boon was elected Chairman [of the Town Council] because the Alliance did not feel it safe without an absolute majority to take the chair. [43] Immediately afterwards quarrels arose in the Party Raayat between Tan Tuan Boon and other officials and between Tan Tuan Boon and Labour Party officials . . . . The disputes went on for a long time, involving other personalities of the party and were exploited by other members of the party . . . . Not only the Chairman of the Socialist Front and the Secretary General but also other members of the National Executive had to come down several times and although there is a temporary withdrawal of the forces, there is no settlement of the dispute . . . .

In Kedah, again because of defeat in the elections, top officials of the Parties began accusing one another This led to the resignation of the Chairman of the Socialist Front . . . . [44]

These are only a few instances of the quarrels between the two parties arising out of the elections. The major problems in this regard have been about finance and Socialist Front policy. Party Raayat, dependent very largely on the support of Malay peasantry, was perenially short of funds and hardly in a position to contribute to the funds of the party. Unlike the Labour Party, its small number of middle-class members and supporters did not contribute much to the party. Also, the party had only four representatives in the state legislatures and the Parliament who contributed a part of their allowance to the party. Another important source of this problem has been the fact that, again unlike the Labour Party, all leaders of the Party Raayat, whether at the state or the national levels, are professional politicians dependent on the party for their livelihood. They have no other sources of income. In the case of the Labour Party most of its English-educated leaders have been professional men of some affluence, medical doctors, lawyers,

[43] The result of the election for the twelve seats in the Town Council was: Socialist Front, five; Alliance, five; Malayan Party, two.

[44] *Annual Report of the Malayan People's Socialist Front, 1961-62*, pp. 10-11.

school teachers, trade unionists, etc., who were not only not dependent on politics for their livelihood but in a position to contribute money to the party funds. Also, the Labour Party membership has been much more substantial and is derived from groups who are in a position to pay membership dues to the party at least.

Consequently, the Party Raayat has always depended on the Labour Party for funds, especially during the elections. It believes that the funds of the Labour Party should be used equally for the benefit of the Party Raayat. This has been a significant cause of trouble between the two parties throughout the period of their link-up.

However, interest in the Socialist Front was to be revived for a short period starting from mid-1961 when the idea of Malaysia was put forward by the Prime Minister, Tunku Abdul Rahman. For some time their common struggle against Malaysia brought them together and strengthened the internal unity of the Front. Both the Labour Party and the Party Raayat, who had initially welcomed the idea, soon came to oppose the formation of Malaysia. Their opposition, however, was not for identical reasons. But it certainly brought the two parties closer.

The Labour Party, now under the substantial influence of the Chinese-educated and through them linked closely to the Chinese chauvinist and ideologically extreme Barisan Sosialis of Singapore, soon reversed its position on Malaysia. The change was not a result of its own independent evaluation of the situation, but almost entirely reflected the views of the Barisan Sosialis, whose position was determined by the internal struggle for power in Singapore between the Barisan and the People's Action Party.

This change in the approach to Malaysia was not fully supported by the English-educated moderates and a large section of the Indian supporters of the Labour Party. They were concerned about the identification of the Labour Party with Communist and pro-Communist organizations within the country and outside. But having no mass base of their own in the party, the English-educated leaders were in no position to influence strongly the party's attitude and as a matter of expediency went along with the Chinese-educated for the time being. Later, when the party adopted a more extreme position, they became inactive or withdrew from the Labour Party altogether.

The Party Raayat's opposition to Malaysia, however, was essentially a reflection of its pro-Indonesian orientation. As we have seen, the leadership of the Party Raayat had always been influenced by Indonesia and it also believed that the salvation of Malaya was only through strong links with that country. And once Indonesia came to oppose the idea of Malaysia the Party Raayat had to go along and support Indonesia. But at the same time, it must be mentioned that, being a radical left-wing party, it had its own reservations about Malaysia as a 'neo-colonial' device.

The first response of the Socialist Front to Malaysia was to send a high-level group of its own to Borneo Territories in November 1961 'to study the situation in the territories'.[45] The delegation consisted of Ahmad Boestamam (the Chairman), Lim Kean Siew (the Secretary-General), Omar Noordin, K. Karam Singh and V. David. It is important to note that the group consisted of Malay leaders of Party Raayat or the pro-Chinese-educated leaders of the Labour Party. None of the English-educated moderates of the Labour Party were included in the group. Nonetheless the mission in its report did not adopt an extreme view on Malaysia. The report maintained that Borneo was neither China nor was it England. 'It belongs to Borneo and Borneo fits into the Malaysian Region of Sumatra, Java and Malaya.' This was Greater Malaysia which they would like to see established in the region. It then asserted:

> ... *we must accept the idea of Malaysia as a logical one and that the Malaysian concept of the Prime Minister of Malaya, which includes only the territories of the Federation of Malaya, Singapore, Sarawak, Brunei and British North Borneo, is but a step towards this Greater Malaysia.* How the concept of Greater Malaysia is going to shape and what form it will take is another question, but there is no doubt that there must be a form of integration which should include all these territories I have mentioned, because geographically, linguistically, and economically we belong to one another.

---

[45] *Report to the Socialist Front, The Bornean Territories*, 16 November 1961 (mimeographed), p. 1.

... the Malaysian concept of the Federation and the North Bornean
States is a proper concept, but it is only part of a greater concept and
must lead towards this greater concept without which there can be no
reality. [46]

Even though the report accepted and welcomed the concept of
Malaysia it emphasized the necessity of three major conditions for
the success of the plan. First, it maintained that 'as long as Malaya
or any Federation of States stands against Indonesia, it will cause
friction with Indonesia which might lead to a clash within the
Malay world itself, of which Malaya is part'. Second,

> ... since the Malaysia as conceived today, consists of only a few
> territories in a vast complex, and since it will cause uneasiness to its
> neighbouring countries if it aligns itself to any power bloc, it must,
> in order to survive in peace and democracy, stand very strongly for
> non-alignment in order not to cause friction within Malaysia so that
> one day we could all get together again as a Malaysian bloc of nations
> having its own independent way of life, without suppression and
> domination from external countries. [47]

Third, the report insisted that the countries forming the new
federation should be brought in 'voluntarily and as equals'. It
maintained that a democratic federation meant self-determination
for peoples involved. And citizenship qualifications should be
changed to include all those who accept Malaysia as their home
and who have lived in the territories for a sufficient number of
years. It also asserted that no special privileges be accorded to any
racial group and that all racial groups be treated on an equal basis.

The Socialist Front soon called for 'a meeting of all progressive
and socialist parties and individuals of the proposed Malaysian
territories' to discuss the proposed formation of Malaysia; it is
important to note that the stated purpose was *not* to oppose Malaysia.

The *Annual Report of the Front for 1961-62* reports:

> ... the first response came from the PAP [People's Action Party
> of Singapore], which offered to assist the Socialist Front in its con-

[46] Ibid. pp. 7 & 8. Emphasis added.
[47] Ibid. p. 8.

ference and, because of this, the Front sent a delegation, led by the Secretary-General, Lim Kean Siew, to Singapore to meet Lee Kuan Yew and Rajaratnam, where *it was agreed that the question of Malaysia, or merger, should not be brought into open conflict and that if there was to be conflict it should at least be in closed session, and that the open session should only deal with matters agreed upon.* It was stressed by the PAP that unity was to be paramount.

If the Malayan Government was obstructive and would not allow the Conference to be held or if certain delegates would not be permitted into Malaya, then the PAP would allow the Conference to be held in Singapore. The PAP would pay one-fifth of the expense involved during the conference and all expenses of delegates, if the conference were held in Singapore, would be borne by the PAP. [48]

The important point to note is that at this time both the Socialist Front and the People's Action Party were willing to cooperate with each other. The Socialist Front, not yet hostile to the concept of Malaysia, was willing to cooperate with the pro-merger PAP and attempt to secure the conditions which it considered necessary for the success of the Malaysia plan. Similarly, the aim of the PAP was to keep the issue out of public political controversy and seek to obtain a mutually acceptable compromise.

But before the conference could take place relations between the Socialist Front and the PAP deteriorated. Earlier, in August 1961, the pro-communist elements had left the PAP and formed a new political organization, the Barisan Sosialis, mainly to oppose the proposals for merger agreed on in principle between the Prime Ministers of Malaya and Singapore in August 1961. [49] The Barisan, as soon as it was formed, established very close links with the Chinese-educated now ascendant in the Labour Party and through them with the Socialist Front. From then on, the Socialist Front policy with regard to Malaysia was almost entirely determined by the Barisan Sosialis. Also, between 13 September and 9 October 1961, after Barisan Sosialis and Socialist Front links had been established, the Prime Minister of Singapore, Lee Kuan Yew, gave

[48] *Annual Report of the Malayan People's Socialist Front, 1961-62,* p. 2. Emphasis added.

[49] Michael Leifer, 'Politics in Singapore', *Journal of Commonwealth Political Studies,* Vol. II No. 2 (May 1964), p. 110.

a series of twelve talks over Radio Singapore where he emphasized that the Socialist Front and the Barisan Sosialis were both linked closely to the underground Malayan Communist Party and that their common aim was to sabotage the formation of the new federation and pave the way for an eventual communist takeover.[50] Nonetheless, the People's Action Party attended the Malaysian Socialist Conference held at Kuala Lumpur from 26 to 28 January 1962 which was attended by the Socialist Front, the Barisan Sosialis, the Partai Raayat of Brunei, the United People's Party of Sarawak, the Party Raayat of Singapore, and the Workers' Party of Singapore. At the Conference, the PAP insisted on their Working Paper being accepted by the Preparatory Committee. When the latter refused the PAP withdrew from the conference.

The Joint Communique of the Conference, 'An Approach to Malaysia', representing the views of all the parties participating in the Conference, put forward the conditions for the success of Malaysia expressed in the *Report to the Socialist Front, The Bornean Territories,* 16 November 1961. But more important, it now implied that the people of the Borneo Territories and Singapore should be asked to make the choice only after they had been granted independence. With regard to Singapore it said:

> Considering the present state of political growth in the Federation. *the Conference realises that the conditions are not favourable for a full and complete merger, and therefore supports the desire of the people of Singapore for full self-determination . . . .* [51]

Speaking generally with regard to all the territories involved, it said: '. . . The people can only decide if representative forms of government are fully established in all the territories'. The Conference also decided to set up a permanent organization of the Malaysian Socialist Conference 'to deal with affairs common to all socialists in Malaysia whether or not Malaysia comes about'. A *pro tem* committee was constituted but it failed to organize the Conference on a permanent basis.

---

[50] Lee Kuan Yew, *The Battle for Merger,* Singapore, Government Press, 1962.

[51] *Annual Report of the Malayan People's Socialist Front, 1961-62,* Appendix A, 'Joint Communique of the Malaysian Socialist Conference, An Approach to Malaysia'. Emphasis added.

Earlier, in December 1961 just before the Conference was held, the Indonesian Communist Party had denounced Malaysia as 'a form of neo-colonialism' which would strengthen 'the position of the imperialists in Southeast Asia in implementing their SEA-TO activities'.[52] Though the Indonesian Government took over a year before committing itself to the Indonesian Communist Party line on Malaysia, it had an almost immediate effect on the Socialist Front and Barisan Sosialis attitude, which now became critical of the concept of Malaysia itself and started moving closer to the Communist line. The entire seven pages of the *Annual Report of the Front for 1962-63* were devoted to Malaysia, and stated that 'we have opposed Malaysia, and we have continued to do so' on the grounds that it would not be to the well-being, peace and prosperity of Malaya.[53] It said:

> Malaysia may yet find in Sarawak and Brunei the Dien Bien Phu of Malaysia, this time not with the French army facing defeat but a British army watched by the 7th Fleet of the American Navy.

It now saw a new danger. Its fear was that the concept of a Greater Malaysia, *Melayu Raya* (including Malaya, Singapore, the Borneo Territories and Indonesia), which it had earlier supported and seen as the only salvation of the whole region and Malaysia as the 'logical' step towards its attainment, was being turned into a racial concept. It said:

> The creation of Malaysia right within the Malaysian region that has been moved by the concept of Melayu Raya as reflected in the demand for Maphilindo would put its non-Malay population at a disadvantageous position. The revival of *Melayu Raya* concept can easily be turned into a racialist cry.[54]

It now feared Malaysia as a racial concept and as a step towards the attainment of a Malay racial Maphilindo or *Melayu Raya* formed

---

[52] *Documents of the Third Plenum of the Central Committee of the Communist Party of Indonesia*, December 1961, pp. 58-61, quoted in J.M. van der Kroef, 'Indonesia, Malaya and the North Borneo Crisis', *Asian Survey*, col. III No. 4 (April 1963), p. 174.

[53] *Annual Report of the Malayan People's Socialist Front, 1962-63*, p. 4.

[54] The reference was to the Maphilindo plan suggested at the Manila conference of Sukarno, President Macapagal and Tunku Abdul Rahman, which had been readily accepted by the three countries.

to protect the Malay communities in Malaya, Indonesia and the Philippines against China and the Chinese in these countries. And in this the Front reflected only the view of the Labour Party and not the Party Raayat.

Malaysia completely dominated the Malayan political scene during this time. The Socialist Front considered no other activity and devoted all its attention to opposition to Malaysia. And this had enabled the two member parties of the Socialist Front to maintain reasonably good relations and cooperate with each other. But as the 1964 general elections drew near the semblance of good relations brought about by their joint struggle against Malaysia was seriously damaged. The issues which had divided the two parties earlier in the pre-Malaysia period came to the fore again.

The first major problem arose with regard to the issue of language and education as the Front had to indicate its position in the manifesto for the elections. The agreement reached between the two in 1960 had proved to be an agreement on paper only and both parties within their organizations had maintained their own conflicting positions on the issue. The situation was well expressed by the Chairman of the Socialist Front Committee to draft the Education Manifesto, V. Veerappan, in a confidential letter to the General Secretaries of the Labour Party and the Party Raayat on 24 January 1964:

> I wish to make the following report and also give my personal suggestions on the above after about six meetings and spending three full days in Kuala Lumpur to resolve the issue.
>
> It is my feeling that we have reached an impasse in the unsolved problem of education which if not solved straight away could lead to a parting of the ways ....
>
> The fear of the Raayat is that the National Language would be pushed aside and relegated to an inferior position and that other languages especially Chinese would also be made an official language.
>
> The fear of the Labour is that the Chinese schools would be slowly made to disappear by being denied state-aid and recognition.
>
> Therefore, our objective must be to emphasize our determination to make Malay the supreme language of the country and Malay schools the main pillars of educational system, whilst Chinese, Tamil

and English are given a proper status and stake in the country and Chinese, Tamil and English schools are given a suitable place in the common educational system.[55]

The final draft for the manifesto submitted by Veerappan on behalf of the Committee asserted:

> The Socialist Front emphasizes that the use of the National Language as the sole official language and the steps taken towards encouraging and fostering such use must not be confused with the aim of education in general. Education in general can be given and obtained in any language that is rich enough. As such and as racialist sentiments are strong in this country, where consideration must be given to the racial composition of the citizens, the Socialist Front believes and declares that education must be given in the Chinese and Tamil languages as well as long as there is a DEMAND for it.

It further maintained that examinations must be conducted in the language of instruction i.e. Malay, Chinese, Tamil and English. Grants to approved independent schools (Chinese and Tamil medium schools) must be provided by the Government 'in order to maintain a proper standard and especially for the teaching of the National Language'. In other details and on the structure of the educational system in the country, it closely followed the Labour Party's statement, *Our Educational Policy, 1961*, which had earlier been submitted to the Socialist Front for consideration but on which no decision had been reached in view of the Party Raayat opposition.

But this was not acceptable both to the Chinese-educated in the Labour Party and the Party Raayat. The Party Raayat in its 'Draft Manifesto on Policy on Education' sent to V. Veerappan on 23 January 1964 put all emphasis on the establishment of a common system of education. It asserted:

> We are convinced that in order to strengthen the forces of national unity and in order to eradicate the colonial influence so widely disseminated through colonial orientated education, it is desirable to have a common national system of education with a common lan-

[55] 'Impasse in Drafting Education Manifesto.' A copy of the original is with this writer.

guage and syllabus. Schools under such a system will ensure that the younger generation of each racial group will not continue to be isolated in schools within their respective stream of education. [56]

What it did not say was significant; it said nothing about Chinese and Tamil languages and education. While the Chinese-educated in the Labour Party were maintaining that the Razak and Rahman Talib reports on education had gone too far and were 'the executioner of Chinese education', the Party Raayat maintained:

> The Alliance, with its Razak and Rahman Talib Reports have utterly failed in redressing the position of Malay schools. Seven years after *merdeka* now, English education has grown into a strength it has never enjoyed before, while Malay education has been utterly neglected and slowly losing confidence of the people. [57]

We have already noted the position of the Chinese-educated in the Labour Party in Chapter III. The election manifesto for the 1964 general elections which was finally drawn and circulated largely ignored the viewpoint of the Party Raayat. It reflected to an extent the views of the Chinese-educated in the Labour Party and went beyond the compromise arrived at between the Labour Party and the Party Raayat in 1960. [58] The main points made by the manifesto were:

1. We shall take into special consideration the failure of the Alliance Education Policy to establish an adequate and proper development of the system of education in the National Language and the suppression of the equal opportunity for development of education in other language media.

2. We will continue state aid to other language schools, like Chinese, Tamil and English.

---

[56] 'National Education Policy, Party Raayat Stand', a letter to V. Veerappan signed by Tajuddin Kahar, Secretary-General, the Party Raayat, 23 January 1964. A copy of the original is with this writer.

[57] Ibid.

[58] See pp. 201-2 above for details of the compromise. The key point of the 1960 compromise was that state aid to Chinese and Tamil medium schools should be continued till 1967 when the whole issue would be reviewed by Parliament. And there was the understanding that in 1967 if a decision was taken not to retain English, instruction in Chinese and Tamil would be treated on the same level and scrapped.

3. We will conduct examinations at all levels in Primary and Secondary schools in the medium of instruction with the National
Language as a compulsory subject.

4. We emphasize the ultimate objective of having a common system
of education with the National Language as the main medium
of instruction. And we guarantee to foster the growth and development of other media of instruction namely Chinese, Tamil
and English within the provision of Article 152 of the Constitution.[59]

Even this statement of policy was not used in the elections by the
Labour Party. The Chinese-educated maintained their extremist
position, and campaigned in the elections on that basis.

The second source of discord was the Labour Party's attempt
in early 1964 to bring the newly formed National Convention
Party of Aziz Ishak into the fold of the Socialist Front. Aziz Ishak,
one of the leading Malays in Selangor and a senior member of the
Malayan Cabinet since Independence, left the UMNO and the
Government because of differences with Tunku Abdul Rahman,
the Prime Minister, and launched the National Convention Party
in July 1963.[60] The Labour Party, conscious of the fact that it had
no support of its own among the Malays and that the Party Raayat
had failed to make any significant impact on the Malay community,
saw a source of strength in the well-known personality of Aziz
Ishak and was inclined to draw him into the Socialist Front to
strengthen its Malay base. But this was vehemently opposed by
the Party Raayat which saw the entry of Aziz Ishak and his party
into the Front as a serious threat to its own position in the Front.
It feared that it would significantly reduce its own bargaining
power. It also believed that the presence of Aziz Ishak would
affect the pre-eminent position in the Front of its leader, Ahmad
Boestamam, which the latter had always enjoyed. But the Party
Raayat was not in a position to oppose the entry of Aziz Ishak and
his party openly, and therefore, the Labour Party was successful
in effecting this on 16 March 1964, just before the general elections
were held. And during the elections, the Labour Party cooperated

[59] *Manifesto of the Socialist Front for 1964 General Election.*
[60] See Chapter VIII for details on the National Convention Party.

more strongly with Aziz Ishak and his party than with the Party Raayat. Being a new and smaller party, the National Convention Party was much less demanding than the Party Raayat and therefore was able to secure more support and cooperation from the Labour Party. And this situation certainly further strained the relations between the Labour Party and the Party Raayat.

As soon as it was announced that general elections would be held in April 1964, some of the English-educated leaders of the Labour Party initiated moves to forge a united front of the opposition parties. Talks were held during February and March 1964 in which the Socialist Front, the National Convention Party, the United Democratic Party and the Party Negara participated. Two important opposition parties, the Pan-Malayan Islamic Party and the People's Progressive Party, which had earlier cooperated with the Socialist Front in their opposition to Malaysia, kept out of the negotiations. The Pan-Malayan Islamic Party, which had cooperated with the Socialist Front in its opposition to Malaysia because of the pro-Indonesian orientation of many of its key leaders, could not sit together with parties with a predominantly Chinese membership. The main basis of its opposition to the UMNO was that the latter by cooperating with the MCA and the MIC, the communal organizations of the Chinese and Indians, in the Alliance had sold out the Malays to the non-Malays. Therefore, it was in no position now to cooperate with the essentially non-Malay parties of the opposition. In the case of the People's Progressive Party there had been a significant shift in its position on Malaysia since the formation of Malaysia in September 1963 and therefore it was not willing to cooperate with parties which were still persistent in their opposition to Malaysia.

Within the Socialist Front, as we have noted, the main desire for the united front had come from the moderate English-educated leaders of the Labour Party, persons like Tan Phock Kin, Tan Chee Khoon and V. Veerappan, who believed that cooperation with other parties would strengthen their position within the Labour Party and would also be a strong check against the Chinese-educated moving the party to an extreme ideological and communal position. Both the Chinese-educated in the Labour

Party and the Party Raayat were opposed to any links with the United Democratic Party. The Chinese-educated, even though they were in sympathy with its pro-Chinese position on the issue of Chinese language and education, had always considered the UDP a *bourgeois* right-wing party similar to the MCA. In a confidential note circulated within the Labour Party in late 1962, its Secretary-General, Lim Kean Siew, asserted that any attempt at a coalition or electoral understanding with parties like the UDP and the PPP would be dangerous because it 'will polarize or split the country into two opposite forces'. Also,

> ... we must never forget that the Socialist Front is struggling for peasantry support. This is a difficult task and any attempt to join up with other parties having an anti-peasantry image will only retard our work... we should not cut our throats in order to be given blood transfusion from sympathisers.

The Chinese-educated were also opposed to any links or understanding with the Party Negara, which to them was essentially a Malay communal party. The Party Raayat, too, was suspicious of the UDP and considered it a Chinese communal party. Both the groups at this time needed the English-educated moderate leaders of the Labour Party and therefore were in no position to reject outright the idea of cooperation sponsored by them. They therefore tagged along. Dr. Rajakumar, representing the Chinese-educated, participated in all the negotiations.

On 9 February 1964, a Draft Agreement was signed in Kuala Lumpur.[61] With regard to Malaysia it significantly said: 'We accept Malaysia as an accomplished fact.' But at the same time in an appendix to the agreement, the Socialist Front insisted on enunciating its own position on Malaysia.

Serious difficulties soon arose between the Socialist Front and the United Democratic Party on the question of allocation of seats, which were specially brought to a head by the Chinese-educated in an attempt to wreck the effort towards a united front. In the meantime, with the decision of the People's Action Party of Singapore to contest the elections across the causeway in

[61] *Draft Agreement, Agreed at Meeting of Opposition Parties on 9 February, 1964 at Kuala Lumpur* (mimeographed).

Malaya, the UDP too had lost interest in the link-up. The leader of the UDP, Lim Chong Eu, was more interested in tying his party eventually to the PAP rather than to the Socialist Front. He knew that any cooperation with the Socialist Front would displease the PAP and would make it difficult to come to any understanding with the latter eventually. Thus the whole attempt fell through and the Socialist Front contested the elections on its own.

Elections seriously put to a test the relations of the Labour Party and the Party Raayat. There was considerable bickering between the two with regard to allocation of seats and selection of candidates. The *Annual Report of the Front* for 1963-4 says: 'In the last elections several disputes arose with regard to constituencies and candidates in the States of Selangor, Johore, Negri Sembilan and Pahang. Consequently, in the electoral constituencies cooperation between the Party Raayat and the Labour Party was not satisfactory.'[62] Much of the trouble was because the Party Raayat wanted a large number of constituencies, both state and parliamentary, as in the 1959 elections, to be allocated to it. But the Labour Party was opposed to this because it believed that the Party Raayat did not have a realistic view of its support. It maintained that the Raayat support was not very extensive and it should field candidates only in those areas where it had adequate support and not in areas where it had to rely on the Labour Party to deliver the votes. Also, the Labour Party, conscious of the fact that eventually it would have to finance the whole electoral campaign and put up the security deposits of most of the candidates, including those of the Raayat, was interested in limiting the number of candidates. However, the Party Raayat went ahead and fielded a large number of candidates. This seriously affected the relations between the two parties. The Labour Party's view was that since the Raayat had not heeded its advice and put up a large number of candidates it could not expect support from it.

---

[62] *Laporan Majlis Kerja Pusat Kepada Kongres Front Sosialis Raayat Malaya* (Report of the Central Council to the Congress of the Malayan People's Socialist Front), 1963-4 (mimeographed). Translated by the author from the original in Malay.

In most constituencies the two parties operated independently of one another.[63] Each party did its own campaigning; the two held their own separate election meetings. Rarely were election rallies addressed by leaders of the other party. Very few election meetings were organized under the auspices of the Socialist Front, participated by both the Labour Party and the Party Raayat. House-to-house campaigns too were conducted separately by the two parties; the workers never included workers of the other party. But in Selangor, leaders and workers of the National Convention Party worked closely with the Labour Party and gave strong support to one another. Aziz Ishak and Datoh Kampo Radjo of the National Convention Party, for example, worked hard to gain Malay support for Tan Chee Khoon of the Labour Party in the Batu parliamentary constituency in Kuala Lumpur. The entire campaign was conducted on a communal basis, the Labour Party concentrating on wooing the Chinese voter and the Party Raayat attempting only to attract the Malay voter. But this was nothing new. The significant point was that the two parties did it exclusively for their own candidates and not for one another.

In the pre-election campaign the ruling party, the Alliance, made Malaysia and Indonesian 'confrontation' as the key election issue.[64] The entire Alliance campaign was geared to prove that the Socialist Front (and the Pan-Malayan Islamic Party) was anti-national and pro-Indonesian. Its loyalty to the country was challenged. Also, the People's Action Party of Singapore, which at the last moment had decided to contest the elections with the chief purpose to fight the anti-Malaysia parties, directed its entire effort to expose the Socialist Front as a pro-Indonesian party.

The reaction of the Socialist Front to this propaganda approach of the Alliance and the PAP was curious. They danced to the tune called by the Alliance. They too made Indonesian 'confrontation' and Malaysia the sole election issue. They put all emphasis on the

---

[63] Interview with Dr. Tan Chee Khoon, Kuala Lumpur, April 1964.

[64] For details of the campaign and the issues, see R. K. Vasil, 'The 1964 General Elections in Malaya', *International Studies*, Vol. VII No. 1 (July 1965), pp. 39-45.

Malaysia issue and their approach to the voters was: 'If you want war, vote for the Alliance, and if you desire peace, vote for the Socialist Front'. They maintained that 'the Alliance is making all efforts to use the war scare that it has created to get back to power. If we do not counter it, they would utilize the situation by telling the people that the country's security and integrity is threatened and that all people must rally round Tunku and the Government.'[65] To counter this, the Socialist Front attempted to pursuade the voters to believe that the Alliance Government, under the influence of the neo-colonialist powers, was pursuing an aggressive policy which was bound to push the country into a war. They put the entire blame for Indonesian 'confrontation' on the Alliance Government and promised in their election manifesto that if they were elected to power they would 'clear up the mess the Alliance Party has made of our country'.[66]

A bulletin distributed by the Penang Division of the Socialist Front during the election campaign entitled 'Where the Alliance has Failed — Its Foreign Policy' said:

It is definitely wrong for our Prime Minister, Tunku Abdul Rahman, to negotiate with the British Government to form Malaysia. Such an action gives other countries an excuse to consider our Government as a neo-colonialist in the sense that it is trying to colonize the Borneo territories. A transfer of power by the British Government to the Malayan Government can be indicative of neo-colonialism. We are not against the formation of Malaysia but we feel that Malaysia can only come about by giving the people in the Borneo Territories the chance of self-determination first. By self-determination we mean that it should be left to the people in these territories to gain their independence from the British colonial government. After they have obtained their independence, then the elected representatives of the peoples in the Borneo Territories can negotiate on an equal footing with the representatives of the Malayan Government to form Malaysia.

[65] Interview with C. C. Yong, a leader of the Party Raayat and the Socialist Front, Johore Bahru, March 1964.

[66] The Front put out many posters with cartoons depicting the Alliance Government as pushing the country into a war with Indonesia.

The leaders of the Socialist Front throughout the election campaign talked mainly of Indonesian 'confrontation'. The party's left-wing socialist character, in terms of economic policy, was not emphasized and no special effort was made to woo the working class vote.

In the elections held in late April 1964, the Socialist Front suffered serious reverses: it was the party most badly hit. The Socialist Front, which had polled 9.7 per cent of the total vote in the 1959 state elections secured 16.2 per cent in 1964.[67] This, however, does not necessarily mean a larger support for the Front, for in 1964 it fielded 167 candidates, as against 124 in 1959. The increase in the vote was much smaller in the parliamentary elections. With only thirty-eight candidates the party had polled 12.8 per cent of the vote in 1959, whereas in 1964 with as many as sixty-three candidates it secured only 16 per cent of the vote. In terms of seats, the organization suffered very serious setbacks: in the state elections, it won only seven seats out of the 167 that it contested in 1964, whereas it had secured sixteen out of 124 in 1959; and in the parliamentary elections, it succeeded only in two constituencies out of the sixty-three in which it fielded candidates in 1964, whereas it had won eight of the thirty-eight seats it had contested in 1959.

The most significant aspect of the election results was that the Party Raayat was completely routed; none of its candidates was returned either in the state or parliamentary elections though it had fielded as many candidates as the Labour Party. The same was the fate of the National Convention Party; all its candidates were defeated. This setback, especially for the Party Raayat, was to prove the end of the Socialist Front. The Front had suffered crushing defeats and thus its *raison d'être* was gone. Immediately, strong pressures were felt within both the Labour Party and the Party Raayat. The inter-communal Alliance, the ruling party, had worked and thrived mainly because it has meant political power for the three communal parties constituting the Alliance, which in-

---

[67] The state elections in 1959 had taken place before the crisis in the Alliance and, therefore, the Socialist Front had secured only a small percentage of the total vote.

dividually none of them could have ever hoped to achieve in view of their communal basis and character. The Alliance, accidentally created before the February 1952 municipal elections in Kuala Lumpur, had several electoral successes which had kept it alive and thriving. Similarly the left-wing alliance, the Socialist Front, was created in 1957 chiefly for the purpose of jointly contesting the 1959 general elections. But unlike the Alliance, it never achieved any significant electoral successes. On the contrary, its serious reverses in the 1964 elections were eventually to lead to its disintegration.

Soon after the elections, important sections in the Labour Party promoted a move for the dissolution of the three parties, the Labour Party, the Party Raayat and the National Convention Party, and the formation of a new single party. On 21 June 1964, the powerful Selangor Division of the Labour Party, at its annual conference, passed the following resolution without any dissent:

> That the Conference bases [sic] on the interest of the struggle of the socialist, resolutely supports the proposal that the Labour Party, Party Raayat and National Convention Party be dissolved and a single party be formed accordingly. [68]

In the Labour Party, both among the English-educated moderate leaders and the Chinese-educated, there was complete disenchantment with the Party Raayat. The Party Raayat had failed to secure any support within the Malay community, the purpose for which the two had been linked up. Further, the Chinese-educated in the Labour Party, who had earlier supported the link-up mainly to strengthen their own position in the Labour Party *vis-a-vis* the English-educated leaders, no longer needed the Party Raayat to boost their position since they were now in complete control of the Labour Party. On the side of the Party Raayat, there was a complete loss of interest in the Front for it had not fulfilled the purpose for which it had been accepted by the Party. The link-up had not helped the Party Raayat at all in the elections. In fact, the leadership of the party had a strong feeling that the association had

[68] Labour Party of Malaya, Selangor Division, *Annual Report, 1963-64* (mimeographed).

done more harm than good. Being linked with an essentially Chinese party, controlled by Chinese chauvinists, it had found it extremely difficult to operate among the Malays. Also, with the later developments in Indonesia which finally resulted in the end of Indonesian 'confrontation' of Malaysia, the last thread binding the Labour Party and the Party Raayat into the Socialist Front was destroyed.

At this time, significant changes were taking place within the Labour Party which were to have a profound impact on the Socialist Front and eventually to contribute to its disintegration. The Chinese-educated, now in full control of the Labour Party, were no more interested in keeping up a show of respectability and a moderate position on communal issues, those of Chinese education and language. Leaders of the Labour Party, both the Chinese-educated (especially Tan Kai Hee and Rajakumar) and the English-educated, with a reasonable position on the issue of Chinese language and education, were either behind bars or had been removed from positions of influence. It was only a matter of time before the new groups controlling the party under the increasing influence of the Barisan Sosialis were to move it to an extreme position on communal issues.[69] This trend in the Labour Party was obvious to the leaders of the Party Raayat who in late 1965 withdrew their party unilaterally from the Socialist Front. Soon, the Labour Party also took the decision 'to disengage' itself from the nine-year-old Socialist Front.[70] Thus came to an end the inter-communal Socialist Front, the one potentially hopeful alliance of ideologically-based parties of the Malays and the non-Malays.

[69] This, as we noted in Chapter III, took place in December 1966 when the Labour Party in an official statement demanded the status of official language for Chinese and Tamil.

[70] *The Straits Times*, 11 January 1966.

VI

THE PEOPLE'S PROGRESSIVE PARTY

THE People's Progressive Party, led by two brilliant lawyers of Ceylon Tamil origin, S.P. Seenivasagam and D.R. Seenivasagam,[1] was founded on 11 January 1953 at Ipoh, Perak, and was then known as the Perak Progressive Party. The inaugural meeting was attended by about thirty important non-Malays of Ipoh, many of whom were lawyers. It was established as a local party with the aim 'to contest all elections to the State Councils or Town Boards when elections are introduced'[2] and 'to further the interests, political, domestic, economic, cultural and aesthetic of the members'.[3] The party was formed in a very casual manner. None of the leaders were keenly interested in politics or had any clear idea of the long-term role of the party. Many of them had studied in England where in a vague way they had become interested in politics. The first secretary of the party reports that he was elected in the following manner:

> I was informed on the morning of the day when the inaugural meeting took place. I was the most talkative and asked the largest number of questions among the people gathered. As a result, they said, well, if you are taking so much interest why not become the secretary of the party. And they promptly elected me.[4]

The key man behind the formation of the party was D.R. Seenivasagam, the younger of the two brothers, who only a few years

[1] The two are brothers.

[2] Elections for the city councils of Penang and Kuala Lumpur had already been held and it was expected that the system would be introduced in Perak also soon.

[3] *The Straits Times*, 8 January 1953. The same objects are mentioned in the present constitution of the party.

[4] Interview with J.R. Devadas, first Secretary of the party, Ipoh, January 1964. This was confirmed by D.R. Seenivasagam, Ipoh, March 1965.

earlier had returned from England after completing his law training and had joined his elder brother in his father's law firm in Ipoh.[5] Before the formation of the party he was one of the founders and a Vice-President of the Perak Labour Party.

Soon after the formation of the Perak Labour Party in October 1952, D.R. Seenivasagam and some others broke away from it and decided to form a party of their own. D.R. Seenivasagam wanted the new party to have a socialist bias and so did the others who came out of the Labour Party with him. However, people who came in from outside did not share this view. They were not inclined towards politics, but had been roped in purely because of their personal relations with D.R. Seenivasagam and others.

The party remained primarily an Ipoh-based group. Its membership was very small, restricted mainly to a small group of professional people, many of them lawyers. The following is a description of the party during those days by its first Secretary:

> The party when formed had no political philosophy. It was completely the creation of the Seenivasagam family, the two brothers and their mother, who played a very important role behind the scenes. At that time it was not dominated by the Chinese. The party's small membership consisted of Chinese, Indians and Ceylonese. There was no preponderance of any one community in the membership. The party did not take up the outstanding issues among the Chinese, *viz.* the issues of Chinese education and citizenship.[6]

On 14 October 1953, in a fifteen-point memorandum sent to the Federal Elections Committee, the party recommended that elections should be held on a non-communal basis.[7] No party or organization which was racial in character or constitution should be allowed to participate in the elections. It demanded that adequate provision be made to safeguard the interests of minorities whose candidates failed in elections. It said that it should be ensured that 'at least two-thirds of the adult population domiciled

---

[5] The elder brother, S.P. Seenivasagam, even today keeps himself away from the limelight, though he carries as much influence in the party, if not more, than his younger brother used to.

[6] Interview with J.R. Devadas, Ipoh, January 1964.

[7] *The Straits Times,* 15 October 1953.

or permanently resident in this country are given the franchise. Otherwise rule of majority by the minority may result.'

However, the very next month the party decided to cooperate with the UMNO-MCA Alliance. On 8 December 1953, it agreed in principle to join the UMNO-MCA Alliance for the purpose of contesting the coming Town Council elections in the State. It stated in a press statement that although the UMNO and the MCA were separate communal organizations, the party believed that the formation of the Alliance indicated that the leaders of the two organizations were resolved to eradicate communalism.[8] At this time the National Association of Perak was very strong in the State. Both the Alliance and the Perak Progressive Party were concerned about their chances against the National Association of Perak in the coming elections. The two parties, therefore, decided to cooperate with the sole aim of beating the National Association of Perak.[9] The Malayan Indian Congress at this time had not yet joined the UMNO-MCA Alliance and was fielding its own candidates against Alliance nominees. The Alliance felt that the Seenivasagam brothers and others of Indian origin in the Perak Progressive Party would be of great help in attracting the fairly significant Indian vote.[10]

In 1954, the party fielded D.R. Seenivasagam as a joint UMNO-MCA-PPP candidate in the Ipoh Town Council elections, where he was successful. This was the first time that a PPP candidate had been successful in any election.

However, cooperation between the two disparate groups was to be short-lived. During the middle of February 1955 the Execu-

---

[8] Interview with D.R. Seenivasagam, Ipoh, March 1965. Seenivasagam felt that he was wrong in his appraisal of the Alliance and its leaders. According to him the Perak Progressive Party had relations only with the Malayan Chinese Association. Its leaders had no contacts with the United Malays National Organisation. Thus, its view of the Alliance was determined primarily through contacts with the MCA.

[9] Interview with J.R. Devadas, Ipoh, January 1964.

[10] Interview with K. Annamalai, a very close friend of the Seenivasagam brothers and a leader of the PPP, Kuala Lumpur, March 1965. It has also been stated by D.R. Seenivasagam (Ipoh, March 1965) that the two most important leaders of the MCA in Perak, Leong Yew Koh and Y. C. Kang, were very keen that the PPP should join the Alliance. They felt that this would strengthen the position of non-Malays within the Alliance as against the UMNO.

tive Committee of the PPP decided to leave the Alliance. 'It was obvious,' announced D.R. Seenivasagam, the Secretary of the party, 'that while the UMNO-MCA are prepared to concede the PPP the right to submit names of candidates for the federal elections they are not prepared to concede the right of the PPP to have representatives on the selection committee in Kuala Lumpur'.[11] Also, the suggestion of the PPP that Alliance candidates should be selected on merit and not on their racial origin was not acceptable to the Alliance, in particular the UMNO.[12] This would have given the PPP an advantage over the Alliance as it had a larger number of professional and educated men in its ranks.

Cooperation with the UMNO-MCA Alliance, while it lasted, was not restricted to electoral understanding only; there was cooperation at the policy level also.[13] The result was that the policy position of the PPP at this time was not very different from that of the Alliance on issues concerning non-Malays. The manifesto of the party for the 1955 elections for the Federal Legislative Council which was issued on 8 June 1955, after the party had left the Alliance, put a great deal of emphasis on the fundamental rights of the people.[14] It demanded a fully-elected legislature and assured that the position of Their Highnesses the Sultans will be maintained as constitutional rulers. It recognized Malay as the national language and stated that

Malay and English as official languages should ordinarily be the medium of instruction in government and government-aided edu-

---

[11] *The Straits Times*, 22 February 1955.

[12] Interview with K. Annamalai, Kuala Lumpur, March 1965.

[13] Interview with S.P. Seenivasagam, Ipoh, January 1964.

[14] These were:
1. Equality before the law: No person shall be denied equality before the law and the equal protection of the laws of the Federation.
2. Prohibition of racial discrimination: There shall be no discrimination against any person on grounds of religion, race or sex.
3. Equality of opportunity: There shall be equality of opportunity for all persons in matters relating to employment or appointment to any office under government...
4. Freedom of speech.
5. Protection of life and liberty: No person shall be deprived of his life or personal liberty except by due process of law.
6. Freedom of conscience and religion.
Federal Elections, 1955, Manifesto, 8 June 1955.

cational institutions. Every community, however, shall have the right to conserve its own language and culture and shall have the right to establish educational institutions of its choice.

On the touchy issue of multi-lingualism the position of the party was the following:

The progressive use of the Malay language for the official purposes of the Federation will be encouraged without, however, restricting the use of the English language for all or any such purposes. While it is agreed that proceedings in the Federal legislature should be conducted in the Malay or English language, as a temporary measure members of the legislature should not be restricted in their choice of their language to give expression to their views. Particularly in the Chinese community there are many able and popular leaders who will be unable to serve the country as Federal Councillors due to this restriction. *It is emphasized, however, that multi-lingualism is recommended purely as a temporary measure and should not be allowed after a period of ten years.*[15]

Further, the manifesto promised:

We shall promote with special care the educational and economic interests of the Malays and shall protect them from social injustice and from all forms of exploitation. Various schemes to encourage and assist the Malays in industry, professions and trade will be established.

Here it should be noted that the party did not attempt to establish a communal image and obtain votes on a communal basis. Its stand on the outstanding and alive communal issues, those of Chinese education and the Malay special position, was a moderate and reasonable one. The party did not write off Malay votes and in an attempt to secure some Malay support committed itself to protecting the special position of the Malays. It attempted to create an essentially non-communal ideological appeal. Hence, the emphasis on people's welfare and rights and socialism in the manifesto. The party had just come out of the Alliance and as yet had not moved very much away from the Alliance position on

---

[15] Emphasis added.

communal issues. The result, consequently, was that it did very badly in the federal legislative council elections of 1955.

The party contested in only two of the fifty-two constituencies and its candidates were D.R. Seenivasagam, who contested in his home town of Ipoh, and Zaharie bin Hassan, a Malay, who contested in the neighbouring Kinta Selatan constituency. Both of them lost their deposits. Later, in November 1955, in the state elections in Perak, the party fielded two candidates for the twenty seats and once again both the candidates lost to the Alliance. One of the candidates again was the party's founder, D.R. Seenivasagam, who contested in the Ipoh East constituency and lost to Yap Yin Fah of the Alliance.[16]

Thus far the party was a genuinely non-communal political party, not exploiting any communal appeal. But the successive defeats in the elections led to a rethinking and reappraisal of the party's appeal and image. It was felt that the strictly non-communal and vague ideological appeal would not take the party very far in securing the support of the masses. If the party was to win any electoral support it had to depend primarily on the non-Malays, in particular the Chinese, who formed a large part of the population in and around Ipoh, the centre of the party's activities. Considering the prevailing communal atmosphere in the country, the leaders of the party felt that the only way to obtain Chinese support was to champion their cause. And the issues of citizenship, Chinese education and multi-lingualism provided the basis of this new and more effective appeal.[17]

Simultaneously, the two Seenivasagam brothers started establishing personal bases of support. They started giving small help like school fees, coffin money, books etc. Also they started appearing in court cases without charge for hawkers, trishaw-riders, small traders and others.[18] Because of these services, D.R. Seenivasagam, during this period, was appointed honorary legal adviser

---

[16] *The Straits Times,* 14 November 1955. Two years later, in November 1957, when the party had adopted a pro-Chinese position, Seenivasagam defeated Yap Yin Fah in a federal by-election in the same constituency by a convincing margin.

[17] Interview with K. Annamalai, Kuala Lumpur, March 1965.

[18] Ibid.

to associations of hawkers, stall-holders, trishaw-riders, petty traders, cycle-repairers etc., which later were to prove very significant sources of support.

The Non-Malay Phase

On 15 March 1956, shouts of *jus soli* echoed in the Perak Library Hall, where the party held its annual meeting. D.R. Seenivasagam declared: 'The Chief Minister speaks of mobilising the people but there will be no mobilisation if there is no *jus soli*. We will not fight if we are not given *jus soli*.'[19] The meeting also resolved to change the name of the party to People's Progressive Party of Malaya.

It should be noted here that the party's manifesto for the 1955 elections had made no reference to the question of *jus soli*, or the citizenship issue in general even though the issue had agitated the Chinese community for many past years.

This was the time when it was becoming increasingly clear that UMNO had emerged as the senior partner in the Alliance and the MCA had lost its position of equality. The MCA found itself in a very awkward position. Its dilemma was that it could not both represent the wishes of the Chinese community and remain as a member of the Alliance. If it attempted to represent the wishes of the Chinese it got into trouble with the UMNO. On the other hand, if it gave emphasis to working in cooperation with the UMNO, which in effect meant playing a secondary role within the Alliance, many Chinese tended to lose faith in it and felt that it was not fulfilling its task of protecting them and their interests.

The issue of *jus soli* was revived in early 1956 at the time of the constitutional talks in London. Demands of *jus soli* immediately reappeared. 'Threats were made by various Chinese associations to withdraw all support from MCA and to set up a rival political organization to it unless it "stiffened" its line on the question of *jus soli*.'[20] In late March 1956, Lau Pak Khuan, a former President

---

[19] *The Straits Times*, 16 March 1956.

[20] Margaret Clark, 'The Malayan Alliance and its Accomodation of Communal Pressures, 1952-1962', unpublished thesis submitted to the Department of History, University of Malaya, for the degree of Master of Arts in History, 1964, p. 103.

of the Perak MCA and the foremost leader of Chinese associations in Perak, warned that unless four specific points were submitted by the MCA in its memorandum to the Reid Commission, the Perak Chinese would break away and submit their own separate views. The four points were:

1. Equal citizenship rights for all non-Malays.
2. Those born in Malaya and those who have lived in this country during the last five years and are loyal to this country should be given full citizenship rights, irrespective of their racial origin.
3. All citizens of independent Malaya should have equal responsibilities and privileges.
4. The principle of multi-lingualism should be accepted and the languages of the various racial groups should be accorded official status.[21]

The MCA convened a meeting of its leaders in Malacca to consider its stand on *jus soli* after accusations by the Chinese Guilds and Associations that the MCA had been indifferent to the issue. Reporting the result of the meeting to the Alliance National Council, T.H. Tan, the Executive Secretary of the MCA, stated in a letter that the meeting had decided 'that the MCA, as the political representative of the Chinese, must support the principle of *jus soli*'.[22] However, this was only a temporary gesture. Very soon the MCA 'found itself embarrassed by the continued vehemence and persistence of their [that of the Associations and Guilds] campaign. Wishing to maintain the good faith of its Alliance partners, the MCA publicly dissociated itself from the Associations and Guilds and claimed their attacks on the MCA were led by die-hard Kuomintang elements.'[23]

The differences between the Chinese Associations and Guilds and the MCA were intensified when in the middle of 1956 the Reid Constitutional Commission, established to make recommendations on a new constitution, visited Malaya. The General Committee of the MCA met on 19 August 1956 and was unable to take a decision on the Alliance draft memorandum which was to be pre-

[21] *The Straits Times*, 29 March 1956.
[22] Ibid. 17 April 1956.
[23] Clark, op.cit. p. 106.

sented as a joint memorandum on behalf of the three parties of the Alliance.[24] Immediately the Guilds and Associations warned the MCA that 'the overwhelming majority of the Chinese in the country' were against the Alliance draft memorandum and wanted the following:

1. Chinese to be one of the official languages.
2. *Jus soli* to be applied unconditionally.
3. No further special privileges to be accorded to the Malays. [They had no objection to the continuation of the existing privileges.][25]

However, the MCA, on 26 August 1956, approved the Alliance draft memorandum with 'minor' changes.[26] The meeting opposed the idea of giving the Malays more privileges than the ones provided for in the Federation of Malaya Agreement of 1948. It rejected those contained in the draft memorandum which reserved for the Malays a proportion of lands, posts in public services, permits to engage in trade or business, government scholarships etc. However, it did not say anything about the issues of *jus soli* and Chinese language.

In May 1957, a three-man delegation consisting of Lau Pak Khuan, Yap Mau Tatt and Tan Kee Gak, representing the powerful Chinese Associations and Guilds, left for London to make representations on Malaya's new constitution to the British Government. However, this last minute effort was fruitless. The Alliance went ahead and with the tacit consent of the MCA refused to make concessions to the Associations and Guilds.

Furthermore, on the issue of Chinese language and education the MCA, in the eyes of many Chinese, had failed 'to protect' their interests. In September 1955, soon after the Alliance had formed the Government following its victory in the Federal Legislative Council elections, the Government of the Federation of Malaya appointed a high-level Education Committee under the chairmanship of the Minister of Education, Dato (now Tun) Abdul Razak bin Hussein. The report of the committee was published during

[24] *The Straits Times*, 20 August 1956.

[25] Ibid. 25 August 1956.

[26] Ibid. 27 August 1956.

the middle of 1956 and later in 1957 legislation incorporating the recommendations was enacted. The main recommendations were the following:

Malay and English would be compulsory subjects in all primary and secondary schools.

Instruction in Kuo Yu and Tamil would be made available in all primary schools maintained in whole or in part from public funds when the parents of fifteen children from any school requested it.

The other language media schools would remain in existence.

All schools conforming to the Government educational policy would be eligible for grants-in-aid.

A common syllabus and time table for all schools was to be enforced.[27]

The main objective of the committee was to establish 'a national system of education acceptable to the people of the Federation'. To the Chinese, however, this meant an attempt to curb the nationalistic (Chinese) orientation of instruction in the Chinese-medium schools. The Chinese concern was centred round the compulsory teaching of English and Malay and the common syllabus and time table.

The enactment based on the Report of the Razak Committee was unanimously accepted by the Federal Legislative Council, which had fifteen representatives of the MCA. However, this did not mean that there was no controversy about the enactment. The opposition to the enactment and its implementation was so great that *The Straits Times* was constrained to write in an editorial:

It [the *Razak Report*] is now being challenged openly by a section of the Chinese community, perhaps a very large section. Everything — even the Emergency — is dwarfed by the threat of communalism.[28]

Mohammad Khir Johari, who took over the Education portfolio in September 1957 and who was primarily responsible for imple-

[27] Federation of Malaya, *Report of the Education Committee, 1956,* Kuala Lumpur, Government Press, 1956.

[28] *The Straits Times,* 13 August 1956.

menting the recommendations, is reported to have described his
task in the following words:

> When I took over the Ministry my office resembled that of a General:
> wall maps and charts with pins showing the location of school strikes
> and riots throughout the country hung everywhere.[29]

Starting from the middle of November 1957 there were serious
disturbances in many of the Chinese schools in Penang, Ipoh,
Kuala Lumpur and Seremban. On 17 November all the Chinese
schools in Ipoh were closed for one week.[30] However, the demonstrations and disturbances continued and a very large number of
young Chinese students were arrested. D.R. Seenivasagam and
his brother, S.P. Seenivasagam, came to the rescue of these students
and bailed them out *en masse*. They were later defended by D.R.
Seenivasagam when formal charges were brought against them
by the authorities.[31]

The MCA again, as a member of the Alliance, was in no position
to take up the issue of Chinese education with the Government,
even though the Chinese community was so agitated about it.

It was in this very highly-charged atmosphere caused by the
Chinese school student riots that the by-election to the Federal
Legislative Council in the Ipoh-Menglembu constituency was
held on 23 November 1957.[32] The PPP scored a major victory
when its candidate D.R. Seenivasagam beat his Alliance rival.[33]
This victory put the party firmly on a new course. The result of
the crucial election was the following:

D.R. Seenivasagam (PPP)	5,911 votes
Yap Yin Fah (Alliance)	4,091 votes

Only two years back, in the 1955 elections, D.R. Seenivasagam
had lost his deposit against an Alliance candidate in the same constituency when he secured only 808 votes.

[29] Clark, op.cit. p. 142.
[30] *The Straits Times*, 18 November 1957.
[31] Interview with K. Annamalai, Kuala Lumpur, March 1965.
[32] The by-election was caused by the resignation of Leong Yew Koh who had been
appointed Governor of Penang.
[33] *The Straits Times*, 24 November 1957.

The by-election of November 1957 witnessed a hard fight. The chief issue was that of Chinese education and the Chinese school students' riots. The Alliance sent its top-ranking leaders, including the Prime Minister, to address election rallies in Ipoh where they were hooted down by the extremely excited, predominantly Chinese, crowds. It was charged by the Alliance that the PPP had instigated student demonstrations.[34]

The leaders of the powerful Chinese Associations and Guilds swung in favour of the PPP candidate. To them the MCA was no more fulfilling its sole function of protecting the interests of the Chinese. They had to look to other political organizations which could be used to project the point of view of the Chinese community and to fight for its interests. On 12 November, only a few days before the crucial by-election, Lau Pak Khuan, the acknowledged leader of the Chinese Associations and Guilds and one of the founders of the MCA, in a letter to D.R. Seenivasagam declared his support for him.[35] At the same time another important leader of the Chinese community and the President of the National Association of Perak, Foong Seong, announced his support for the PPP. The PPP used these two letters in the by-election campaign and distributed thousands of copies of them. This support proved crucial. The present Secretary-General of the party, Chan Yoon Onn, gave the following reasons for Seenivasagam's victory in the by-election:

1. D.R. Seenivasagam was elected a Town Councillor in Ipoh in 1954. This had given him the opportunity to build himself up as a leader of the people of Ipoh.

[34] However, S.P. Seenivasagam said in a statement: 'The Progressives refute categorically the utterly false and mischievous insinuations made by the Prime Minister and other Alliance men that there is some connection between the student situation in Ipoh and the pending federal election . . . . We have never had anything to do with organizing the campaign.' He added that the student demonstrations had come as a 'complete surprise to us. However, once the demonstrations commenced, it was clearly our duty to concern ourselves with the way in which the students were treated by the police.' *The Straits Times*, 22 November 1957.

[35] *The Straits Times*, 13 November 1957. Lau Pak Khuan had earlier sent his resignation to the MCA.

2. Chinese education trouble just before the elections and the support given by party to the movement.
3. Personal service to the people.
4. Support from Chinese Associations and Guilds.[36]

Encouraged by his success in the by-election, D.R. Seenivasagam announced his party's intention to extend its activities on a Malaya-wide basis. He also said that one of the first things he would do when he took his seat in the Federal Legislative Council would be to raise the issue of the education policy of the Alliance Government.

D.R. Seenivasagam, who from the time of his debut in the Federal Legislative Council was to become a stormy petrel of Malayan politics, in his maiden speech in the Council crossed swords with Prime Minister Tunku Abdul Rahman. In a short speech on 7 December 1957, which was very mild compared to many of his speeches in the later years, he criticized the Alliance Government for not allowing the people of Malaya to visit the Soviet Union or China.[37] He alleged that the people of Malaya had no personal knowledge of what was going on in China or Russia and that they

> ... were forced to listen to a stream of propaganda emanating from America.... The people of Malaya are not allowed to see Chinese or Russian newsreels while, on the other hand, American propaganda discrediting China and Russia are freely circulated in this country ... the dignity of a country cannot be maintained in international affairs if it seems apparent to the world that the international affairs of a free nation are being conducted or steered by another country — in this case, I say, the United States of America.

He suggested that the Alliance Government should seriously consider sending to China an all-party delegation 'to see for themselves and come back and report to the people of this country'.

With regard to the Emergency he charged that 'it has been the policy of the Alliance Government to introduce a certain state of affairs to enable the continuance of the Emergency Regulations in

[36] Interview with Chan Yoon Onn, Ipoh, March 1965.
[37] Federation of Malaya, *Legislative Council Debates — Official Report*, 7 December 1957.

this country'. He added: 'We must realize that terrorism and communism are two different things . . . in all civilized countries, in all democracies, people are given the right to preach their political beliefs, and one of the political beliefs of this world is communism.' Making a plea for the recognition of the Communist Party as a legal organization, he asked: 'Has the Alliance Government ever considered the fact that communism if legalized in this country may be chucked out, may be thrown out, by the people at the elections and that will be the end of the preachings of communism in this country?'

Finally, with regard to the recommendations of the Razak Committee on Education he asserted:

> I do say that the recommendations made by that Committee did not reflect the views of the majority of the people in this country. As for the parents, I would only draw the attention of this House to the existence of the Emergency Regulations, to the existence of the banishment laws of this country. Parents of Chinese students are, in the large majority, uneducated, who dare not open their mouths because they feel that if they do something, Emergency Regulations Sec. 24, will be applied and they will be arrested, detained and possibly put on the next boat to China.

Tunku Abdul Rahman, the Prime Minister, was not used to this sort of strictures and suggestions. D.R. Seenivasagam was the first elected non-Malay representative to sit on the opposition benches of the Federal Legislative Council of independent Malaya. The Prime Minister, in an unprecedented outburst, at the next sitting of the House on 9 December, told Seenivasagam: 'I could have you arrested.'[38] He said: 'Can you find a country more democratic than this country? . . . if he can, then I say clear out of here and go there.' Countering the charge that the police had been unduly severe in controlling the Ipoh students he asserted that they 'were lenient when compared with what the students did on the occasion . . . because the police used canes, as a correction on an age-old adage: spare the rod and spoil the child — they were called brutes by the Honourable Member . . . .'

[38] Ibid. 9 December 1957.

However, this episode pushed Seenivasagam into the limelight and he became a hero. He emerged as the sole champion of the rights and interests of the non-Malays.

The party now moved farther in the direction of an essentially non-Malay party championing the cause of the non-Malays. Its leaders became more vocal. The President of the Penang Division, Jagjit Singh, declared that if the party was elected to power it would immediately recognize China and Soviet Union.[39] The Secretary of the party, D.R. Seenivasagam, in a campaign speech for the Ipoh town council elections in December 1958, asserted that the Constitution of Malaya was unfair.[40] In Singapore, Malays were only a small minority whereas the Chinese formed a large majority, yet the Chinese and Indians in Singapore had accepted Malay as one of the official languages. But in Malaya although there were more than two million Chinese their language was not accorded the status of an official language. Touching on the ban on the import of certain goods from China, he stated that he wanted to know why there should be a ban on cheap and good articles from China only. Why not ban goods from Japan, United States, England and India if Malayan industries were to be protected?

This approach of the party paid immediate dividends. In early December 1958, in the Ipoh town council elections, the party was able to capture all the four seats for which elections were held.[41] Its candidates defeated the Alliance and National Association of Perak candidates with comfortable margins. This was a very crucial victory and gave the party control of the Ipoh Town Council. Jubilantly, D.R. Seenivasagam declared: 'In the 1954 elections the Alliance got its first 100 per cent victory in the town council elections in Perak with the help of the PPP. Today the Progressives have given the Alliance their first 100 per cent defeat.'[42] Significantly, one of the defeated Alliance candidates was Too Joon Hing, the Secretary-General of the MCA. PPP control of

[39] *The Straits Times*, 10 September 1958.

[40] Ibid. 3 December 1958.

[41] Ibid. 8 December 1958.

[42] Ibid.

the Ipoh Town Council was to prove of great significance. As will be seen later, a substantial part of the support for the party in and around Ipoh was a result of the extremely honest and efficient management of the Ipoh Town Council, which is recognized as the best-administered town in Malaya.

Soon after assuming control of the Ipoh Town Council, the party officially sponsored and secured approval of a proposal to introduce multi-lingualism in the council. This had great impact, for this was the first time when the languages of the non-Malays, Chinese and Tamil, could be used for any official purposes.

With its changing orientation, the party made attempts to gain support outside Ipoh. However, such attempts were unsuccessful. In the City Council elections in George Town, Penang, the party fielded four candidates, all of whom lost.[43] Its candidates in the Council elections in Tapah (Perak) and Kuala Lumpur too were defeated by the Alliance nominees.[44] In the other states of the Federation, the party fielded no candidates for it had no organization. The major bases of the party's appeal being the personality of its two key leaders, the Seenivasagam brothers, and its control of the Ipoh Municipal Council, it failed in its attempt to extend itself beyond Ipoh.

On 6 August 1959, the party issued its manifesto for the 1959 general elections which was called *Blueprint for Equality and Progress*.[45] It declared that the basic objectives of the party were 'democracy and a welfare state based on socialism'.

Its position on some of the important issues was as follows:

Equal Rights and Privileges: Every citizen of this land should have equal rights and privileges in return for the equal obligations which he owes to King and country. This is a fundamental principle of democratic socialism and to obtain this equality the People's Progressive Party of Malaya will strive to amend the Constitution. Any semblance of special treatment to any one race will inevitably lead

---

[43] *Singapore Standard*, 15 December 1958.

[44] *The Straits Times*, 8 and 21 December 1958.

[45] Election manifesto of the PPP, Ipoh, 6 August 1969. It is intersting to note that the party's manifesto for the 1955 elections was titled *Federal Election Manifesto*.

to frustration, suspicion and disappointment of the other citizens and the establishment of a true Malayan nation will be retarded.

Citizenship Laws: The party will seek to amend the laws relating to citizenship to establish for all time in this country only one class of citizens — all enjoying the same rights, privileges and security and owing the same obligations.

It accepted Malay as the sole national language, but at the same time demanded that the languages of the non-Malays, Chinese and Tamil, be accorded the status of official languages. On the vital issue of education policy the manifesto declared:

> The People's Progressive Party of Malaya condemns the Razak Education Policy and the manner of its implementation and will call for the immediate setting up of an independent committee consisting of education experts free from political attachment to devise and recommend a fresh education policy for the children of the Federation.

It further demanded:

a. That the medium of instruction in all vernacular schools be in the mother tongue.

b. That the medium of examination be the same mother tongue as the medium of instruction.

c. That Malay shall be a compulsory subject in all schools but the medium of instruction and examination shall be the mother tongue.

d. That all educational institutions of the various communities be accorded fair and equal treatment.

e. That the education provided in vernacular schools be recognized as part of the educational system of the country.

f. That grants-in-aid be on a fair and equitable basis for all institutions irrespective of community.

g. That all teachers, vernacular or otherwise, be treated equally.

h. That students from all recognized schools after completion of studies be treated equally on merit in relation to the question of employment and no discrimination should exist.

The manifesto, on the whole, put the greatest emphasis on issues of language and education and equality for all citizens of the country though formal homage was paid to socialism and welfare of the people. The position taken by the party was aimed entirely at securing the support of the non-Malay communities, especially the Chinese. Its chief aim was to build itself up as the sole representative of the Chinese community. And in view of the failure of the MCA to protect Chinese interests, the party was successful in projecting this image. It virtually became a Chinese communal party. It might be of interest to recall here that in October 1958, when the Chinese community was extremely agitated about the Government's educational policy, D.R. Seenivasagam had moved the following resolution in the Federal Legislative Council:

> That this Council is gravely concerned over the dissatisfaction which exists over the present Education Policy of the Government and resolves that a Committee be immediately appointed by the Government to review the present policy and to make recommendations for its improvement or replacement by a policy which will meet with approval of the people of Malaya.[46]

The interesting point is that Dr. Lim Chong Eu, the President of the MCA, opposed the resolution and refused to believe that there was 'widespread dissatisfaction'. He suggested that Chinese views 'with regard to education have sometimes appeared to be more vehement than otherwise but I am certain . . . that these views can be collated and can be channelized into fruitful views which can find common understanding and common unity with the other communities in this country and which will together strengthen our educational policy. . . .'[47]

The party did well in the elections: it captured four seats in the Parliament and eight in the Perak State Assembly. All the four parliamentary seats were also in Perak. In the parliamentary elections the party fielded candidates only in four States: Johore one, Penang two, Selangor three and Perak thirteen. In the state elections it put up candidates in three States: Penang eleven, Selangor four and Perak twenty-four. In Perak, the party emerged as the main opposition and secured as much as 24.3 per cent of the

[46] Federation of Malaya, *Legislative Council Debates, Official Report*, 22 October 1958.
[47] Ibid.

total vote. It was obvious that the bulk of the party's support was in the State of Perak. Further, the party had failed to secure any support among the Malays; all its support had come from the Chinese and Indians. The single Malay candidate who had been successful in the elections was soon to leave the party and join the UMNO.

Following these significant successes in the 1959 elections, though only in Perak, the party was full of hope and vigour. In October 1959, D.R. Seenivasagam made a bid to introduce multi-lingualism in the Perak State Assembly.[48] The motion, however, was defeated.

In February 1960, the Alliance Government appointed the Education Review Committee under the chairmanship of the Minister of Education, Abdul Rahman bin Talib, an UMNO extremist. The PPP submitted an eleven point memorandum to the committee in which it reiterated its position on the issues of Chinese language and education which had been formulated in its manifesto for the 1959 elections. Later in March 1960, following serious anti-Chinese measures in Indonesia which caused concern among the Chinese in Malaya, D.R. Seenivasagam called upon the Government to sever diplomatic relations with Indonesia because of its 'inhuman treatment of non-Indonesians'.[49]

In the by-election to Parliament in the Kampar constituency in Perak the party made a gain when its candidate, Chan Yoon Onn, polled 11,314 votes against 9,315 polled by the Alliance candidate, Liew Whye Hone, a very prominent leader of the MCA in Perak.[50] Here again, the PPP propaganda was that the MCA had betrayed the Chinese cause. It was the PPP which was the champion of the rights of the Chinese.[51]

In the early 1960s, however, the party suffered from a lack of interest and activity on the part of its leaders and members. Speaking at an Annual General Meeting of the party, D.R. Seeni-vasagam asserted:

[48] *The Straits Times*, 6 October 1959.

[49] Ibid. 29 March 1960.

[50] Ibid. 19 May 1960.

[51] Interview with K. Annamalai, Kuala Lumpur, March 1965.

We started in 1954 and by 1959 we were a very strong party. But as soon as we became strong some top leaders of the party became too confident. Other leaders of the party would not do anything. Everything, writing of letters, arranging meetings etc. was all pushed on to one man, the Secretary-General. No work was done at the branch level with the result that they began to disintegrate. So when the elections [Local Council] came last year [1963] there were no strong and well-organized branches to work for the party.[52]

It has been suggested to this writer that following the 1959 general elections some leaders of the party took more interest in building up their personal fortunes than in party work.[53] The party's control of the Ipoh Town Council and representation in Parliament is said to have come in handy in pursuing this activity.

Then came the 1964 general elections in which the entire opposition, primarily because of the issue of Indonesian confrontation and Malaysia, suffered serious setbacks. However, the PPP came out with much less damage done to its position. The party, unlike the Socialist Front, was able to avoid a crushing defeat by changing its position on Malaysia soon after the inauguration of the new Federation in September 1963 and by not associating itself with the anti-Malaysia activities of the other opposition parties.[54] The leaders of the party, earlier, had been signatories to statements and memoranda issued by the opposition parties condemning the way Malaysia was being brought into existence by the Alliance Government. They had all demanded that the establishment of the larger federation should be preceded by a determination of the wishes of the people in Singapore and the Borneo territories. But as soon as Malaysia came into existence, the PPP promptly changed its position. It accepted Malaysia as a *fait accompli* and withdrew its opposition to it. It did not participate in the rallies and meetings organized by the Socialist Front to register opposition to Malaysia. It was obvious to the leaders of the party that a large part of the Chinese population in the country, because of the harsh treatment

---

[52] Ipoh, 13 September 1964. Record kept by this writer.

[53] Interview with a top-ranking leader of the party, Ipoh, September 1964.

[54] See R.K. Vasil, 'The 1964 General Elections in Malaya', *International Studies*, Vol. VII No. 1 (July 1965), p. 50.

of Chinese in Indonesia, was very hostile to Indonesia. Therefore, the party was not willing to adopt an anti-Malaysia position which in effect meant being pro-Indonesia and supporting it in its confrontation of Malaysia.

In the first of its two manifestos for the 1964 general elections, both significantly issued only in the Chinese language, it asserted with regard to its policy on Indonesian confrontation and Malaysia:

> Our party has always opposed the Indonesian anti-Chinese and xenophobic policies and the policy of opposing Malaysia. The Socialist Front and the Islamic Party [PMIP], on the other hand, are supporting Indonesia in her anti-Malaysia stand and would even merge Malaysia with Indonesia.[55]

The second manifesto stated:

> Today some among you or among your children may already have been conscripted under the labour mobilization to guard against the Indonesian agression. Of course, resistance against the enemy and defence of the country constitute a responsibility that every citizen should and must fulfil. But let us reflect on this a little further: who is the villain responsible for creating the disorders of war, terror, and trouble? Without the least doubt it is Indonesia as well as fellow-travellers in the Socialist Front and the Islamic Party.
>
> It is perfectly clear that Greater Malaysia is a fact, and whether attempts are made to oppose it or crush it, the end result must be confusion, terror and unsettled conditions. Consequently, support of the Socialist Front and the Islamic Party amounts to supporting Indonesia.[56]

As in the 1959 general elections, the party once again put emphasis on the issue of equality in its election campaign. However, it helped only marginally for the Alliance had been successful in making Indonesian confrontation and Malaysia as the sole election issue. Communal issues, by and large, were relegated to the background. The following is a short speech by D.R. Seenivasagam at Sitiawan, Perak, on 20 April 1964 during the election campaign:

---

[55] *The First Election Manifesto of the People's Progressive Party of Malaya*, 1964 general elections. Translated from the original in Chinese.

[56] *The Second Manifesto of the People's Progressive Party*, translated from the original in Chinese.

In Malaya there is an equal number of Malays and non-Malays but equal treatment is not given to the non-Malays. Take Singapore where 75 per cent of the population is Chinese. Malays are a very small minority. But the 75 per cent Chinese have such a big heart that they have given the Malays an equal treatment. Take language in Singapore. Although the Chinese constitute 75 per cent of the population, Malay, Tamil and Chinese are given an equal status. But here in Malaya there are about three million Chinese but their language is given no status.

All over this country your parents and grandparents, rich or poor, gave money to build Chinese schools. Why did they do this? They did this to preserve your language, culture and heritage. But what has the Tunku Government done? They have destroyed your language and culture. A boy from a Chinese school can get no job. But in Singapore a boy from a Chinese school has no difficulty in securing a job.

When the Tunku Government behaved horribly with Lim Lian Giok, the well-known Chinese educationist, the Malayan Chinese Association did not do anything. Lim Lian Giok only asked for the right of the Chinese people to use their language. What did the government do to him? They took away the license to teach from a man who taught for twenty years. They went further and said that he was not a good man and took away his citizenship. Lim Lian Giok would remain a symbol of our fight for equality.[57]

S.P. Seenivasagam said in a speech on 18 April at a Menglembu, Perak, election rally: 'Under the anti-Chinese Government of the Tunku they are taking the money from the Chinese and spending in Malay *kampongs*.'

The party's leaders, knowing full well that the bulk of the support for the party was only in and around Ipoh, the city administered by the party, and their attempts to extend its influence outside Perak had failed in the past, showed keeness just before the elections to come to an electoral arrangement with the People's Action Party of Singapore which had at the last moment decided to contest elections across the causeway in Malaya. It has been suggested that the Seenivasagam brothers, being non-Chinese, had serious apprehensions if they would be able to secure the support of the

[57] Record kept by this writer.

Chinese for long in the future, especially if they had to compete against the People's Action Party to secure this support.[58] Therefore, they seemed keen to link their party with the PAP. In this they were supported by the more pro-Chinese group led by Khong Kok Yat, which had the support of at least half the Executive Committee of the party. Others, Chan Yoon Onn, C.H. Yin etc. were not very keen to link the party with the PAP. Their fear was that the better organized PAP would eventually take over the PPP.

The party, however, did establish an electoral understanding with the PAP and as a result the latter did not field any candidates in Perak. On its part the PPP supported PAP candidates in other states. This link had an important impact on the PPP election campaign. The PAP leadership, in view of its strong desire not to alienate the Malay leadership, suggested to the PPP leaders that they should soft-pedal their opposition to Malay privileges and their demand for the recognition of Chinese and Tamil as official languages. This was the condition on which the PAP was willing to cooperate with the PPP and allow the fusion of the two parties at a later date. However, this did not very seriously affect the position of the PPP in the elections because of the personal position of its leaders, mainly the Seenivasagam brothers, in and around Ipoh. There was no substantial difference in the votes gained by the party. But it did lose, though only by narrow margins, some of the seats it had won in the 1959 general elections. It won only five seats in the Perak State Assembly as against the eight that it had secured in 1959. In the parliamentary elections, it captured only two seats, losing two that it had won in 1959.

Following the elections, with the increasing hostility shown by the Alliance towards the PAP and the UMNO propaganda that the PAP was attempting to gather Chinese support on a communal basis, the PAP leadership started showing only a lukewarm attitude towards a fusion of their party with the PPP. This was reciprocated by the PPP leadership who were discouraged by the poor showing of the PAP in the elections; and any chance of a PAP-PPP link-up disappeared when Singapore was forced out of Malaysia in 1965.

[58] Interview with a senior leader of the PPP, Ipoh, April 1964.

Organization

The constitution of the party, *Rules of the People's Progressive Party of Malaya*, has remained unchanged since the inception of the party in 1953. It is a short and simple document.

The membership of the party is open to persons of either sex, not less than 18 years of age who are ordinarily resident within the Federation of Malaya. The significant point is that non-citizens resident in the country are eligible for membership. Though the party has a mass membership, the constitution provides that every application for membership must be submitted to the Secretary of the party and the General Committee shall have the right to reject any such application without assigning reasons.

The officers of the party are a President, a number of Vice-Presidents (not exceeding four), a Secretary, a Treasurer and a General Committee. All officers are elected for a period of one year in annual meetings.

The executive of the party is the General Committee which consists of the officers and eight others elected each year at the annual general meeting. The General Committee is supreme and controls the party.

The constitution provides for an annual general meeting for which the quorum is twelve members. The general meeting receives and passes the annual report presented by the General Committee, receives and passes the Treasurer's account for the the year, and elects officers and the General Committee for the following year. An extra-ordinary general meeting, which again could be convened by twelve members, comprising a three-fourths majority of those present could vote to dissolve the organization.

This constitution has allowed the party to be completely controlled from the city of Ipoh. All annual general meetings have been held in Ipoh. Number 7, Hale Street in Ipoh, the residence of the Seenivasagam brothers, is the headquarters of the party. Fifty yards away, across the road, are the offices of the Ipoh Muncipal Council controlled by the party. Number 7, Hale Street and the offices of the Muncipal Council are the main centres of party activity. Most leaders of the party make daily visits to these offices where no particular activity takes place. The atmosphere is more like a Moghul *darbar*.

The party is completely controlled by the two brothers. If they were to leave it, it would immediately collapse. For the annual general meeting, trusted key men bring their own supporters who vote according to prior instructions or instructions whispered on the spot in the midst of the deliberations. The meeting lasts only for two or three hours. Members, all from Ipoh and around, who attend the meeting do not come to discuss the policy of the party or bring issues to the notice of the general body of the members but are brought there to maintain a certain leadership of the party.

Membership, Party Activity and Branches

The bulk of the membership of the party comes from the Chinese New Villages and the city of Ipoh. There are some prosperous businessmen who are leaders of the party. But a very large part of the membership is of working class origin and is Chinese-educated. In Ipoh, for example, membership very largely consists of Chinese trishaw-riders, hawkers, stall holders, petty traders, cycle repairers, etc. [59] As mentioned earlier, D.R. Seenivasagam was the honorary legal adviser to the associations of these groups.

A vast majority of the membership is Chinese. The Malay membership is very small and consists generally of disgruntled young men who joined the party for personal advantage or because they had been obliged to the Seenivasagam brothers. Some of them are family friends. In towns there is a sizeable Indian and Ceylon Tamil membership. These are generally younger men with a grouse against the older and more prosperous leadership of the Malayan Indian Congress.

The relations between the Chinese membership and the Indian and Ceylon Tamil membership are not very friendly and close. 'The extreme Chinese group in the party has no regard for the Indians. They do not mix much with the others.'[60] The Chinese

---

[59] Interview with Chan Yoon Onn, Secretary-General of the PPP, Ipoh, March 1965.

[60] Interview with a top-ranking leader of the PPP, Kuala Lumpur, May 1964.

attack on India in October 1962 sharpened the differences between the two within the party. Many Indians left the party at the time because of its neutral stand on the issue and its declared opposition to the fund started by Prime Minister Tunku Abdul Rahman in an effort to help India.

Two distinct groups have formed the leadership of the party:

1. The two Seenivasagam brothers and a small number of Indians, Ceylon Tamils and Chinese who are completely loyal to the two brothers. The prominent Chinese in this group is Chan Yoon Onn, the present Secretary-General of the party.
2. The extremist Chinese group led by Khong Kok Yat and Chan Swee Ho, former members of Parliament.

The two brothers have attracted considerable mass support. But this support 'has no depth. If they were not lawyers they would be nowhere in politics. They are supported because the Chinese rank and file gets something out of them. If the same service and help could be provided by a Chinese they would kick them out the next day.'[61] No other leaders of the party have a mass appeal and base.[62]

Most of the Chinese leaders have large business interests: not many of them come from the professions. 'They are not sincere. Their hearts are not in working for the party. Now at the time of the elections they are working very hard but once the elections are over they forget the party and do not take any interest in politics in general and party work in particular. They are too busy with their businesses and making money.'[63] Another important leader has suggested that had the two Seenivasagam brothers joined the Alliance, the Chinese leadership would have been happier for that would have given them greater opportunities to make money. He further suggested that the Chinese leaders joined the party primarily for the reason that it wins elections in Perak and has, in particular, controlled the Ipoh Municipal Council for many years.

[61] Interview with a senior leader of the PPP, Ipoh, April 1964.
[62] Interview with Chan Yoon Onn, Ipoh, March 1965.
[63] Interview with a top-ranking leader of the PPP, Ipoh, April 1964.

Over half the party branches are to be found in Chinese New Villages. The following is a breakdown of the branches:

New Villages in Perak	27 branches
New Villages outside Perak	3 branches
Towns in Perak	15 branches
Towns outside Perak	6 branches
Malay *kampongs*	2 branches

Almost all the active branches are in Perak. Many of the branches outside Perak have become inactive. For example, the list provided by the Secretary-General of the party does not mention the branch in George Town (Penang) at one time a strong one, which has now gone out of existence. Also, branches in Klang (Selangor) and Malacca are no longer functioning.

In both towns and New Villages party activity is entirely based on the municipality or local council. Party slogans refer to proper drainage systems, roads and electricity. The party tries to provide financial support in cases of sickness and death. Free legal aid is arranged. It helps people in obtaining visas to go abroad, identity cards, citizenship, etc. As the Secretary-General of the party, Chan Yoon Onn, put it: 'Most of the activity is in terms of service to the people — getting things done for them.'[64] He added: 'The ideology and party programme are not enough to draw the people to the party and therefore we have to do something to prove our sincerity. Even for the Chinese members it is not enough that the party fights for their rights.'

Electoral Support and Party Appeal

The result of the 1964 general elections clearly indicates that the party thrives only in the town of Ipoh and the areas around it, where the influential Seenivasagam brothers have been held in great respect.[65] In 1959, in an attempt to extend itself outside the

[64] Interview with Chan Yoon Onn, Ipoh, March 1965.

[65] It may be of interest to note that in the 1964 parliamentary elections out of the five sitting members of the party only two, the Seenivasagam brothers, were re-elected; the three Chinese sitting members were not re-elected by a very predominantly Chinese electorate.

state of Perak the party fielded many candidates in other states with large Chinese electorates. But it failed to obtain any electoral successes and in 1964, therefore, it fielded very few candidates outside Perak.[66] The party has never contested any elections in the states of Malacca, Perlis, Kedah, Kelantan, Trengannu and Pahang, all very predominantly Malay.

More, the party has never fielded candidates in constituencies with a large Malay vote. All its candidates, both in the 1959 and 1964 general elections, contested in constituencies with a very large non-Malay vote.

The appeal of the party is two-fold: first, the party has been successful in projecting an image as the champion of the cause of the non-Malays; and second, the Seenivasagam brothers have built up a powerful personal appeal through services rendered by them to the people in and around Ipoh. According to Chan Yoon Onn, the following are the bases of party's support:

1. The PPP is an opposition party and thereby is able to gather some protest votes against the Alliance.

2. Our party has always been very particular in fulfilling all the promises made by it in various manifestoes issued by it.

3. Our party is non-communal and has always fought for equality for the different racial groups in the country.

4. The personal appeal of the leaders, in particular that of the Seenivasagam brothers.[67]

S.P. Seenivasagam however, feels that 'the party's support is primarily because of the personal services rendered by us, two brothers. If we were to leave the party it would collapse immediately.'[68]

In attracting members the personal appeal of the two brothers plays a more important part. Chan Yoon Onn told this writer:

Trishaw-riders, hawkers, petty traders etc. have acquired a certain freedom and status *vis-à-vis* the police in Ipoh. They feel that there

[66] See Vasil, op.cit.

[67] Interview with Chan Yoon Onn, Ipoh, March 1965.

[68] Interview with S.P. Seenivasagam, Ipoh, March 1965.

are powerful people behind them and in case of any trouble with the law they could always go to the brothers for support and help.[69]

It would be useful to recall here a conversation that took place between D.R. Seenivasagam and a Chinese hawker. This particular person was selling his goods outside the Ipoh market in a prohibited area when he was asked by a policeman to move away from there. A heated exchange took place between the two and soon the hawker was to beat up the policeman, according to the police report. The man had been arrested and proceedings against him had been started by the police. On release on bail he came to see D.R. Seenivasagam, the honorary legal adviser of the hawkers' association, who heard the whole story through an interpreter and then told him that he would be glad to appear in court on his behalf. Then he asked him if he was a member of the PPP. Learning that he was not a member he told him that this time he would take up the case without any charge but in case he got into trouble again in future he would not be able to do anything for him unless he was a member of the party. This is said to take place quite often.

The following is another incident witnessed by this writer, which took place in the Municipal Council office of S.P. Seenivasagam, the Chairman of the Council. An old Chinese woman, accompanied by some six or seven others, was ushered into the office. At the head of the group was a PPP local leader who came from the same area as the woman. Seenivasagam was told by the party leader that the woman's only son, a young man, had been killed by a truck the same morning in an accident. She had nobody else. On hearing the story Seenivasagam asked what she wanted immediately. The party leader spoke to the woman and then told Seenivasagam that she had no money to buy a coffin. Thereupon, Seenivasagam asked them to call a coffin man. As soon as his words had been translated into Chinese a middle-aged gentleman stepped forward from the group and said that he was a coffin man and what could he do for them. Seenivasagam asked him to supply a coffin worth about one hundred dollars to the woman and to charge Seenivasagam for the same. He also told the woman that later, if

[69] Interview with Chan Yoon Onn, Ipoh, March 1965.

she wanted to claim damages from the truck driver who had killed her son, she could come to him and he would file a suit on her behalf and would do it free. This again was said to be not a rare incident.

Not many join the party as members because of its position on some of the communal issues, but they do support the party in elections. The party uses its communal appeal more effectively in gathering votes. The bulk of the propaganda literature issued by it is in the Chinese language. Party slogans are: *Equality and Progress, Vote PPP for Equality and Justice, PPP Opposes Special Privileges for Malays* (translated from the original in Chinese). It puts all emphasis on equality for all the racial groups.

VII

THE UNITED DEMOCRATIC PARTY

THE United Democratic Party was established on 21 April 1962.[1] The chief sponsors of the new party were a group of leaders of the Malayan Chinese Association whose position within the party had been made 'untenable' at the time of the crisis in the Alliance in 1959, and who, therefore, had to leave it.[2] The more prominent of these were Dr. Lim Chong Eu (President of the MCA), Too Joon Hing (Secretary-General), Ng Ek Teong, Chin See Yin, Quek Kai Dong, Lawrence H.C. Huang, and Tan Suan Kok.

Following the 1959 crisis in the Alliance, many left the MCA. However, Dr. Lim Chong Eu wavered. On 3 July 1959, he submitted his resignation as the President of the MCA and announced in a press conference in Penang, his home town, 'I am resigning primarily for health reasons'. But he was immediately to add that 'my position as MCA President has been rendered untenable by the political events leading to the MCA crisis'.[3]

Soon after the crisis there were reports that the dissidents were planning to establish a new political party.[4] There was strong pressure on Dr. Lim to lead the formation of a dissident MCA. Dr. Lim, however, went away to England for medical treatment which was to keep him out of politics for some time. He returned to Penang during the middle of 1960 and was once again approached by many to form a new political party. He, however, declined to do so at the time, for 'these approaches were based on communal

---

[1] The inaugural meeting was attended by S.P. Seenivasagam, D.R. Seenivasagam and three others as representatives of the People's Progressive Party. This was because of the identity of aims of the two parties.

[2] See above pp. 27-32 for the details of the crisis.

[3] *The Straits Times*, 31 July 1959.

[4] *The Standard*, Singapore, 15 July 1959.

issues and a fight on these issues would have stirred up very strong and bitter feelings'.[5] He was still a member of the MCA. It was only on 6 January 1961 that he finally resigned from its membership.[6] This attitude of Dr. Lim's disappointed many who had left the MCA in 1959 and had looked towards him for leadership.[7] Chin See Yin, one of the leaders of the group, alleges that Dr. Lim asked them to quit the MCA and contest the 1959 elections as independents and promised support. But Dr. Lim did not lend support to them and went to the extent of asking the people to vote for the Alliance.[8]

The placid Malayan political scene suddenly became alive when in 1961 Tunku Abdul Rahman, the Prime Minister, announced the Malaysian plan in Singapore. In a later major speech on 10 March 1962, Dr. Lim Chong Eu, referring to the formation of the UDP, was to state:

> Therefore, when the Tunku announced in May of 1961 that the Government was planning to create Malaysia by achieving some sort of merger with Singapore and bringing in the North Borneo territories of Sarawak, North Borneo and Brunei, we considered that the time had come for us to take not the kind of negative action as we had done in the past but the positive step of creating a new party which can challenge the Alliance Party in the further amendments to our Constitution which we anticipated will come with the creation of Malaysia.[9]

Also, Dr. Lim told this writer that 'when the Tunku decided to form Malaysia, I thought that this was the time to look into the unresolved communal issues [the questions of racial equality,

[5] Interview with Dr. Lim Chong Eu, Penang, May 1965.

[6] *The Straits Times,* 7 January 1961.

[7] Interview with Too Joon Hing, Ipoh, March 1965. Dr. Lim waited about three years after the Alliance crisis before he formed the UDP. According to Too Joon Hing, Dr. Lim's view was that the demand for the new party should come from the people. Too considers this delay to be the most serious mistake. He maintains that by waiting for so long Dr. Lim spoilt all chances of success for the new party. The right time, according to him, for the formation of the UDP would have been 1961, the time of the key Parliamentary by-election in Teluk Anson, when Too defeated a candidate of the MCA.

[8] Interview with Chin See Yin, Seremban, July 1964.

[9] *Straits Echo,* 11 March 1963.

education, language, Malay special position etc.] on a wider basis.'[10]

Chin See Yin, one of the founders of the party, in a press statement on 18 April 1962 announced that 'a get-together' of 'the independent Councillors [of the Seremban Town Council], their supporters, and persons who are interested in the political development of the Federation of Malaya in the context of the coming formation of Greater Malaysia' would be held at the Seremban Town Hall on 21 and 22 April. He added:

> This get-together will provide us with an opportunity to discuss fully the political problems arising in the Federation and other territories involved and to consider the desirability of forming a new party to solve the problems . . . . The new party will be formed on a strictly non-communal basis and based on a policy, which will be acceptable to and benefit all sections of the people of the country as a whole.[11]

Because of the serious differences among the leaders on the approach to these problems, the party's position remained vague and highly generalized. What kept the divergent groups together was the feeling each one had that it would be able to use the other one and eventually commit the party to its own viewpoint. Chin See Yin, one of the important leaders of the extremist elements, announced that the new party's stand on the controversial issues such as education and citizenship would be 'in the interest of the nation on a long term basis'. But he told this writer that the party was 'formed for the protection of non-Malays, in particular the Chinese'.[12]

Dr. Lim Chong Eu, who led the moderates, declared at the inaugural meeting of the party: 'We are forming a truly patriotic national organization in which all citizens will enjoy equal rights . . . It will not think in terms of communalism but will work positively as a united nation.'[13]

---

[10] Interview with Dr. Lim, Penang, May 1965.

[11] *The Malay Mail,* 19 April 1962.

[12] Interview with Chin See Yin, Seremban, July 1964.

[13] *The Straits Times,* 22 April 1962.

He praised the Alliance for developing a sense of racial harmony in the country and the establishment of a stable government. But he doubted if the foundation for further progress had been laid and said that the recent actions of the Government could seriously jeopardize the future. In particular he referred to the Government's education policy and the amendments made to the Constitution of the country. Concluding, he asserted that 'one pervading principle — of equal rights or equality — had to be upheld'.

In an interview with this writer, Dr. Lim outlined the following as the dominant urge for the formation of the UDP:

1. Equality is the cardinal factor. Our experience in the Alliance indicated that the Alliance was fraught with danger. If fundamental issues came up in the Alliance the cleavage would be on communal lines whereas in a truly Malaysian type of organization if there was any cleavage it would be on economic and social lines. To create a balance rather than build up a new society is the basis of the Alliance policy. But to us the building up of a new society is of the greatest importance and this can be done only on the basis of equality.

2. Experience of the Indian National Congress in India and the Kuomintang in China is an indication of the process of the petrification of a national party. The building up of a loyal opposition which could eventually take over is imperative. Parliamentary democracy in Malaysia as a result of the petrification of the national party, the Alliance, has become less and less viable. To make it viable the United Democratic Party had to be formed and the establishment of the new federation, Malaysia, was the right time for this.[14]

Talking more from a personal view, Dr. Lim added:

Essentially the drive towards a non-communal Malaysia is a drive for identity and security. Colonialism did bring many benefits to this country. But at the same time it uprooted the cultural patterns of the various communities living in the area. Many of them today belong nowhere — East or West. They want the feeling of being accepted. They want facilities for the flowering of their genius. To them the

[14] Interview with Dr. Lim Chong Eu, Penang, May 1965.

new Malaysian nation represents the fulfilment of a basic human need. Communal politics denies this human need.

The Straits Times, however, doubted the professions of the party leaders that the new party would be a non-communal one when it said:

> ... It is more than likely, however, that the preponderant appeal of the United Democratic Party will be felt by a single community, bearing in mind the political background of most of its leaders and their past espousal of issues on which their political reputations have been built.[15]

The inaugural meeting of the party constituted a *pro tem* committee which was completely dominated by those who had left the MCA in 1959. These were Dr. Lim Chong Eu, Chin See Yin, Quek Kai Dong, Tan Suan Kok, and Ng Ek Teong, all of whom had been important leaders of the MCA until 1959. They held all the important positions in the committee; only the three vice-presidents were non-Chinese and had never been associated with the MCA. These were political non-entities from Seremban roped in by Chin See Yin to give the party a non-communal facade.

Also, it is not insignificant that the inaugural meeting was held in Seremban, a stronghold of Chinese chauvinists, and not in Penang, the home town of Dr. Lim and a more enlightened and cosmopolitan city. It is clear that Chin See Yin, who was appointed Secretary-General and who had been one of the more extreme leaders of the MCA, dominated the show with the help of his Seremban group. Quek Kai Dong, the Assistant Secretary-General, was also from Seremban and was a close associate of Chin See Yin.

The party largely failed to evoke the response that its leaders had expected. For one year, from the time of its formation until the first meeting of its Central Assembly in April 1963, it witnessed no substantial activity. Very few branches were opened. No considerable membership was attracted. The leadership showed no drive and the party definitely had a slow start. The major factor was the serious disagreement among its leaders on the character,

---

[15] 24 April 1962.

appeal and policy orientation of the party.[16] Though all the important leaders had come out of the MCA in 1959, they were very sharply divided into two groups: the ultras, led by the Seremban group and the moderates, with Dr. Lim Chong Eu as the leader. The relations between the two deteriorated when in late 1962 and early 1963 Dr. Lim showed a desire to form an anti-Alliance united front of the opposition parties, including the radical Socialist Front.

It was in the midst of these mounting differences that the first Central Assembly of the party met in Kuala Lumpur on 14 April 1963, where the local party machine was controlled by Lawrence H.C. Huang and Ng Ek Teong, close associates of Dr. Lim and moderate in their views. In the showdown that took place Chin See Yin and Quek Kai Dong, the two leaders of the ultras, were ousted from the important positions they had held. They were not only not re-elected the Secretary-General and Assistant Secretary-General but also were not named to the Executive Committee. Significantly, Dato Zainal Abidin bin Haji Abas, a very prominent Malay, was unanimously elected the President. Dato Zainal had been a close associate of Dato Onn bin Jaafar and had been one of the very few Malays who believed that there was no necessary contradiction between the interests of the Malays and non-communal political parties. His appointment was a victory for the moderates who believed that 'a national organization should indicate as soon as possible that it has no racial distinction within the party'.[17]

The keen interest of the UDP in Malaysia has already been noted. It was the decision of the Alliance Government to establish the new federation which had determined the timing of the formation of the party. In fact, before the party was launched, Dr. Lim and his associate, Too Joon Hing, had made a special trip to the Borneo Territories and Singapore to ascertain the wishes of the people in those areas and to find out what sort of policies would

---

[16] Dr. Lim, however, maintains that the party had little activity outside its membership solely because of the Emergency in the country brought about by Indonesian confrontation. Interview, Penang, May 1965.

[17] Dr. Lim ni a personal communication to this writer, 12 March 1966.

be suitable for the proposed party.[18] Consequently, Malaysia was
one of the first issues on which the party came to have an unambiguous policy position. Speaking before the Central Assembly on
14 April 1963, Dr. Lim outlined the party's approach to Malaysia
as the following:

> I would like to emphasize that the *pro tem* committee of the party has
> openly advocated our support for the principles of Malaysia. We are
> not anti-Malaysia. Nevertheless we are against the scheme put for-
> ward by the Alliance Party on how they intend to establish Malaysia.
> We are against the Alliance schemes for many reasons, but chiefly
> it is our opinion that the establishment of Malaysia should only be
> made with the full consent of the people in the Federation of Malaya
> as well as the people in the other territories which are to comprise
> Malaysia. In the case of the Federation of Malaya, in view of the large
> number of important amendments to our Constitution which will
> have to be made because of Malaysia, we advocate that the people
> must be consulted more thoroughly, their opinions sought and their
> consent obtained for the finalized Malaysia plan. If possible we should
> hold another General Election before we finally approve of the Ma-
> laysia plan ... Further we oppose the Alliance plan for Malaysia
> because we consider that by recklessly forcing the pace of their plans
> the Alliance Party will strain the democratic institutions provided
> for by our Constitution to the very extreme. Further ... [it] may
> jeopardize the independence and freedom of our nation ... [It] will
> undoubtedly mean that the Federation of Malaya will become more
> and more obligated and dependent upon other countries over these
> matters.[19]

With regard to the important communal issues the party gave no
expression to its views. In his address to the Central Assembly,
Dr. Lim had said:

> What are the policies of the party? To this question we have invari-
> ably replied that the policies of our party will be established in accor-
> dance with the principal aims and objects of our party as laid down
> in the Constitution of our party and through the democratic process
> of debate and decision in the Central Assembly ... Our political
> party has undergone this long gestation period simply because we

[18] Interview with Too Joon Hing, Ipoh, March 1965.
[19] *The Straits Times,* 15 April 1963.

fully uphold the principles of democratic action. We believe that the policies of our party should develop and grow with the membership of our party, and that they should not be framed arbitrarily by a few founding members.

Within a few days of the meeting of the Central Assembly the six Councillors of the party in the Seremban Town Council resigned. Also, Quek Kai Dong, a member of Parliament and the first Assistant Secretary-General of the party, announced his resignation.[20] Chin See Yin, the leader of the group, announcing his exit, declared on 18 April 1963 that he did not share the views of Dr. Lim on forming a united front with the opposition parties. He maintained that in early 1962, when Dr. Lim had gone to him with the idea of forming a new political party, the following was agreed upon:

1. To fight for the rights of non-Malays, especially in education which should be based on a more reasonable policy than the Razak Report.
2. While recognizing Malay as the national language, multi-lingualism should be allowed in all councils.
3. To fight for fair distribution of land, and equal employment in the administration and the defence of the country.[21]

He further said:

Sometime in the later part of 1962, like a bolt from the blue, there appeared a newspaper report stating that Dr. Lim had discussions with Party Negara, the PMIP and the SF [Socialist Front] with a view to forming a united front.

Since that time Dr. Lim and I have not agreed with one another's views. I was also amazed to receive a telephone call one night from Dr. Lim asking me to attend an all-opposition parties' meeting in Penang to oppose the Alliance concept of Malaysia and condemn the arbitrary arrest of Inche Boestamam . . . .

The choice of a former deputy President of Party Negara [Dato Zainal Abidin bin Haji Abas] as the new President of the UDP clearly shows the reincarnation of the Party Negara in the body of the UDP.

[20] *The Malay Mail*, 18 April 1963.
[21] *The Straits Times*, 19 April 1963.

Dr. Lim maintains that Chin See Yin wanted to make the party 'a Chinese communal organization'.[22] This writer was told by Chin that the UDP was formed 'for the protection of the non-Malays, in particular the Chinese. Communalism and chauvinism are a fact. Any one who says that he is non-communal and not chauvinistic is a hypocrite.'[23] He further observed that when a Malay talks of Malays it is said to be nationalism and not communalism. But when a Chinese talks of Chinese he is branded as a communalist. Chin believes that Malayan society is in a state of confusion because of the inadequate system of education. The education system in Malaya placed no emphasis on 'moral education and filial piety. Education system must be made to mould the younger people through each community's culture.' In a free society any education system should not be curbed. His goal is 'a Malayan society based on equality and justice and an educational system which will bring up the younger generation on good moral outlook, civic mindedness and a sense of responsibility towards the country on a democratic basis'.

Soon after the exit of the extremist leaders the party was able to cooperate with the Socialist Front in a limited manner. The result was the establishment of coalitions to assume control of the Town Councils of Seremban, Taiping and Bentong in July 1963.[24]

The second Central Assembly of the party was held at Segamat (Johore) on 12 January 1964 and in the absence of the ultras it was able to adopt a more progressive and less communal position. In a resolution it declared that it would endeavour to establish through constitutional means an egalitarian society based on the principle of justice for all. It asserted, as part of its new progressive posture: 'We will not permit foreign powers to establish more military bases in our country and will eliminate those that are already in existence and rely on our own resources and on our membership of the United Nations and the Commonwealth for our defence.'[25] In

---

[22] Interview with Dr. Lim Chong Eu, Penang, May 1965.

[23] Interview with Chin See Yin, Seremban, July 1964.

[24] *The Straits Times*, 16, 18 and 24 July 1963.

[25] United Democratic Party, *Resolutions passed by the meeting of the Central General Assembly* (mimeographed), 12 January 1964.

an obvious reference to the Malays, it promised that it will 'promote and ensure the economic and cultural upliftment of all races particularly to improve the economic position of all workers and peasants and those who are economically backward'.

On the vital issue of education another resolution stated: 'We shall take into special consideration the failure of the Alliance educational policy to establish an adequate and proper development of the system of education in the national language and the suppression of the equal opportunity for development of schools teaching in other language media.'

The vague pledge to 'take into special consideration ... the suppression of the equal opportunity for development of schools teaching in other language media' was certainly not all that certain sections of the rank and file and the leadership of the Chinese community had expected from the UDP which had been established by leaders who had fought for the Chinese cause and had left the Malayan Chinese Association in 1959. These sections, who formed a large part of the Chinese community and for whom the new party was expected to have a strong appeal, had expected a clear and strong stand in favour of the right of the Chinese community to operate its own particular system of education. It was the realization of this that made the party adopt a more definite and unambiguous position in its manifesto for the 1964 general elections. The party was in no position to disregard this large area of support in the first national elections that it was to contest.

In a resolution on Malaysia it declared, unlike the Socialist Front, its acceptance of Malaysia 'as an accomplished fact' and pledged to support and sustain it. But at the same time it asserted that 'we will continue to maintain our principle that the right of the people of the Borneo Territories to self-determination of their own destiny be respected and that they be given the opportunity to decide to remain in Malaysia or secede after their first free direct general elections have been held'.

As a result of the announcement by the Government that general elections would be held in April 1964, the party revived its efforts to effect a united front of the opposition parties against the Alliance. Dr. Lim played a leading role in this attempt. Consultations took place between the Socialist Front and the UDP during February and early March. Devising an agreed common programme did not prove to be the most serious problem. On 9 Feburary the two parties adopted a Draft Agreement.[26] The urge to avoid splitting the opposition vote was strong enough to make the two parties forget the substantial differences in their policies and programmes and to arrive at a joint compromise programme. But soon serious difficulties arose between the two on the question of the allocation of seats, and the issue was used by both the parties as an excuse to suspend the talks. The real reason for the failure of the move, however, was that on the side of the Socialist Front there was a tremendous pressure from the extreme left wing of the party not to have any understanding or cooperation with the *bourgeois* right-wing UDP. The UDP on its side lost all interest in the move the moment the People's Action Party of Singapore announced its decision to contest the elections across the causeway.[27] Dr. Lim was more interested in linking his party with the PAP, closer to the UDP in its policy and programme, rather than with the Socialist Front. Also, Dr. Lim had great attraction for the dynamic leader of the PAP, Lee Kuan Yew. However, at that time the PAP, as part of its overall strategy, did not want to alienate the Malay leadership and the UMNO; in fact their major attempt was to replace the MCA as a member of the Alliance.[28] Any link with the UDP was bound to be viewed suspiciously by the UMNO. And therefore, the PAP leaders did not encourage a tie-up between their party and the UDP. The UDP thus had to contest the elections on its own.

In its manifesto for the general elections in 1964[29] the party generally moved to a more progressive position and committed itself to 'a form of national democratic socialism'. With regard to foreign policy it asserted that the party 'will ensure that our

[26] See *Draft Agreement concluded at a meeting of Opposition Parties on 9 February 1964* (mimeographed).

[27] This information was given this writer by two leaders of the Socialist Front and the UDP who had participated in the talks.

[28] For details of the PAP strategy in the elections see R.K. Vasil, 'Why Malaysia Failed?', *Quest* (Spring 1966), pp. 51-9.

[29] United Democratic Party, *Election Manifesto — 1964 Parliamentary Elections*.

country is fully independent, completely divested of all the vestiges of the colonial past, and we will ensure that it will be non-communist and non-aligned'. It pledged to establish an independent foreign policy based on the country's national interest, to work for peaceful cooperation with 'all the independent nations in Southeast Asia', and resolve the problem of Indonesian and Filipino non-acceptance of Malaysia through direct negotiations.[30] And it added: 'We are opposed to the 'Macapagal Plan' for the establishment of Maphilindo because of the racialist and communal concepts embodied by that plan.'[31]

It also promised to review the Internal Security Act 'with the object if possible of doing away with it' and to 'give fair trial' to all political prisoners under detention. It maintained that it would not permit the establishment of military bases by foreign powers and 'will eliminate those that are already in existence'.

On the controversial issue of education the manifesto made the party's position clearer and more explicit. It went significantly beyond what it had said in the resolution passed at the meeting of the Central Assembly on 12 January 1964. The manifesto maintained:

> The United Democratic Party's Policy is to establish a unified and integrated system of education for our country with a common syllabus for all schools adhering to the true spirit and meaning of Article 152 (1) of the Constitution which provides:
>
>> The national language shall be the Malay language and shall be in such script as Parliament may by law provide:
>>
>> Provided that —

[30] Though the party accepted Malaysia 'as an accomplished fact', it did not, unlike the People's Progressive Party, adopt an anti-Indonesian posture. At this time chiefly because of the ill-treatment of Chinese in Indonesia most of the Chinese in Malaysia were hostile to Indonesia. Realizing this the PPP, just before the elections started demanding severance of diplomatic ties with Indonesia. It was an attempt to undo the pro-Indonesian image of the party which had resulted from its opposition to Malaysia. However, the UDP did not take this important step. It still demanded direct negotiations with Indonesia and the Philippines to solve the Malaysia issue. It refused to condemn Indonesia.

[31] The idea of Maphilindo was opposed by all the non-communal parties in the country, including the Singapore-based People's Action Party which had worked for the establishment of Malaysia.

(a)   no person shall be prohibited or prevented from using (otherwise than for official purposes), or for teaching or learning, any other language; and

(b)   nothing in this clause shall prejudice the right of the Federal Government or of any State Government to preserve and sustain the use and study of the language of any other community in the Federation.

All Malay schools and all Chinese, Tamil and English schools accepting Malay as a compulsory subject shall be entitled to equal treatment by Government and the medium of instruction shall be the medium of examination.

The objective of making Malay a compulsory subject is to achieve the aim of making Malay the unifying and National Language of the country.

School Leaving Certificates, whether obtained in the National Language or in other media, shall be accepted as of equivalent status in the seeking of employment and livelihood.

In this, as against its resolution on education of 12 January 1964, the party had gone a long way to meet the position of the extremists within the Chinese community. It demanded that all schools, Chinese, Tamil and English medium, which accepted Malay as a compulsory subject should be given equal treatment. It further made the demand that the medium of instruction be the medium of examination and that the School Leaving Certificates, whether obtained in the National-type schools or the non-National-type schools, be treated as equivalent for purposes of employment.

It also pledged to 'ensure that equal opportunities for securing employment and livelihood will be given to all citizens . . . .' This was an indirect criticism of the special position accorded to the Malays by the Constitution.

This programme, however, did not prove very effective in vote catching. The party, which put up a large number of candidates, did badly in the elections. It found most of its support in the States of Penang, Perak, and Negri Sembilan, all with sizeable non-Malay electorates. It won little support in Johore and did not field any candidates in Selangor, the two states with a large non-Malay population where the Labour Party, especially its Chinese-educated sections, had considerable influence. The party's five electoral successes were all in Penang, the home State of Dr. Lim. Dr. Lim himself was elected to Parliament from a city constituency, defeating his Socialist Front and Alliance rivals. The other successful candidates were four Chinese elected to the Penang state legislature from predominantly Chinese constituencies.

None of the Malay candidates of the party was successful though it had put up so many as 36 Malay candidates. What is more, the votes secured by them were much smaller than those by the non-Malay candidates. In the parliamentary elections the 8 Malay candidates secured only 11,450 votes while the 19 non-Malay candidates secured as many as 76,773 votes. The biggest setback for the party, as far as its Malay support was concerned, was the defeat of its Malay Chairman, Dato Zainal Abidin, in the parliamentary constituency of Parit, his home town in Perak. In fact, the Dato lost his deposit, securing only 1,138 votes.

The party's poor showing in the elections was very largely a result of the lack of clarity in its position on important issues of Chinese language, education and culture. It was also handicapped by a lack of proper organization and adequate funds. In its attempt to win some support among Malays (to strengthen the party's non-communal character) it lost the support of many Chinese who had seen it as a champion and protector of their interests.

Organization

The lowest unit or organization established by the party is at the level of the Division, which normally covers a parliamentary constituency. Members are admitted and registered only at this level. Each Division has a Divisional Assembly which meets once in six months. All members registered in a particular Division are entitled to attend the Divisional Assembly and from amongst themselves they elect an Executive Committee.

The Divisional Assemblies send delegates to a State Assembly which meets at least once in six months and elects from among its members a State Executive Committee. The State Assemblies in turn elect delegates to the Central General Assembly, held at least once a year. However, this is not the exclusive privilege of the

State Assemblies. The constitution empowers the Divisional Assemblies to elect and send directly their own delegates to the Central General Assembly. In fact, in any General Assembly there are more delegates from the Divisions than from the States for the constitution provides that whereas the State Assemblies would send one delegate for every complete 1,000 members the Divisions would be entitled to send one delegate for every 250 members. The Central General Assembly is the supreme authority in the party and its powers and functions are spelled out in detail in the party constitution. As it is constituted, Divisions have a much greater influence over its working than the State Assemblies. The state organizations are relatively powerless.

The party has three types of members, viz., Ordinary Members, Associate Members, and Corporate Members. Any federal citizen over 18 who is resident in the Division through which he seeks membership is qualified to be a member. Non-citizens are debarred from membership. However, if the person is over 18 and intends to be a federal citizen 'as soon as he or she is eligible'[32] he can apply for associate membership.

Membership, Branches and Party Activity

The membership of the party is chiefly derived from the Chinese community. There are very few non-Chinese members. Most of the Malays who have joined the party were at one time with the UMNO and left it for personal reasons. They generally came out of the UMNO because of personal dissatisfaction. Also, some of the Malays have joined because of their personal relations with the Malay leadership, especially Dato Zainal Abidin. However, these Malays enjoy little support and influence within the Malay community.

The bulk of the membership is Chinese. It largely comes from the middle class, educated sections of the population. A fairly sizeable part of it is Chinese-educated. English-educated Chinese represent only a very small percentage of the membership. The party has found support mainly among the white-collar non-

[32] *The Constitution of the United Democratic Party,* 21 May 1962.

industrial workers, especially shop assistants, and small business-men, in cities and towns in the west coast States. It has little appeal for the manual workers of Chinese origin. Its support in the New Villages, inhabited by Chinese of the working class, is very limited. Many Chinese who support the party now were at one time sup-porters of the MCA. Also, a large part of the membership is re-latively young, in the age-group of 25 to 35.

Most of the branches are to be found in the states of Perak, Penang, Negri Sembilan, Malacca and Johore. All these states have large Chinese populations. As is the case of all the non-communal parties in the country, it has no organizational base in the predo-minantly Malay states of the East Coast, Kelantan, Trengganu, Perlis, Kedah and Pahang. The main reason why most of the party branches are to be found in the States of Perak, Penang and Negri Sembilan is that the leadership is derived mainly from these States. In other States it has no important leaders who could organize branches and support for the party.

Party activity at the branch level is restricted primarily to 'pu-blic service', which is the case too with the People's Progressive Party. Party workers strive to help the general public in sorting out citizenship problems, identity card difficulties, rectifying errors in birth certificates etc. Also, through its councillors in the city and local councils, it attempts to push through projects of public interest, such as drains, facilities for water supply, electri-city, roads etc.

The party also puts some emphasis in its activities on the pro-motion of Chinese culture and language. However, this part of its activity in not thus far well organized. But as the party moves fur-ther towards a more pro-Chinese position these activities would increase.

There is a tremendous gap between the present national lea-dership of the party and its rank and file. Its national leadership, consisting of people like Dr. Lim Chong Eu, Dato Zainal Abidin, Ng Ek Teong, Too Joon Hing, Lawrence Huang, etc. has been able to moderate significantly the pro-Chinese beginnings of the party. In early 1964, as was noted earlier, they were able to get rid of the Chinese extremist leaders who had played a leading role in the formation of the party, and move it along a more genuinely non-communal path. But soon, conscious of the ineffectiveness of this posture in securing electoral support, it gave in significantly to extremist Chinese sections within the party in its manifesto for the 1964 general elections. The rank and file is still very largely committed to securing for Chinese language, education and culture its rightful place, which to them is the most important aspect of equality for all races. And it may be only a matter of time when the rank and file would be able to assert its position and force the moderate leadership (as eventually happened in the Labour Party) to commit the party to a pro-Chinese posture. The moderate leadership will either have to give in or go.

VIII

THE NON-COMMUNAL PARTIES OF PERSONAGE

THE main non-communal parties of personage, formed at different times, have been the National Association of Perak, the Malayan Party, and the National Convention Party. All of them were organized by locally influential leaders of different racial groups and remained in existence while these leaders were active. Their support was restricted only to a small region; none of them ever became an all-Malaya party. Their appeal was very largely dependent on the personality of the leaders. And, as it will be seen later, they never thrived because of the special racial situation in the country.

National Association of Perak

The National Association of Perak grew out of deliberations in early 1953 (after the experiment of the Independence of Malaya Party had failed) among the close associates of Dato Onn bin Jaafar and some prominent supporters of the IMP. At a meeting of this group on 12 February 1953, it was thought that the proposal of Dato Panglima Bukit Gantang (Mentri Besar of Perak from 1948 to 1957) that he should form a political organization in Perak 'on the lines discussed at this meeting was reasonable and should be treated as a pilot organisation'.[1] At the same time this group had decided to establish 'a central political body' to take the place of the IMP which had declined.[2] This new body was seen as an alternative to the inter-communal Alliance, which had taken away the leadership of the Malayan national movement from Dato Onn bin Jaafar and his associates. It was in this context that in May

[1] Notes on Meeting held at the house of Yong Shook Lin, Kuala Lumpur, 12 February 1953.

[2] This was eventually launched as Party Negara.

1953 Dato Panglima Bukit Gantang initiated moves for the formation of 'a strong national political organization' in Perak.

Towards this end a group of community leaders met in the Perak Council Chamber on 2 May 1953. Dato Panglima Bukit Gantang described the meeting in the following words: 'A number of my friends had got together and discussed the political situation in Perak with regard to the impending elections to the Town Council and eventually to the State Council.'[3]

The meeting appointed a ten-man working committee headed by the Federal and State Councillor, C.M. Yusuf bin Sheikh Abdul Rahman, to make recommendations about the steps to be taken with regard to the formation of the new party.

Towards the end of September 1953, the committee recommended the formation of a strong non-communal political party in Perak which would promote the interests of each community generally and work for the good of the whole country.[4] It asserted: 'The rapid political changes demand that members of all communities should combine in one association to take responsible part in the government of the country.'

The draft rules mentioned the following as the objects of the party:

Promote unity among the people by inculcating in them loyalty to the State of Perak and its Sultan.
    To integrate all communities into one Malayan nation with a Malayan outlook and strive for responsible self-government within the British Commonwealth.[5]

The new organization, the National Association of Perak (NAP) was formally launched on 4 October 1953 at Ipoh. The inaugural meeting was attended mostly by Indians and Malays.[6]

In late February 1954, Dato Panglima Bukit Gantang told a meeting of the party that members could also join the newly formed Party Negara. He further announced that the NAP was seeking

[3] *The Straits Times*, 3 May 1953.
[4] Ibid. 30 September 1953.
[5] Ibid.
[6] Ibid. 5 October 1953.

affiliation with the new party.[7] However, the formal affiliation was never effected and the NAP led its independent existence; but it maintained close links with the Party Negara. In fact, the NAP operated more or less as a Perak State branch of the Party Negara. And it was for this reason that the latter never set up any branches of its own in Perak even though it had established branches in most of the other States.[8]

The party suffered a serious setback in the first elections that it contested. In mid-1954, it fielded a large number of candidates for the thirty contested seats for the Town Councils of Ipoh, Taiping and Teluk Anson in Perak. None of its candidates was successful. Even in Taiping, a stronghold of the party, it was not able to capture a single seat, and many of its candidates lost their deposits.[9] The party was convincingly beaten by the Alliance, which had effected an alliance with the Perak Progressive Party with the sole purpose of defeating the NAP.

The general belief among the people was that the NAP was an official organization; it was a party of Dato Panglima Bukit Gantang, the Mentri Besar, and was supported by some senior civil servants[10] and a large number of *penghulus* (headmen in Malay *kampongs*). The party had also attracted a small number of non-Malays from professions and business who joined it because of the Mentri Besar's association with it. In fact, in early 1954, the Perak Progressive Party charged that people were being told that they should join the NAP because its leader was the Mentri Besar of Perak.[11] It alleged that they were being told that if they joined the NAP 'the Mentri Besar would be very pleased'. To off-set this image, in late 1955, just before the Perak state council elections, Dato Panglima Bukit Gantang quit as the leader of the party. The party announced that 'one of the reasons why the Dato has stood down as leader of our party is to show to the people that we are not a government party'.[12]

[7] Ibid. 22 February 1954.
[8] See Chapter II, note 123, p. 84.
[9] *The Straits Times*, 17 August 1954.
[10] At this time all senior civil servants were either Malays or expatriates. Non-Malays were not appointed to the upper echelons of the service.
[11] *The Straits Times*, 23 February 1954.
[12] Ibid. 1 October 1954.

In late July 1955, the party issued its manifesto for the federal legislative council elections. This was the first time that it had given some idea of its policy position and political orientation. The one-page manifesto declared *inter alia* that,

(a)   The party shall work for the attainment of self-government in the shortest possible time as an eventual step to independence.
(b)   The status of the Malay Rulers shall be preserved.
(c)   The improvement of the economic position of the Malays shall receive special attention.
(d)   The party shall work for the immediate tightening of the immigration laws.

The party further pledged itself to the Malayanisation of the public services, a measure of rural development and free primary bilingual education with Malay as a compulsory language. It would be useful to note that there was no significant difference between the manifestoes of the NAP and the Party Negara, except that on the issue of national language the NAP did not state its position explicitly while the Party Negara committed itself to Malay as the sole official language of the country.

In the Federal Legislative Council elections held in late July 1955 the party fielded 9 candidates for the 10 constituencies in Perak; 8 of these were Malays and 1 Chinese. None of them was returned and they together were able to secure only about 2 per cent of the total vote. Five of the candidates lost their deposits.[13] It should be noted that the Party Negara, which had contested 30 of the 52 constituencies in the country, did not put up any candidates in Perak. This was because of the close links between the NAP and the Party Negara and its leaders, Dato Panglima Bukit Gantang and Dato Onn bin Jaafar.

In early November 1955, following the federal elections and just before the Perak state elections, the party decided to support non-Alliance candidates in constituencies where the party was not contesting.[14] In the state elections for 12 seats (8 had been se-

[13] See Federation of Malaya, *Report on the First Election of Members to the Legislative Council of the Federation of Malaya*, Kuala Lumpur, Government Press, 1955.
[14] *The Straits Times*, 8 November 1955.

cured by the Alliance without contest) it put up 8 candidates, all
of whom were Malays. None of them again was successful; 5 of
them lost their deposits. The party suffered the same fate as the
Party Negara.

The first and last success achieved by the party was in the Ipoh
town council elections of 1957 when one of its candidates was returned.[15] In late 1958, knowing full well that the party had achieved no success and that Dato Panglima Bukit Gantang was no more
the Mentri Besar of the State, it decided to join forces with the
Alliance Party, its chief enemy, to contest town council elections
in Taiping. At the same time a party spokesman announced that
it had been decided that the name of the party would be changed
to National Association of Malaya and extend its activities to the
whole country.[16] This ironically was the beginning of the end
of the party. Once it decided to cooperate with the Alliance most
of its leaders and members joined the Alliance knowing full well
the advantages of belonging to the ruling party. To them the party
had been formed mainly to provide an alternative to the Alliance
and if it had come to a position where it had to cooperate with the
Alliance for its survival, there was hardly any reason for its separate existence. The death of Dato Panglima Bukit Gantang in 1959
led finally to the disappearance of the party though in June 1959
after strong rumours that it was to be scrapped, a top-level meeting
of the party unanimously decided that it should continue to exist.[17]
However, it very soon ceased to function. It was unable to put up
any candidates for the 1959 general elections and soon disappeared
altogether from the Malayan political scene. Most of its members
and supporters soon after switched their loyalties to the Alliance
Party.

The Malayan Party

The Malayan Party was inaugurated in Malacca on 24 October
1956, United Nations Day. The date was no mere coincidence,

[15] Ibid. 8 December 1957.
[16] Ibid. 12 November 1958.
[17] Ibid. 22 June 1959.

for the first and major aim of the organization was 'to promote and defend by all lawful means the aims and objects set out and specified in the Universal Declaration of Human Rights of the United Nations Organisation'.[18] But in actuality the party was sponsored by the leaders of the Malacca Chinese Chamber of Commerce and the Federation of Chinese Guilds and Associations in response to their serious dissatisfaction with and concern over the Alliance view of the new Constitution for independent Malaya. The chief founder of the new party and its first President, Tan Kee Gak, was at the time the President of the Malacca Chinese Chamber of Commerce.

The party had attracted the conservative communal Chinese and a small number of locally prominent non-Malays from the professions, who were keen to preserve their status as 'subjects of the Crown' which they had enjoyed as residents of the Crown Colony of Malacca. As residents of the Crown Colony (both in Penang and Malacca) non-Malays had enjoyed a better position and more freedom than non-Malays in the Malay States of the Federation where sovereignty lay with the Malay Sultans and the British had only a protectorate relationship with the Sultans.

The chief reason for the formation of the party was given in its annual report for 1956 as the following:

> The Founder Members were stimulated to form the Party ... because the UMNO-MCA-MIC Alliance Memorandum to the Reid Constitutional Commission was put forward as representing the agreed views of all the communities whereas the Founder Members, themselves belonging to all communities, felt that this was not the case.
>
> No other party intended to contest the Malacca Municipal elections and there was the certainty of an unqualified Alliance victory if there was no opposition. At such a time and in the special circumstances of the case an unqualified Alliance victory in Malacca would have had consequences far beyond the normal scope of municipal elections as it would have been used by the Alliance leaders to support their claim that their manifesto (which recommended introduction of racial

---

[18] *Manifesto of the Malayan Party*, Malacca Municipal Elections, 1956.

privileges in the Settlement) enjoyed the unqualified support of the people of Malacca.[19]

The party opened its membership to people of all races not less than 21 years in age. The Rules of the party did not provide for a set of officials, except a President. It established a Committee of Management which was to be the chief organ of the party. With regard to its policy the party announced that it was contained in the Universal Declaration of Human Rights and that a more detailed policy would be worked out as the party progressed.

In brief it can be said that the Malayan Party policy is to promote a multi-racial socialist property-owning democracy, a composite political and economic structure of the lines of Switzerland.

The Committee believes that government by one party, however eminent and unselfish the leaders, results inevitably in dictatorial methods, secrecy and corruption and therefore looks confidently to the public to welcome the Malayan Party first as the nucleus of a democratic opposition to the Government and later as an alternative Government to be in readiness at any time required.[20]

It maintained that, 'Culture of the community is to be participated in freely as in Switzerland where the different races speak their own languages, have their own radio stations, schools and universities.' With regard to the system of education it asserted that it was the exclusive right of the parents to choose the sort of education they wanted for their children. The State had nothing to do with it.

It put great emphasis on the equality of rights of all the people of Malaya, irrespective of their racial origin. It opposed immediate transfer of sovereignty in Malacca:

Sovereignty should remain with the present rulers. If Her Majesty the Queen wishes to surrender her sovereignty it should be surrendered to the people of Malacca who would then be at liberty to seek to be administered (if necessary, under United Nations Trusteeship) as part of the Federation of Malaya.

It was for this reason that Tunku Abdul Rahman, the leader of the Alliance and the Chief Minister, alleged that the new party's aim

---

[19] The Malayan Party, *Annual Report for 1956* (mimeographed), p. 1.
[20] *Manifesto of the Malayan Party*, op.cit.

was to hinder independence for Malaya. Denying this charge, one of the candidates of the party for the Malacca municipal elections asserted that his party was not concerned with independence, which everyone knew would come on 31 August 1957. They were interested only in the new Constitution of the country.[21] He maintained that the Alliance Memorandum to the Reid Commission 'menaces the equality before the law previously enjoyed by all in the Settlement'.

The Malacca municipal elections of December 1956 were fought entirely on the issues of the Constitution for independent Malaya, the Alliance Memorandum to the Reid Commission and the position of Malacca. One of the party candidates had stated in an election speech:

> Malacca has lost its true port and also its railway. It is now threatened by the Alliance with the loss of its equality and brotherhood. The physical losses can be restored but should the spiritual quality of equality and brotherhood once lost can never be recovered.[22]

Expecting serious opposition, the Alliance sent most of its top-ranking leaders, including Tunku Abdul Rahman, for the election campaign.

The Malayan Party did badly in the elections despite its high hopes. Only one of its candidates was returned though the party polled a large vote. In comparison, in the other Settlement, Penang, the Labour Party, with a broader economic and political programme, had achieved a significant success when it was able to win 5 of the 8 seats for which elections were held in late 1956.

Later in 1957, the party joined hands with the powerful Federation of Chinese Guilds and Associations in expressing its disapproval of the Constitution finalized by the Malayan Government, which had deviated significantly from the recommendations made by the Reid Commission. In May 1957, Tan Kee Gak represented the Malayan Party in a Chinese Guilds and Associations mission to London to make representations to the British Government against provisions in the proposed Constitution of Malaya relating

[21] *The Straits Times*, 28 November 1956.

[22] *The Malay Mail*, 29 November 1956.

to the official language, the state religion, citizenship and the special position of the Malays.[23]

In the December 1957 elections for the Malacca municipal council the party was able to win 3 seats out of the 6 for which elections were held.[24] The Alliance was able to secure only 2 seats. In spite of the fact that the party had failed to attract mass support outside the city of Malacca it contested the 1959 general elections. It fielded 6 candidates in the State elections; 5 in Malacca and 1 in Selangor. In the parliamentary elections it fielded 2 candidates, 1 each in Malacca and Selangor. The only successful candidate was the party's pre-eminent leader, Tan Kee Gak, who defeated the Alliance nominee in the Malacca city constituency by a small margin.

The party survived for a few years, but only in name. The end came in March 1964 when its sole representative in the Malaysian Parliament and its most important leader, Tan Kee Gak, decided to rejoin the MCA just before the 1964 general elections.[25] In a joint statement with Tan Siew Sin, the President of the MCA, he announced:

> President Sukarno, under pressure from communists, is endeavouring to crush Malaysia, which was established on the principle of self-determination.
>
> The most important task facing us is to unite the Chinese of Malaysia under the leadership of MCA.

And he successfully contested the 1964 general elections as an Alliance (MCA) candidate from the Malacca city parliamentary constituency.

The National Convention Party

Abdul Aziz Ishak,[26] the founder of the National Convention Party, has been a controversial figure from the beginning of his

---

[23] *The Straits Times*, 6 May 1957.
[24] Ibid. 8 December 1957.
[25] Ibid. 5 March 1964.
[26] His elder brother is the President of the Republic of Singapore and his younger brother is a Minister in the Singapore Government.

political career. He came to the limelight in 1952 as a young Malay journalist who had the courage to cross swords, at the height of the Emergency in Malaya and during a period of severe repression, with the very powerful British High Commissioner, General Gerald Templer. General Templer publicly called him 'a rat'. He began his political career with the UMNO, later going over to the Independence of Malaya Party in late 1951. He unsuccessfully contested the Presidentship of the Kuala Lumpur branch of the IMP against the founder of the party, Dato Onn bin Jaafar. He also contested the Kuala Lumpur municipal elections of early 1952 as an IMP candidate, but was defeated by an UMNO nominee in a predominantly Malay area. Because of his differences with Dato Onn his association with the IMP was shortlived. He rejoined the UMNO and soon emerged as an important leader of the organization and a regular member of its Central Executive Committee. Following the 1955 Federal Legislative Council elections, in which he was returned as an Alliance (UMNO) candidate, he was included in the first cabinet formed by Tunku Abdul Rahman as the Minister for Agriculture, a post he retained right through to mid-1962. As the Minister for Agriculture, strongly pursuing schemes for the benefit of the Malay peasantry, he landed himself in serious trouble not only with well-entrenched Chinese middlemen and powerful British and other foreign interests, but also with Tunku Abdul Rahman and Tun Abdul Razak who suspected that his activities were geared mainly to promote his own personal popularity and support within the Malay community.

Aziz's efforts to establish cooperative rice mills in the States of Perak and Penang brought him into direct clash with the Chinese rice millers and through them with the MCA. Aziz had been successful in pursuading the State Governments of Penang and Perak to grant a monopoly over rice milling in these two States to cooperative mills. This decision was eventually reversed at the insistence of the Malayan Government, which pointed out to the two State Governments that the action was unconstitutional in that they had refused to renew licences already in possession. The Constitution of Malaya had provided this as an important protection for the non-Malays. Also, in 1958, after a visit to India, Aziz

Ishak initiated a Community Development Programme for the uplifting of the rural masses within his Ministry of Agriculture. The programme attained some success and certainly gained some popularity for Aziz among Malay peasants, though to the discomfiture of some of the other top-ranking leaders of the UMNO interested in the question of who ultimately would succeed Tunku Abdul Rahman. Consequently, in late 1959, the Community Development Programme, the brainchild of Aziz, was quietly shifted from the Ministry of Agriculture to the Prime Minister's Office and then almost immediately to the Ministry of Rural Development headed by Tun Razak (arch-rival of Aziz) where it died in early 1960. Later, in 1961, Aziz Ishak attempted to build an urea fertilizer plant in Malaya which incurred the great displeasure and hostility of some of the politically influential British firms which had a monopoly over the supply of fertilizers to Malaya. The Government of Malaya refused to put up the money for the fertilizer plant, even though Aziz insisted that the plan had been approved by international experts and was a very sound proposition economically. Thereupon, Aziz went round collecting money from Malay peasants in order to establish the factory as a cooperative venture. But later developments made it impossible for him to go ahead with the project.

In early 1960, an important committee of the UMNO had recommended some far-reaching changes in the UMNO Constitution. The most important of these related to divesting the State branches of the UMNO of most of their powers and according to Tunku Abdul Rahman this was aimed at safeguarding the party and preventing it from 'chaotic disintegration into State organizations'.[27] The major opposition to these changes had come from the Selangor UMNO whose Chairman was Aziz Ishak. In fact, when the new constitution was put to vote in the UMNO General Assembly in April 1960, Aziz Ishak, one of the three Vice-Presidents of the party, was the only one in the top leadership to abstain. His abstention on the vote was greeted by shouts of 'resign'.[28] He had again ventured to cross swords with Tunku Abdul Rah-

[27] *The Straits Times*, 17 April 1960.
[28] Ibid. 18 April 1960.

man. In fact, this was not the end of the confrontation. The next year, in 1961, the Tunku made critical references to the urea fertilizer factory scheme in his presidential address before the UMNO General Assembly and for this Aziz's supporters in Selangor decided to censure him. They attempted to amend a motion of thanks to the Tunku for his presidential speech by deleting any reference to the proposed urea factory. The amendment was defeated by ninety-nine votes to forty-four, which was certainly still an impressive vote against the Tunku since rarely had so many voted against him within the UMNO.[29]

The final showdown took place when the Tunku asked Aziz in a telegram to give up his portfolio of agriculture and take over health and then characteristically went abroad.[30] Aziz refused to do so and said in a statement:

> There are so many schemes and projects in hand designed to help uplift the living standards of the people. We cannot just change horses mid-stream without adversely affecting their interests.
>
> I, therefore, propose to ask the Prime Minister on his return the reasons for making the switch.
>
> I had not at any time been consulted about this change of portfolio and I became aware of it only on Saturday on my return from my tour of Borneo, Sarawak and Brunei.[31]

The Selangor State UMNO immediately lent its support to Aziz and said in a statement that it was 'greatly perturbed' and added:

> Like ourselves, our constituents are also anxious to know the reasons for the transfer especially when we are aware of the attitude of certain middlemen groups arising out of the implementation recently of some cooperative schemes such as *padi* purchasing and marketing by the cooperatives in North Malaya.[32]

At the UMNO General Assembly held in late August 1962 the Tunku used strong words against Aziz in his presidential speech when he said:

[29] Ibid. 8 May 1961.
[30] *The Malay Mail,* 17 July 1962.
[31] Ibid.
[32] *The Straits Times,* 18 July 1962.

When any Minister wishes to seek a good name for himself alone and blames his colleagues in the cabinet his loyalty diverges from his party and he breaks his oath to the cabinet. If that Minister is allowed to go on his way, the cabinet will be divided and this state of affairs will impair the party and government in power. [33]

This was the end of Aziz Ishak in the Cabinet and the UMNO. He was not re-elected as one of the three Vice-Presidents though he was to retain his seat in the Central Executive Committee. In late January 1963, Aziz finally left the Cabinet. At a press conference he said that the strained relations between Malaya and Indonesia were absolutely 'senseless and purposeless' and were to the benefit only of the British.[34] With regard to the Alliance Government's attitude towards the peasantry he said:

It is not fair to judge the position of our rural people by simply looking at the privileged few who have joined the class of prosperous and the wealthy after *merdeka*.

What is the use of having new roads and new buildings if the rural people are to continue living from hand to mouth?

According to him such projects were only to benefit the urban contractors by way of huge profits while the poverty of the rural people would not change. He added:

Despite difficulties, I pursued a policy of cooperative expansion [*sic*] with great zeal. I was always aware that with the expansion of co-operative activities, especially into the fields of marketing and processing and business and industry, there would be a corresponding retraction of the activities by the middlemen and businessmen which they were certain to resent in the strongest possible terms.

Recently the Deputy Prime Minister proudly declared that the Government stood for capitalism and free enterprise. The rural folks, in particular the Malays, are unsuited for the cut and thrust of a capitalist society. They are used to the *gotong royong* [mutual help] society of cooperative effort.

[33] Ibid. 24 August 1962.

[34] Ibid. 28 January 1963. Aziz was well-known for his strong anti-colonial views and in this differed strongly from the pro-Western views of Tunku Abdul Rahman and other leaders of the UMNO.

Thus came to an end the long association of Aziz Ishak with the UMNO.

The beginning of the Indonesian confrontation in December 1962 delayed the formation of the new party. But as soon as the Indonesian confrontation subsided a little (in April and May 1963) Aziz Ishak and his close associate, Dato' Kampo Radjo, travelled all over the country and discovered that 'the desire for the formation of this party had come not only from leaders, but there was a clear and genuine wish on the part of the masses, especially among the peasants and fishermen living in the villages'.[35]

Encouraged by the interest among the people Aziz launched the new party, National Convention Party (Parti Perhimpunan Kebangsaan), on 14 July 1963 at Kuala Lumpur. The inaugural meeting was attended by thirty-three close associates of the founder, all belonging to the Malay community.

The party was looking only towards the ordinary Malay peasants and fishermen in the *kampong* for support. *The Straits Times* said in a leading article, 'Vehicle for Aziz': 'The NCP will seek directly to organize what may broadly be called the "Malay left" — the poorest peasants, the most insecure fishermen and other discontented rural dwellers'.[36]

These were the people in whose interest Aziz had chiefly worked as Minister for Agriculture and Cooperatives for many years and it was therefore natural that he looked for support. The major economic aims of the party were also directed at the betterment of the position of these people. It took no notice of the urban proletariat, mostly non-Malay. Also, the party's aim to establish a democratic state based on principles in accordance with the teachings of Islam was not designed to attract non-Malays, most of whom are not Muslims.

Aziz Ishak had always been known as a radical in the UMNO who had not reconciled himself to the pro-British posture of the Alliance Government. In an election meeting during the 1964 general elections Aziz alleged: 'I found that by the Merdeka Agree-

[35] *Penyata Tahun, 1963-64* (Annual Report), Parti Perhimpunan Kebangsaan, p. 1.

[36] 16 July 1963.

ment signed in London in 1956, the Tunku had made an unwritten agreement with the British Government whereby the wealth and economy of this country continued to be controlled by Britain'.[37]

Consequently, two months after independence, he submitted his resignation from the ministry and the Tunku took over his portfolio for a week. But according to Aziz, the Tunku later persuaded him to return with the assurance that when the British expatriate officials left Malaya their influence would fade away and the Government would be able to reshape policies.

Aziz's sympathies with the Afro-Asian world were also well-known. This orientation of Aziz had found expression in the new party's aims. It committed itself to the creation of a 'completely independent Federation of Malaya' and to the eradication of colonialism. This by implication accepted the Indonesian view that Malaya was neo-colonial. These pronouncements were to attract a small number of radical and pro-Indonesian elements in the Malay community. But on the whole, the party's only effective appeal was the personality of its leader, Aziz Ishak. Most of the people who joined and supported it did so because of Aziz Ishak. The party did not succeed in establishing a wider ideological appeal.

The leaders of the party were conscious of this limitation and it was for this reason that it was explicitly stated that one of its aims was to 'cooperate with political parties and such organizations with similar objects'. *The Straits Times* commented in a leading article soon after the formation of the party:

> The name of Inche Abdul Aziz Ishak's new political party is conspicuously neutral. There are no overtones either of race or of class in 'National Convention Party'. It is the sort of roof under which a variety of tendencies may shelter. Perhaps that is why the name has been picked. A rigidly dogmatic image might hinder the formation of partnerships and alliances....[38]

Even before Aziz launched his new party he began to cooperate with the parties in opposition to the Alliance, especially on the issue of the formation of Malaysia. In March 1963, all the oppo-

[37] *The Straits Times*, 13 April 1964.
[38] 16 July 1963.

sition parties in the Malayan House of Representatives formed a common front under his leadership to oppose the formation of Malaysia in the manner it was being effected by the Alliance Government.[39] The party also participated in the unsuccessful attempts in early 1964, before the 1964 general elections, to forge a united front against the Alliance.

The fact that the NCP appealed essentially to the Malay rural dweller should not mean that it was necessarily a Malay communal party. It allowed full membership, unlike the UMNO, MCA and the MIC, and the PMIP, to persons of different racial origins. It was a party very much like the United Democratic Party and the People's Progressive Party, interested chiefly in the problems of one racial community, but not to the exclusion of the other communities. The party's political programme did not explicitly commit it to protect the interests of one community against the others. Its chief aim was to 'improve the economic and cultural levels of the people in the rural areas'.

It was unfortunate for the party that it was formed at the time of the establishment of Malaysia and Indonesian confrontation. The party opposed the formation of Malaysia. It believed that Tunku Abdul Rahman had played into the hands of the British in accepting the Malaysia plan. It maintained, as did all the other opposition parties, that the new federation should be formed only after the peoples of the territories involved were consulted. This position of the party was extremely effectively exploited by the UMNO to brand the party and Aziz Ishak as being anti-national and pro-Indonesian.

Just before the 1964 general elections, the party's decision to join the strongly anti-Malaysia Socialist Front strengthened the UMNO propaganda against it. On 16 March 1964, Aziz Ishak told the press at the Socialist Front headquarters in Kuala Lumpur:

> In the interests of the unity of the socialist movement, with which I have been identified since the very beginning of my political career, I have decided to lead my party into the Socialist Front. The Front

[39] *The Straits Times*, 12 March 1963.

will now consist of my party, NCP, the Party Raayat and the Labour Party.[40]

The party knew that it could not expect any support among the non-Malay communities. It was imperative that to achieve any electoral successes it would have to work in cooperation with a party with some hold on the non-Malays.

Immediately the UMNO blast against Aziz and his party, in particular against him personally, was intensified. On the one side they told the Malays that he was anti-national and pro-Indonesian, and on the other side they told the Chinese that he was the man who, as the Minister for Agriculture and Cooperatives, had 'confiscated all the licences held by the Chinese in Perak, Province Wellesley and Penang. He did this to hand them over to the Malays so as to win the Malays in his cunning scheme to contest my leadership.'[41] Tunku Abdul Rahman further said:

This is the man which the Socialist Front now has. This is the man who denounced capitalism at one time. Yet he wanted to make himself the head of a capitalist organization in the manufacture of urea — a company having a capital of about $50 million.

In the general elections of 1964, the party fielded several candidates, none of whom was returned. Significantly, all the candidates of the party were Malays and were fielded in the State of Selangor, the home State of Aziz Ishak. Aziz Ishak contested both the parliamentary and state elections in his own home area. In the two preceding elections in the country, 1955 and 1959, Aziz had been returned from the same constituencies with large majorities as an UMNO candidate. The same electorate which had elected him twice with large majorities did not support him now that he had left the UMNO, the communal organization of their community, and had formed a party of his own. By leaving the ranks of the Malays he had become a 'traitor' to their cause. The same had happened to Dato Onn bin Jaafar. It is not that the UMNO has a very strong political machine, an organization which is effective

---

[40] Socialist Front Press Statement (mimeographed), 16 March 1964.

[41] A statement by Tunku Abdul Rahman, *The Straits Times*, 29 March 1964.

in gathering votes; it is essentially a question of loyalty to the Malays and their communal organization, the UMNO.

In spite of the crushing defeats suffered by the party in the general elections it held its first annual General Assembly meeting in late September 1964, at which it reiterated its policy position more explicitly. It demanded laws to protect the interests of the country from exploitation by foreign capitalists and to wipe out middlemen and landlords so that the peasants, fishermen and workers could secure the fruits of their labour.[42] It further demanded that the defence treaty with Britain be scrapped and no foreign troops be allowed to use Malaysia as a base.

By this time the party had been able to establish its Divisions (corresponding to a parliamentary constituency) in the following places:

Selangor: Kuala Langat, Klang, Kuala Selangor Selatan, Langat.
Pahang: Raub and Temerloh.
Perak: Larut Selatan.
Johore: Muar.[43]

However, the party was not to last long. In late 1965, Aziz Ishak was arrested and imprisoned under the Internal Security Act for alleged pro-Indonesian activities. Other leaders, Zailani Sulaiman and Dato' Kampo Radjo, were also detained. They were all released only in early 1967, after Indonesian confrontation was over, under the condition that they would not indulge in any political activity. The party having thus lost all its important leaders, went out of existence.

Such non-communal 'parties of personage' have little chance of success in a plural society, more so in Malaysia, a multi-racial society of an extreme kind. It is only those parties of personage which champion the cause of a single community that can thrive in such societies.

These parties, by their very nature and bases, appeal only to the politically inarticulate; they are hardly expected to attract the educated and the politically sophisticated members of society.

[42] Statement by the Central Executive Committee of the NCP (mimeographed), 26 September 1964.
[43] *Penyata Tahun, 1963-64,* Parti Perhimpunan Kebangsaan, p. 10.

But the politically inarticulate have a stronger sense of loyalty to their community than to an individual leader, however brilliant or powerful he may be. They would be attracted by an individual leader only if he is a communal leader, fighting for the exclusive interests of his community. They would not support an individual leader on the basis of his personal appeal if he attempts to build up a non-communal image and is not willing to fight strongly for the interests of his community. This was to an extent the reason for the failure of Dato Onn bin Jaafar and his Independence of Malaya Party. Dato Onn, who was the father of Malay nationalism, was a very powerful charismatic personality. His hold on the Malay masses during 1946 to 1950 was even stronger than Tunku Abdul Rahman, the present *Bapak Malaysia,* has ever had. But this lasted only so long as he acted as a communal leader of the Malays fighting to protect their position in their fatherland. As soon as he started seeing himself in the role of a national leader, committed to look after the good of all the people of the country, irrespective of their racial origin, the Malay *raayat* completely withdrew their support from him. When he left the UMNO and formed the Independence of Malaya Party in 1951 only a handful of his close Malay friends and admirers came out with him. His tremendous charismatic appeal for an ordinary Malay was no more. The ordinary *raayat* owed a much stronger loyalty to their community.

This is what happened to Dato Panglima Bukit Gantang, the founder of the National Association of Perak. He was a powerful personality with considerable charismatic appeal and influence in Perak. As an UMNO leader in Perak he had been unshakeable. But once he went out of the UMNO he lost all his appeal and influence among the Malays. The loyalty of the Malay *raayat* was stronger to their community and its communal organization, the UMNO, than to him. As for the ordinary Chinese and Indian he would rather support a communal organization representing his own community than a non-communal party based on the personality of a Malay.

In the case of Tan Kee Gak and the Malayan Party, some support was forthcoming from non-Malays around the time of Malayan independence mainly because of the special circumstances in Malacca mentioned earlier. But soon after independence the Chinese and Indians in Malacca were concerned more with their position as Chinese and Indians than as residents of Malacca. Naturally, they were attracted more to their communal organizations than to the Malacca-based Malayan Party, established mainly to save the separate identity of Malacca. And this shift led to the decline of the party.

Aziz Ishak, though he had not given up his basic pro-Malay orientation, was unsuccessful because he had come out of the UMNO after it had successfully promoted the Malay interest for about two decades. If the Malay *raayat* was to support the National Convention Party on the basis of its pro-Malay position, then why not support the older, larger and more powerful UMNO?

This fate of the non-communal parties of personage is further confirmed by the position of non-party candidates in elections in Malaysia. In the 1955 Federal Legislative Council elections only eighteen non-party candidates had contested for the fifty-two seats for which elections were held and secured a total of only 31,642 votes. It is not surprising that none was returned and fourteen of them lost their deposits. As many as sixteen of these were Malays. By this time the Pan-Malayan Islamic Party had not emerged as a powerful and more extreme Malay communal party and therefore many Malays who were unhappy with the role of the UMNO in the Alliance fielded themselves as independent candidates in predominantly Malay areas and sought the support of extremist Malay elements. However, once the PMIP emerged as

TABLE 9

VOTES POLLED BY INDEPENDENTS IN THE 1959 AND
1964 GENERAL ELECTIONS

	Number of votes polled		Seats contested		Seats won	
	1959	1964	1959	1964	1959	1964
State Elections	63,387	22,164	82	39	5	—
Parliamentary Elections	74,194	13,509	27	8	3	—

a powerful political force very few Malays are tempted to contest elections as independent candidates and those who do secure little support.

The position of non-party candidates in the 1959 and 1964 general elections is given in Table 9 on p. 288. The large number of independent candidates and a fairly sizeable vote secured by them in 1959 was entirely a result of the crisis in the Alliance which had resulted in many MCA leaders leaving the party and contesting as independents. In 1964, as expected, not a single independent candidate was returned either in the State or Parliamentary elections. On the other hand, in countries like India, independents have always secured a large vote. In the 1967 general elections in India, a total of 342 independents secured over 17 million votes (11.5 per cent of the total) and 25 parliamentary seats. In the state elections, 2,504 independent candidates secured over 21 million votes (15.2 per cent of the total) and captured as many as 310 seats.[44] This is so in India because the major parties are non-communal and comprise locally influential candidates of groups, which do not have their own communal organizations, or in cases where the communal organizations are unable to field their own candidates, they successfully contest the elections on the basis of their own personal appeal or as representatives of a particular communal or religious group.

---

[44] Norman D. Palmer, 'India's Fourth General Elections', *Asian Survey*, Vol. VII No. 5 (May 1957), pp. 283-4.

IX

CONCLUSION

NON-COMMUNAL political parties appear to have little future in Malaysia. As long as politics operate on the basis that Malays, as the only *bumiputras* (the sons of the soil), have a special right over the country and that they must have a pre-eminent position in the government and administration of the country in order to off-set the non-Malay control over the economic and commercial life, it will be extremely difficult for non-communal political parties to thrive.

The object of the Alliance Party and the Malay leadership (which rules the country) is not so much to achieve an integration of the different racial groups in Malaysia on the basis of equality[1] as to maintain a racial balance and communal peace through a sort of separation of powers. This has meant that the Malays, as the only indigenous people, enjoy a pre-eminent position in politics, government and administration, and the non-Malay communities are given a more or less free play in the economic and commercial sphere, the purpose for which these communities in the first place had emigrated to Malaya. It is a kind of *quid pro quo* between the leadership of the United Malays National Organisation and the property-owning leadership of the Malaysian Chinese Association (the Malaysian Indian Congress just tags along) that the non-Malays do not make too many encroachments into the preserves of the Malays and the Malays in return would not make serious

---

[1] Dato Syed Jaafar Albar, a former Secretary-General of the UMNO, once when asked if he believed that integration of the different racial groups in Malaysia was at all possible gave an emphatic negative answer. And then, asked if integration was not possible, what was the solution of the communal problem, promptly replied: *Maphilindo*. And to him Maphilindo meant a strong and formal link with Indonesia as a means of solving the Chinese problem in Malaysia (Kuala Lumpur, August 1964.) Ali bin Ahmad, a former Assistant Secretary-General of the UMNO, told this writer (Kuala Lumpur, August 1964): 'If we have to choose between Indonesian masters and Chinese masters we would of course choose the Indonesian masters, who practice the same religion, belong to the same race and speak the same language.'

incursions into the spheres of activity of the non-Malays. It is not an absolute separation of power and activity. Each community has to be given some share in the sphere of influence of the other to keep it happy. It is for this reason that the Malaysian Chinese Association does not make much fuss when some half-hearted attempts are made by the Government to promote Malay participation in trade and commerce. These attempts are made by the leaders of the UMNO chiefly to hold the Malay demand of a share in the economic life of the country in check. UMNO leaders know full well that if they promoted Malay participation in trade and commerce too strongly it would seriously impair the *quid pro quo* and prompt the MCA to make demands for an increased share in the politics, government and administration of the country. When Aziz Ishak during the early 1960s as the Minister of Agriculture and Cooperatives had attempted to promote Malay participation in trade and commerce with greater zeal there was an outcry from the MCA and he was forced to leave the Ministry of Agriculture. UMNO leadership felt that if such activities continued the Chinese would inevitably come to demand a larger share in political power which would be worse.

As we noted earlier, a great emphasis is put by the Malays and their leaders on Malay unity. They believe that Malay unity is of supreme importance; only through unity can they protect themselves and their interests.[2] This emphasis has been strongly asserted in the post-independence period when the threat to Malay interests has been more real and when the protective power of the British has been dismantled. The result has been that very few Malays have dared to come out and join non-communal political parties. And when some of them did so they soon found themselves completely cut off from the rank and file of the Malay community so as to be without any popular Malay support, and they became politically ineffective. In fact, they became outcasts of the

[2] As part of this, disunity and divisions within the ranks of the non-Malay communities are encouraged. It has been suggested, for example, that the decision to allow the opening of a Formosan Consular and Trade Agency in Kuala Lumpur in 1965 was essentially to bolster the declining influence of Kuomintang groups in Malaysia and thus strengthen at least one divisive force among the Chinese.

Malay community. The case of Dato Onn bin Jaafar has already been referred to. Soon after Dato Onn left the UMNO, its new President, Tunku Abdul Rahman, asserted that Dato Onn by leaving the UMNO and forming the non-communal Independence of Malaya Party had sold away Malay rights and heritage to other races.[3] One could also cite the cases of Dato Zainal Abidin bin Haji Abas, until recently the Chairman of the United Democratic Party, and Aziz Ishak. Then there is the case of Osman Siru, one time founder and leading light of the Labour Party, who because of a complete lack of support from people of his own community found his position untenable within the Labour Party and quietly left it.

The crucial consequence has been that non-communal political parties have assumed over a period of time the character of essentially non-Malay parties, parties with a predominantly non-Malay leadership and rank and file. This is what happened to the non-communal parties during the mid-1950s when prospects of independence became clear. And once the process began, the parties got caught in a disastrous vicious circle: the lack of support from the Malays started turning them into essentially non-Malay parties (in terms of leadership and rank and file, though not necessarily, initially, in terms of policy and programme) and thus made them even more unattractive to the Malays who anyway were not keen to join non-communal parties, parties which were not specially committed to safeguard the interests of their community. But to join such parties was unthinkable. What is more, as a result of the complete lack of support from among the Malays the leaders of these non-communal parties, many of whom had a genuinely non-communal orientation, found it increasingly difficult to face the pressure from the non-Malay rank and file and lower level leadership to convert the parties essentially into instruments for the protection of the interests of the non-Malay communities. Over the years, they succumbed to the pressure and were unable to stop the parties from championing mainly the cause of the non-Malays. In some cases, they did this for the sake of their own survival within the party. Those who did not wish to go along with this were

[3] *The Straits Times*, 1 July 1952.

forced out of the parties. If Malay support had been forthcoming in significant numbers, they could have put forward the view that promoting the cause of the non-Malays in an extreme manner would cost the party its entire Malay membership and support. But unfortunately, they have never been in a position to do so in the post-independence period, except in the case of the Labour Party where its non-communally orientated national leadership was able to hold in check the excessive demands of Chinese extremists by suggesting that acceptance of these demands would threaten the existence of the Socialist Front. For example, so long as the Labour Party was joined with the Party Raayat in the Front it never officially supported multi-lingualism even though many of its leaders and members were of the view that Chinese and Tamil should be accepted as official languages. But soon after the Party Raayat left the Socialist Front in late 1965, the Labour Party committed itself officially to support the demand for official language status for Chinese and Tamil.

In the case of the United Democratic Party, Dr. Lim Chong Eu's genuine attempt to strengthen his party's non-communal character and appeal through the election of a well-known Malay, Dato Zainal Abidin bin Haji Abas, as Chairman of the party and the nomination of a large number of Malay candidates in the 1964 general elections would possibly have succeeded if the party had gained some significant support from the Malay community in the elections. Unfortunately, none of the party's many Malay candidates, including Dato Zainal Abidin, was successful and the party failed to secure any support from the Malays. This naturally weakened the position of the non-communal elements. It also made the position of the Malay leaders untenable within the party, most of whom soon became completely inactive or left the party. Proponents of a moderate policy position on communal issues could no longer convert many to their viewpoint in the party for such a policy not only was not able to obtain the support of the Malays but made it difficult for the party to project a strong appeal for the Chinese community.

As the non-communal political parties were being turned into 'non-Malay parties' during the mid-1950s a critical change was taking place within the Alliance which was to have a decisive impact on the non-communal parties. As we noted in Chapter 1, by the mid-1950s the UMNO had come to enjoy a position of pre-eminence within the Alliance; the Alliance was no more to be based on the principle of equality of the three partners. In fact, starting from this time the Alliance was to be converted into an instrument of Malay supremacy. This meant a secondary position for the MCA and the MIC.

The role of the MCA during constitution-making in 1956-7, and with regard to the issues of Chinese language and education, gave many Chinese the feeling that their communal organization had failed them and their cause. This was the basis on which in 1958 a group led by Dr. Lim Chong Eu and others had been able to challenge the leadership of Tan Cheng Lock. In view of the widespread disenchantment with the leadership of the MCA, it was not a surprise that these people were able to wrest the leadership of the organization. But the treatment meted out to this new and more popularly-based leadership by the UMNO and Tunku Abdul Rahman during the Alliance crisis of 1959 was a traumatic experience to many in the Chinese community, who now lost faith in their communal organization as a protector of their interests. The position of the MCA was so seriously undermined that never again was it to assume the unchallenged leadership of the Chinese community.

The result of this was that communal elements and people seeking equality for all races, who had pinned their hopes of safeguarding the interests of their communities on the communal organizations, the MCA and the MIC, felt frustrated, and many of them at different times left the parties. Such an exodus from the MCA took place on a large scale in 1959 following the crisis in the Alliance. On coming out they either joined the existing political parties which, because of the special communal situation in the country, had already become 'non-Malay parties', or they established new political parties of their own. But when they joined the existing parties they attempted to swing them into a communal direction. And in this they were successful. This is what happened in the case of the People's Progressive Party and the Labour Party.

Diagrammatic Representation of Party Politics in Malaysia

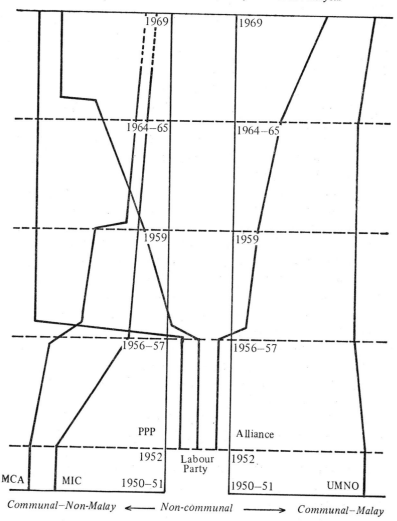

Communal–Non-Malay ← — Non-communal — → Communal–Malay

1952 : Formation of the Alliance.
1956–7 : Time of independence.
1959 : Alliance crisis and general elections.
1964–5 : Polemics between Singapore and Kuala Lumpur; exit of Singapore;
intensification of communal contradictions.
1969 : General elections and the communal explosion.

Moreover, once the communal parties, the MCA and the MIC, accepted a secondary position to the UMNO in the Alliance and conceded concessions in matters of vital concern to the non-Malays, the issue of equality for all races became the supreme issue, especially among the non-Malays. And non-communal political parties found it very difficult, from the point of view of practical politics, not to exploit it, this being the major effective source of appeal among the non-Malays. They began emphasizing this in their propaganda and built up their appeal mainly around it. Here the example of the People's Action Party of Singapore is of interest. Before the formation of Malaysia, in Singapore the party had found its appeal based on its non-communal and socialist character adequate in attracting substantial mass support. But, after the creation of Malaysia, the party discovered during the 1964 general elections that this was not good enough and soon began using the demand for equality for all races as the basis of its new appeal. That is when the slogan 'Malaysian Malaysia' was devised and played up by Prime Minister Lee Kuan Yew. The party now demanded a Malaysian Malaysia 'where people, regardless of their race, religion and different cultural backgrounds, should get a just share of the good things of life as citizens of equal worth', which, according to the leaders of the UMNO, was only another way of saying what the Chinese extremists of parties like the People's Progressive Party, the United Democratic Party and the Labour Party, had been asking for.

The failure of non-communal political parties to maintain their non-communal character and appeal is of the greatest significance, for it may well be that it is only the success of these parties that can provide viability to the political system, make representative government a success, and resolve the basic communal contradiction in Malaysia. Thus far, it has been possible for Tunku Abdul Rahman to maintain a position of political supremacy for the Malays without, by and large, endangering communal harmony or straining constitutional democracy too much.[4] This is a measure of his great personal influence. Also, it has been a result of his being able

[4] The following pages are based on R.K. Vasil, 'Man for Any Job', *The Dominion*, Wellington, 11 April 1967.

to impose moderation on the Malays and making them concede minor concessions to the non-Malays. Only once has the Tunku found the situation beyond his control and doubted the effectiveness of his appeal. This was the threat posed by the suspected more effective appeal of Lee Kuan Yew over the Chinese through his slogan of 'Malaysian Malaysia' and the Tunku had to take desperate action and force separation on Singapore in mid-1965. The fear was, firstly, that if Lee Kuan Yew was allowed to continue he would eventually rally most of the Chinese to his banner and thereby pose a most serious threat to the Malays and their position in Malaysia, and secondly, that he and his style of politics would give rise on the opposite side to a strong rallying point to Malay extremists, both within and outside the UMNO, and thus threaten the very existence of the Alliance system.

The problem with this arrangement based on the *quid pro quo* mentioned earlier and Tunku Abdul Rahman's personal influence is that first, the Tunku is a mortal being and would take with him one significant element of stability, and second, which is more important, this arrangement does not aim to solve the fundamental contradiction between the Malay insistence on a position of political supremacy and the non-Malay quest for equality for all races. Thus by its very nature it is only transitory. The relative calm in the country and the attempts by the ruling leadership to de-emphasize the seriousness of the situation[5] may make the problem seem remote. It is not so; it is immediate and urgent. Tunku Abdul Rahman has several times indicated that his deputy, Tun Abdul Razak bin Hussein, would succeed him. And at least once in the past Tun Razak has acted as the Prime Minister. Recently, at a party in Kuala Lumpur to celebrate his sixty-fourth birthday, the Tunku urged all Malaysians to give Tun Razak the same cooperation, support and help they had given him. He said: 'Back Razak as you have backed me . . . . In Tun Razak you have a good man, an honest and conscientious man. Give him any job and he is capable of completing it.'[6] The Tunku said this not just to please

[5] Tunku Abdul Rahman has always insisted on making people believe that he is the happy Prime Minister of the happiest country in the world.

[6] *Suara Malaysia* (Ministry of Information and Broadcasting, Kuala Lumpur), 23 February 1967, p. 3.

Tun Razak (who is a close and trusted friend); it was not meant as a formal gesture. This call to the people of Malaysia, in particular to the non-Malays, was a result of the Tunku's fear and doubt that Tun Razak would be able to maintain communal harmony and constitutional democracy after he left. Tun Razak is just the opposite of the Tunku. He is basically the efficient administrator who keeps his staff on the alert, but

> ... he gives rise to a good deal of criticism that his methods are mechanical, his standards arbitrary, and his disposition despotic. The criticism, it seems, comes less from the traditionally relaxed Malays, whom one might expect to be upset by his demand for efficiency, than from the energetic Chinese, who appreciate his drive but mistrust his motives .... Widespread misgivings about Tun Razak among the Malayan Chinese, misgivings which he fully reciprocates, lead to a good deal of speculation whether the Alliance and the Alliance Government can hold together when and if Tun Razak actually does succeed the Tunku. [7]

Large numbers of Chinese and Indians fear Tun Razak and suspect him of being anti-Chinese and anti-Indian. He lacks the Tunku's considerable personal appeal and influence among the non-Malays. It is not important whether the non-Malay fears of him are genuine or ill-founded. The crucial point is that they are held by large numbers of non-Malays. And this would make it almost impossible for Tun Razak to maintain Malay political supremacy without resorting to a blatantly authoritarian system of government. Also, without significant support amongst the non-Malays Tun Razak would be forced to give in far more than Tunku Abdul Rahman to the extremist demands of the Malays.

The future of non-communal political parties depends to a significant degree on the emergence of a numerous and strong Malay middle class, medical doctors, lawyers, accountants, engineers, journalists, teachers, etc., who are willing to accept the non-Malay peoples in the country as citizens of equal status and having as much right over the country as the Malays. It is only these Malays who would be willing to go beyond the present dominant attitude

[7] W.A. Hanna, *Eight Nation Makers: Southeast Asia's Charismatic Statesmen*, New York, 1964, p. 106.

amongst the Malays that the country has to be dominated by one racial group or the other (there is no alternative to this; if it is not controlled by the Malays the Chinese would dominate it) and think in terms of a new Malaysian nation where people irrespective of their racial origins enjoy full and equal rights. Only then would it be possible for genuinely non-communal political parties to maintain their non-communal character and appeal and thrive. And that in turn would make representative government viable.

X

POSTSCRIPT

SINCE this study was completed in 1967 important political events have taken place in Malaysia. The Labour Party has opted out of constitutional politics and decided to seek power through 'mass struggle'. The United Democratic Party has been disbanded. Their place has been taken by two new non-communal political parties, the Democratic Action Party and the Gerakan Rakyat Malaysia (Malaysian People's Movement). And, following the 1969 general elections and the bloody communal explosion of 13 May, representative government has been suspended for an indefinite period and the country is being governed by an all-powerful National Operations Council headed by Tun Razak. However, none of these events has necessitated a reappraisal of the main thesis and broad conclusions of this work.[1]

In mid-1965, Singapore was forced out of the Malaysian federation and as a result the People's Action Party of Singapore had to withdraw itself from Malaysia.[2] But interestingly, one of its principal leaders and its lone representative in the Malaysian Parliament from Malaya, C.V. Devan Nair, was left behind in Malaysia because of the accident of his birth. At first, under his leadership 'a completely Malaysian-based PAP took over, in a much more modest fashion, of course, from where the largely Singapore-based PAP had left off'.[3] But the Malaysian Government was unwilling to allow the party to operate in Malaysia on the ground that it now was foreign-based. As a result Devan Nair decided to

---

[1] It is for this reason that the Conclusion prepared in late 1967 has been retained unaltered while later developments have been dealt with in this Postscript.

[2] For a full analysis of the separation see the author's forthcoming *The 1969 General Elections in Malaysia*, Chapter 3.

[3] Democratic Action Party, 'Central Executive Committee Report to the First Party Conference', 17 March 1968, in *Who Lives if Malaysia Dies*, Kuala Lumpur, 1969, p. 53.

launch a new party, the Democratic Action Party, which was given registration by the Government on 19 March 1966.

At first, the new party presented itself in general as the champion of Malaysian Malaysia, the slogan introduced by Lee Kuan Yew. It did not attempt to fully define the vague but effective slogan and seemed mainly interested in exploiting it to build up a mass base among the non-Malay communities. But as the general elections drew near the party began to define the slogan in order to make it more effective. And in this attempt it went beyond the position earlier taken by the People's Action Party when the latter participated in Malaysian politics.[4] Here the underlying basis of the thinking of the party leadership was that in the existing communal circumstances in the country it was impossible for any non-communal political party to attract significant support from among the Malays.[5] They believed that the party, in order to emerge as a viable and effective entity, had first to build up a mass base, even if it meant only among the non-Malay communities. The attempt to attract Malays to the party was only to be effected later over a period of time, once the solid support of the non-Malay communities had been secured. Hence it wished to present the party's policy and programme in terms mainly having an appeal for the non-Malays. Unlike the Gerakan Rakyat Malaysia, no special effort was made to create an appeal for the Malays.

The party's 'basic guiding policy and principles' were contained in *The Setapak Declaration* announced on 29 July 1967. It placed a great emphasis on the principle of racial equality and demanded its implementation 'at all levels of national life and in all fields of national endeavour — political, social, economic, cultural and educational'.[6] It rejected the idea of racial hegemony

[4] This was based on the experience of non-communal political parties in general and that of the PAP in particular.

[5] The PAP had gone through the same process earlier. When it first entered Malaysian politics in early 1964, just before the general elections, it placed the utmost emphasis on not alienating the Malays and seeking cooperation with their leaders in the UMNO. But following the communal riots in Singapore in mid-1964 and the severe attacks by the UMNO on the party and its foremost leader, Lee Kuan Yew, it decided to concentrate its efforts on securing the support of the non-Malay communities. This is when the slogan of 'Malaysian Malaysia', with a special appeal for the non-Malays, was devised.

[6] Democratic Action Party, *The Setapak Declaration*, p. 4.

by one community for it was not only undesirable but also impracticable because of the composition of the population in Malaysia. It maintained that the Malays did not constitute a national majority and that any single community, by itself, is outnumbered by the rest so as to make the idea of racial domination completely impractical. It took exception to the categorization of citizens into *bumiputras* and non-*bumiputras* and rejected discrimination against citizens in matters of 'appointments and promotions, particularly in the public sector and now increasingly in the private sector, on grounds of race'.[7] This was an attack on the special position of the Malays as inscribed in the Constitution of Malaysia. This was one of the important issues on which the party had deviated from the position of the PAP which had never attacked the special position of the Malays as guaranteed by the Constitution.

Later, the party in its manifesto for the 1969 general elections, *Towards a Malaysian Malaysia,* put forward its three objectives as: political democracy, social and economic democracy, and cultural democracy. By political democracy it meant that all citizens, regardless of race, language and religion, must enjoy equal political status, rights and opportunities. Under the concept of social and economic democracy, it sought to eradicate exploitation of man by man, class by class and race by race. But it placed the primary emphasis on cultural democracy for it related to issues of vital interest and concern to the non-Malay communities. It alleged that the policies of the Alliance Government had caused a deep feeling of 'cultural insecurity' among the non-Malays and offered as solution the models of such multi-racial and multi-lingual states as Switzerland, Canada and the Soviet Union. It put forward the following *inter alia* as its major objectives:

(i)   Official status for the Chinese, Tamil and English languages, and acceptance of Malay as the national language to serve as the common language of expression and communication among Malaysians.

(ii) Free use of Chinese, Tamil and English in the Parliament, State Assemblies, and in public notices and government correspondence.

[7] Ibid. p. 5.

(iii) Abolition of the distinction between national and national-type schools.

(iv) Adoption of an integrated education system, where schools using the major languages as media of instruction and examination are recognised as National Schools, provided the content of education imparted is Malaysian-orientated and the National Language is taught as a compulsory second language.[8]

In all, the party's aim was to project itself as the main protector of the rights and interests of the non-Malay communities. It was the only major party, among those contesting the elections, which demanded official status for the languages of the non-Malay communities. In this again the party had significantly moved away from the position of the PAP. Its entire election campaign was geared to present itself as the sole representative of the non-Malay communities. And in attempting to achieve this it had fully adopted the position of the Chinese-educated Chinese. There was little difference between its position and that of the extremist elements in the non-Malay communities on vital communal issues.

While the Democratic Action Party was emerging as the main champion of the non-Malay communities, the Gerakan Rakyat Malaysia was inaugurated in March 1968 as a genuinely non-communal party. The main sponsors of the party were Dr. Tan Chee Khoon and V. Veerappen (both former leaders of the Labour Party), Dr. Lim Chong Eu (the founder and foremost leader of the United Democratic Party), and a few well-known non-party men, Professor Wang Gungwu (Professor of History, University of Malaya), Professor Hussein Alatas (Professor of Malay Studies, University of Singapore) and Dr. J.B.A. Peter (President of the Malaysian Medical Association). The nucleus of the new party was provided by the English-educated moderates of the Labour Party and the non-chauvinist Chinese of the United Democratic Party.

In the mid-1960s the Labour Party had been taken over by the Chinese-educated Chinese who converted it into an essentially Chinese communal and pro-Peking party. This had made the

[8] *DAP General Elections Manifesto.*

position of the English-educated moderates untenable and over a period they withdrew from the party. Similarly, as noted in Chapter 7, the rank and file of the United Democratic Party

> ... is still very largely committed to securing for Chinese language, education and culture its rightful place, which to them is the most important aspect of equality for all races. And it may be only a matter of time when the rank and file would be able to assert its position and force the moderate leadership, as eventually took place in the case of the Labour Party, to commit the party to a pro-Chinese posture. The moderate leadership will have either to give in or go.[9]

With the inauguration of Malaysia and especially the circumstances under which Singapore was forced out of the federation communal contradictions had become far more intense in the country. And this had strongly affected the UDP. More, the lack of any significant success by the party in the 1964 general elections (especially the defeat of all its large number of Malay candidates) had strengthened the position of the pro-Chinese elements who argued that with its non-communal image the party was not getting anywhere. It had not only failed to attract support from the Malay community but, in the process, had failed to establish itself as a representative body of the non-Malay communities. This had created serious pressures within the party and had weakened the position of the moderates led by Dr. Lim Chong Eu. And in the worsening communal situation in the country it seemed certain that Dr. Lim Chong Eu would not be able to maintain the non-communal character of the party for long in the future. Therefore, when the English-educated moderates withdrew from the Labour Party, Dr. Lim saw his opportunity and established contact with them. And this eventually led to the dissolution of the United Democratic Party and the inauguration of the Gerakan Rakyat Malaysia.

The circumstances which had led to the formation of the new party by Dr. Lim and the former English-educated moderates of the Labour Party had caused the leadership to place the utmost emphasis, unlike the DAP, on building the new party as a strictly

[9] See p. 268 above.

non-communal party. Since it was the takeover of the Labour Party by Chinese chauvinists and a similar threat of a takeover of the United Democratic Party which had made these leaders form a new party, they were especially keen not to allow the process to repeat itself. The leadership of the new party did not share the DAP view that the party, in order to emerge as a viable and effective entity, had first to build up a mass base (even if it meant only among the non-Malay communities) and only later attempt to attract Malay support. Consequently, the Gerakan placed considerable emphasis on presenting its policies in such a way as not to alienate the Malay community and with the positive aim of attracting them. It elected a well-known Malay intellectual, Professor Syed Hussein Alatas, as the first Chairman. Five of the sixteen members elected to the *pro tem* committee were Malays.

The new party attempted to build its appeal mainly on three bases — non-communalism, moderate socialism, and democracy. Its political programme issued on 15 April 1968 recognized the need to accord 'special attention and emphasis on the economically weak Malays and other indigenous peoples' and maintained that they should be protected from exploitation and assisted to enable them to compete with other communities 'on a just basis' in business, trade and the professions. Unlike the DAP it did not reject the special position of the Malays as guaranteed by the Constitution.

On the contentious issue of language and education, the party, seeking a compromise between the demands of the non-Malays and the position of the Malay community, advocated the following *inter alia* to solve the problem:

(i) To recognize School Certificate and Higher School Certificate examinations in Chinese and Tamil.

(ii) To increase higher secondary educational institutions in the national language.

(iii) As it is in Indonesia, the promotion of the national language is achieved without competitive conflict with regional ethnic community languages such as Javanese, Sundanese. Similarly in Malaysia the promotion of the national language in the fields of education should not be considered in the light of conflict with other languages.

(iv)   It is our conviction that the existence of Chinese and Tamil education up to Higher School Certificate will not conflict with the aim of promoting the national language and unifying the Malaysian communities. We see no reasons for Government not to grant aid to Chinese Schools, and if there are Tamil Secondary Schools, without them giving up their Chinese and Tamil mediums of instruction. Given the national syllabus and proper leadership, pupils from these schools can be as good and patriotic Malaysians as those from existing Government schools.[10]

Even though the party did not advocate official status for the languages of the non-Malay communities, which to the non-Malays was of vital importance, it made a concession to them when it stated that the continued existence and support by the State of Chinese and Tamil education up to the Higher School Certificate level was not inimical to the aim of creating a united Malaysian nation and the development of Malay as the sole national language. Its basic approach to these problems was:

We strive for a Malaysian nationhood evolved out of the existing communities in Malaysia. The process of formation should be left to historical growth. The state participates in its formation by eliminating obstacles to harmony and inter-community accultration. It should not impose cultural elements or indulge in artificial experiments such as introducing a common dress, dance, ritual and ceremony without regard to the receptivity of the communities in Malaysia. We emphasize common experience and the sense of a common destiny as the decisive essentials of nationhood rather than cultural, religious or ethnic uniformity.[11]

All in all, the party's aim was to present itself as a genuinely non-communal organization. And conscious of the fact that its non-communalism would be difficult to sustain unless it established some contact with the Malay community it placed a great emphasis on winning Malay support.

One significant result of the formation of the two new parties and the refusal of the Labour Party to participate in elections was

---

[10] Minutes of the 3rd Working Committee meeting of the Gerakan Rakyat Malaysia, 24 August 1968.

[11] A mimeographed document circulated by the party on 15 April 1968.

that the non-Malay opposition in West Malaysia emerged as a far more homogeneous group than ever before. There were no fundamental differences with regard to ideology and political programme among the major parties, the DAP, the Gerakan Rakyat Malaysia and the PPP. The differences were mainly with regard to the intensity of their commitment to the interests of the non-Malay communities and the value attached by them to the necessity of establishing contact with the Malay community. In addition, there were minor conflicts of personalities. The affinity was underlined by the common support of a mildly socialist programme and representative government. More, the fear of the Alliance, especially the growing authoritarianism of the Government and its tendency to use its over two-thirds majority in the Parliament to amend the Constitution,[12] encouraged them to de-emphasize their differences and seek cooperation. Following prolonged negotiations, in February 1969 a three-way electoral arrangement between the DAP, the PPP and the Gerakan was approved. They entered into separate agreements, each one of them with the other two, to allocate both the parliamentary and state constituencies to each of the three parties on the basis of its organization and an estimate of electoral support in the constituency. The crucial result was that there was little dispersion and waste of the opposition vote in the general elections; the Alliance had to face straight contests.

The campaign strategy of the Alliance, dominated by the UMNO, was largely determined by the fear that the PMIP now posed a much greater threat to the UMNO than ever before. The period following the exit of Singapore from the Malaysian federation had seen a considerable worsening of communal relations in the country. This had been largely a result of the greater awareness and articulation among the non-Malay communities and the resultant increase in the fear of the non-Malays among the Malays.

[12] Addressing an election eve meeting in Kuala Lumpur, Dr. Tan Chee Khoon, a key leader of Gerakan Rakyat Malaysia, said:

> The simple message that I wish to put across to the voters of this country is this: *Deny the Alliance Party the two-thirds majority it needs to change the Constitution.*

Text of the speech supplied by Dr. Tan. Emphasis in the original.

Malays in the northern and east-coast states had come to believe that the Alliance, based on the principle of inter-communal co-operation, had failed to protect them against the non-Malays. The disillusionment with the Alliance, and consequently with the UMNO, was very considerable and the Malays had started looking for alternatives to protect their community and its vital interests. This is when the PMIP assumed a greater attraction for the Malays than before for they had come to feel it was this party, not the UMNO, which went to the root cause of the grave problem faced by them.

A grave consequence of this emphasis on the threat from the PMIP was that on the whole the Alliance attempted to present its appeal, past achievements and promises for the future in terms chiefly of attraction to the Malays. It did not make any special effort to woo the non-Malay voter and the communal organizations of the Chinese and Indians, the MCA and the MIC, were generally left to fend for themselves. But that created a serious problem, as the Alliance, because of its emphasis on maintaining Malay support for the UMNO, had begun acquiring an increasingly pro-Malay image. The secondary position of the MCA and the MIC in the Alliance was further underlined and the non-Malays, by and large, became convinced that the Alliance had become an instrument of Malay supremacy and was primarily committed to promoting and protecting the interests of the Malays. And if the non-Malays were to protect and further their interests they would have to look for other political organizations than the communal ones, the MCA and the MIC.

It was under these circumstances that the general elections took place in May 1969. In spite of the advantageous electoral arrangement, the opposition parties did not face the elections with a great deal of confidence. But the Alliance, by contrast, was full of optimism: there was no indication of the panic that was to grip it as soon as election results were announced.

The Alliance suffered serious reverses and a crushing blow was dealt to the Malaysian Chinese Association.[13] In the State elections

---

[13] For a full analysis of the results see R.K. Vasil, *The 1969 General Elections in Malaysia*.

the Alliance secured a total of 162 seats and 47.95 per cent of the total vote whereas it had won 206 (55.52 per cent) and 241 seats (57.62 per cent) respectively in the 1959 and 1964 elections. Similarly, in the Parliamentary elections, it won 66 seats (48.41 per cent of the vote) out of a total of 104 whereas it had captured 74 (51.78 per cent) and 89 seats (58.37 per cent) respectively in the 1959 and 1964 elections. The MCA losses were even more staggering: in the state elections it secured only 26 seats as against 59 and 67 seats respectively in 1959 and 1964, and in the parliamentary elections it won only 13 seats when it had captured 19 and 27 seats respectively in 1959 and 1964.[14] This was clear evidence of the complete lack of confidence on the part of the non-Malay communities in their communal organizations, the MCA and the MIC. Even the Malay voter had given an indication of his disenchantment with UMNO and an increasing preference for the more extreme Pan Malayan Islamic Party. This was reflected in the losses suffered by the UMNO in the northern and east-coast states.

The opposition parties, which had begun the election campaign without a great deal of confidence, were surprised at the results. They all made significant gains. The best performance was that of the DAP, which emerged as the largest opposition party in the Parliament. It won 13 seats in the parliamentary elections and secured 13.73 per cent of the total vote. In the State elections it won 31 seats and 11.76 per cent of the vote. However, a large part of this support for the party came in the states of Selangor, Perak and Negri Sembilan, where non-Malays outnumber the Malays and form a significant majority of the electorate. Out of the 13 seats won by the party in the parliamentary elections as many as

[14] The losses suffered by the MCA in the predominantly non-Malay States were even more shattering. For example, the position of the MCA in the state elections in five states was as follows.

State	Seats won		
	1959	1964	1969
Johore	7	11	9
Negri Sembilan	7	9	4
Penang	6	6	—
Perak	9	12	1
Selangor	8	9	1

11 were in these states. Similarly, in the state elections out of the 31 seats won by it 23 were in these states. In the other two states with a large non-Malay electorate, Johore and Penang, it did not put up many candidates chiefly because it had no important local leaders and the party organization there was very new and weak.

The success of the DAP was mainly a result of its effective utilization of the slogan of Malaysian Malaysia. The party's programme and policy proved extremely effective in attracting non-Malay support and it emerged as the main spokesman of the non-Malay communities in Malaysia.

The Gerakan Rakyat Malaysia, which had very zealously guarded its non-communal posture and had avoided making any significant concessions to extremist elements in the non-Malay communities during the election campaign and in its policy and programme, also did very well in the elections. The party had concentrated its effort in the two States of Penang and Selangor, especially in the former where its aim was to capture the state government. The party won 8 seats in the parliamentary elections and polled 8.57 per cent of the total vote. In the state elections it won 26 seats and secured 8.78 per cent of the vote. It achieved its greatest triumph in Penang where it won 16 of the 24 seats in the state legislature, thus capturing control over the state government. This was of utmost significance for this was the first time in the history of Malaysia that a party representing mainly the non-Malay communities had assumed control of a State government. The success of Gerakan was very largely based on the personal stature and popularity of several of its leaders and the support it was able to secure from the trade union movement in the country. In Penang, it was the personal appeal of Dr. Lim Chong Eu and several other important leaders, such as Tan Phock Kin and V. Veerappen, which had enabled the party to capture control of the state government. It has been suggested by a prominent leader of the party that the announcement that if the party was voted into power in Penang it would appoint Dr. Lim as the Chief Minister had attracted considerable support.[15] Moreover Penang, which had been a Crown Colony directly ruled by the British, has been well-

[15] A personal statement to this writer by V. Veerappen, 15 August 1969.

known for its more cosmopolitan atmosphere and its people, of all races, have shown greater interest in non-communal politics. Generally, non-communal parties have been more successful in Penang than elsewhere in the country. The Gerakan was also helped by the fact that neither of the other opposition parties, the DAP and the PPP, had organizations in Penang strong enough to collect the anti-Alliance vote.

The Alliance saw the election results as a very serious challenge to its claim that it represented the nation through its three constituent communal organizations, the UMNO, the MCA and the MIC. In the case of the UMNO, its position as the representative communal organization of the Malays which it had used to build itself as the dominant partner in the Alliance, was threatened by the PMIP. The undermining of the position of the MCA and the MIC was even greater; both the communal bodies, more or less, once and for all lost the basis of their claim that they represented the Chinese and the Indians in Malaysia and thus the *raison d'être* of their very existence was destroyed. This situation was seen by the Malays and their leadership in the Alliance as the beginning of the end of the Alliance system and the position of pre-eminence enjoyed by the Malays in the politics, government and administration of the country under the *quid pro quo* arrangement between the UMNO and the MCA. Thus far they had accepted the Alliance arrangement, less extreme than the solution offered by the PMIP, and representative government because their political domination had been ensured within its framework. But once it became obvious, after the 1969 general elections, that this crucial condition could not be sustained for long in the future they had no more any interest in representative government and the Alliance arrangement. They saw no option but to look for a drastic remedy. This is how following the communal explosion of 13 May the leadership of the UMNO under Tun Razak over-reacted to the situation and suspended representative government and introduced the all-powerful regime of the National Operations Council.

The general elections and the events following it have gravely worsened the communal situation in Malaysia and made it that

much more difficult for non-communal political parties to exist
and maintain their non-communal character and appeal. The little
progress that had been made in the country since independence
in creating a measure of trust and confidence among the different
racial groups was all destroyed over a period of a few days by the
riots and by the Government's handling of the situation. Communal antipathies have intensified and the whole atmosphere has
been brought to a point where it is impossible for any significant
number of Malays to think (or dare to think) in terms of non-
communalism and for non-Malays not to be attracted by extremism. Non-communal political parties now are bound to be confronted with a much greater pressure than ever before within their
organizations from their rank and file and lower level leadership
to consider the promotion of the interests of the non-Malays as
their primary task. And in this they may have to suffer the same
fate as the non-communal political parties in the past.

Here the examples of the Gerakan Rakyat Malaysia and the
DAP are extremely interesting. As we noted earlier, the Gerakan
places strong emphasis on maintaining its non-communal character
while the DAP believes that in the present communal conditions,
the party in order to survive has to promote strongly the interests
of the non-Malays and establish itself as their representative organization. In the circumstances, even though the Gerakan did
well in the last general elections and captured control of the state
government in Penang, it is the DAP alone which may emerge as
the representative body of the non-Malay communities, especially
the Chinese, who would increasingly look towards it (among the
parties participating in the legal political process) for the protection of their interests.

The Gerakan in order to have appeal for the Malays and retain
its non-communal character would have to maintain its moderate
position on communal issues. As a result it should be able to avoid
severe repression by the Government but in the process it would
fail to establish itself as a powerful and representative political
organization. In the atmosphere existing in the country, the more
it is tolerated by the completely Malay-dominated Government
the less would it be acceptable to the non-Malays who would sus-

pect it and have a decreasing faith in its intent and capacity to protect their interests. However, the party's control over the Penang state government and its growing links with the trade union movement may save it. If it is successful in providing an efficient and honest administration and obtaining rapid economic progress in Penang it may be able to add a new and more effective dimension to its present non-communalism and the personal appeal of its leaders and establish itself as a viable non-communal political organization.

In the case of the DAP, ironically, its emergence as a representative organization of the non-Malay communities may prove to be its undoing, for the more it gains support from the non-Malays the more it would be mistrusted by the Malays and the greater the repression it would have inflicted upon it by the Malay-dominated government. Already, following the elections, Lim Kit Siang, one of the key leaders of the party and the main architect of its electoral success, has been under detention. C.V. Devan Nair, the founder of the party, remains in neighbouring Singapore, not daring to enter Malaysia, for he suspects that as soon as he sets foot on Malaysian soil he would be arrested. Several other leaders are either under detention, or, since the May riots, have been evading arrest. All this may strengthen the party's mass base among the non-Malay communities, especially the Chinese, but at the same time it would make it more difficult for it to participate effectively in the legal political process.

All in all, recent events have seriously impaired the faith of large numbers of non-Malays in the constitutional and legal processes. Many are arriving at the shattering realization that all that they had gained through the ballot box in the last general elections has been wrenched away from them by the bayonet and the bullet. Increasingly it is going to be felt 'that parliamentary democracy is phoney and that justice can only be secured through armed revolution'.[16] Extremism is bound to thrive with a new vigour and vehemence on both sides, and the tragedy is that the one feeds on the other.

---

[16] A personal statement to this writer by one of the most perceptive leaders in the region, 7 June 1969.

BIBLIOGRAPHY

I. *Political Party Documents*

The Alliance Party
1. Statement by the UMNO-MCA Alliance on the report and recommendations of the Working Committee of the *mentri-mentri besar-*sponsored National Conference, 31 August 1953.
2. Undang2 Tuboh (Constitution), United Malays National Organisation, 16-17 April 1960.
3. Constitution of the Malayan Chinese Association, 12 November 1963.
4. Constitution of the Malaysian Alliance Party, 16 April 1965.
5. Minutes of the Central Working Committee Meeting, Malayan Chinese Association, 7 April 1957, 7 July 1956, 4 May 1957, 6 July 1958, 9 July 1959.
6. Minutes of Central General Committee meeting, Malayan Chinese Association, 12 July 1959.

Independence of Malaya Party and the Party Negara
1. Resolution moved at the inaugural meeting, 16 September 1951.
2. Rules of the party.
3. Election manifesto for the Kuala Lumpur municipal elections, February 1952.
4. Confidential memorandum on the 1952 Kuala Lumpur municipal elections by Yong Pung How, party's election agent in the Petaling Ward.
5. Report of the Working Committee of the Malayan National Conference, 1953.
6. Report of the proceedings of the Malayan National Conference, 1953.
7. Declaration by the sponsors of the Malayan National Conference, 1953 and the draft prepared by Malcolm MacDonald, British Commissioner General.
8. Letter from Dato Onn bin Jaafar to the members of the Branch Committee of the Kuala Lumpur Branch, 21 July 1952.
9. Press statement by the Communities' Liaison Committee, March 1949.

10. Personal letter dated 2 July 1952 by Dato E.E.C. Thuraisingham to Dato Onn bin Jaafar.
11. Motions and resolutions at the first meeting of the Central National Council, 16 September 1952.
12. Letter by Dato Panglima Bukit Gantang to Dato E.E.C. Thuraisingham, 24 December 1952.
13. Rules of the Party Negara.
14. Party Negara, election manifesto, 1955.
15. ——Objectives and platform, approved by the National Council, 15 August 1954.
16. ——Objectives and platform, approved by the National Council, 29 August 1960.
17. *Negara* (an English language organ of the Party Negara), August & September 1954.

Labour Party of Malaya

1. *Towards a New Malaya* — policy statement of the Pan Malayan Labour Party, adopted on 14 September 1952.
2. *Towards a New Malaya*, 1952, the draft submitted to the party.
3. First Annual Report of the Pan Malayan Labour Party, 9 July 1953.
4. Proceedings of the Second Annual Conference of the Pan Malayan Labour Party, 5-6 June 1954.
5. Proceedings of the extra-ordinary conference of the Labour Party, Ipoh, 7 May 1955.
7. Memorandum to the Reid Constitutional Commission, 25 September 1956.
8. *Annual Reports:* 1956-63.
9. *Labour Plans for Malaya*, 24 August 1958.
10. *Our Educational Policy*, 1961.
11. Memorandum on the *Educational Review Report* by the Johore Division of the Labour Party to the National Congress of the Party, 1960.
12. Constitution of the Labour Party.
13. Penang Division, *Annual Report*, 1963.
14. Selangor Division, *Annual Reports*, 1961-3.
15. The UDP and the PPP, a note by Lim Kean Siew, 1962.
16. *Selangor Divisional Committee*, a report by the State Secretary, 1964.

17. *Malaysia,* a study paper for the Labour Party members, Johore Division, October 1962.
18. Regarding the 'Problems of Chinese Education', speech by Dr. Wee Lee Fong, Secretary-General of the Labour Party, January 1964.
19. 'Our Economic Policy', speech by Tan Phock Kin, January 1964.
20. Working paper for the Malaysian Socialist Conference, 1962.
21. Statement on language policy, 1967.
22. 'We most resolutely oppose the language bill', (undated; 1967?) statement by the Central Secretariat of the party.
23. The Resolution of the 13th National Delegates' Conference, 1967.

The Malayan People's Socialist Front

1. Constitution of the Malayan People's Socialist Front.
2. *Annual Reports,* 1957-64.
3. Election manifestos, 1959 and 1964.
4. Approved draft policy statement, 25 January 1959.
5. *Towards a New Malaya:* policy statement, May 1963.
6. Draft agreement agreed at meeting of opposition parties on 9 February 1964 — Socialist Front, United Democratic Party, Party Negara and the National Convention Party.
7. Ooi Thiam Siew, Chairman, Socialist Front, Penang, *Post Mortem on the Elections in Penang,* 1964.
8. *Our Educational Policy,* prepared by a high-level Socialist Front committee, 1961.
9. 'Proposal for a Draft Educational Policy and Programme of the Socialist Front', a draft submitted by Lim Kean Siew, 1961.
10. Report to the Socialist Front on the Bornean Territories by a team of Socialist Front leaders, 16 November 1961.
11. 'Impasse in drafting education manifesto', a letter by V. Veerappan to the General Secretaries of the Labour Party and the Party Raayat, 24 January 1964.

Party Raayat

1. Anggaran Dasar Party Raayat.
2. Party Raayat policy, undated (1958?).
3. *National Education Policy, Party Raayat Stand:* signed note by Tadjuddin Kahar, Secretary-General, 23 January 1964.
4. Peringatan Congress Ke-IX (Minutes of the 9th Congress), 8-10 November 1963.

Parties of Personage
1. Manifesto of the Malayan Party, 1956, Malacca municipal elections.
2. *Malayan Party*, Annual Report for 1956.
3. Press statement by Aziz Ishak giving the aims of the National Convention Party — issued on the day of the formation of the party, 14 July 1963.
4. Statement by Aziz Ishak announcing the decision to join the Socialist Front, 16 March 1964.
5. Constitution of the National Convention Party.
6. Speech by Aziz Ishak at the First Annual Meeting of the National Convention Party, 20 September 1964.
7. Statement by the Central Executive Committee of the National Convention Party, 26 September 1964.
8. National Convention Party, *Annual Report*, 1963-4.

People's Action Party
Our First Ten Years, Tenth Anniversary Souvenir.

The People's Progressive Party
1. Manifesto, federal elections, 1955.
2. Election manifesto of the People's Progressive Party, 6 August 1959.
3. The First election manifesto, 1964.
4. The second manifesto, 1964.
5. Rules of the People's Progressive Party.

The United Democratic Party
1. Constitution of the United Democratic Party, 21 May 1962.
2. Election manifesto, 1964, parliamentary elections.
3. Resolution passed at the meeting of the Central General Assembly, 12 January 1964.

II *Books and Articles*

Published Works

ALLEN, JAMES de VERE, *The Malayan Union*, New Haven, 1967.
CARNELL, F.G., 'Communalism and Communism in Malaya', *Pacific Affairs*, Vol. XXVI No. 2 (June 1953).
——'Constitutional Reforms and Elections in Malaya', *Pacific Affairs*, Vol. XXVII No. 3 (1954).

EMERSON, R., *Malaysia: a Study of Direct and Indirect Rule*, Kuala Lumpur, University of Malaya Press, 1964.

FEDERATION OF MALAYA, ELECTION COMMISSION, *Report on the Delimitation of Parliamentary and State Constituencies under the Provisions of the Constitution of the Persekutuan Tanah Melayu, 1960*, Kuala Lumpur, Government Press, 1960.

——*Report on the Parliamentary and State Elections, 1959*, Kuala Lumpur, Government Press, 1960.

FEDERATION OF MALAYA, *Malayan Constitutional Documents*, 2nd edition, Vol. I, Kuala Lumpur, Government Press, 1962.

——*Report on the First Election of Members to the Legislative Council of the Federation of Malaya*, Kuala Lumpur, Government Press, 1955.

——*Report of the Registrar-General on Population, Births, Deaths, Marriages and Adoptions for the Year*, Kuala Lumpur, Government Press. Various issues.

——*Report of the Education Committee, 1956*, Kuala Lumpur, Government Press, 1956.

——*Report on the Introduction of Elections in the Municipality of George Town, Penang*, Kuala Lumpur, Government Press, 1951.

——*Report of the Education Review Committee, 1960*, Kuala Lumpur, Government Press, 1960.

FEDERATION OF MALAYSIA, *Official Yearbook*, 1963 and 1968, Kuala Lumpur, Government Press.

GINSBURG, N., ROBERTS, C.F., et al. *Malaya*, Seattle, University of Washington Press, 1958.

HAMZAH SENDUT, 'Urbanisation' in Wang Gungwu (ed.), *Malaysia: a Survey*, London, Pall Mall Press, 1964.

HANNA, W.A., *Eight Nation Makers: Southeast Asia's Charismatic Statesmen*, London, St. Martin's Press, 1964.

——*Sequel to Colonialism: the 1957-1960 Foundations for Malaysia*, New York, American Universities Field Staff, 1965.

HANRAHAN, G.Z., *The Communist Struggle in Malaya*, New York, Institute of Pacific Relations, 1954.

ISHAK BIN TADIN, 'Dato Onn: 1946-1951', *Journal of Southeast Asian History*, Vol. 1 No. 1 (March 1960).

KENNEDY, MALCOLM, *A Short History of Communism in East Asia*, London, Weidenfeld & Nicolson, 1957.

LEE KUAN YEW, *The Battle for a Malaysian Malaysia*, Singapore, Government Press, 1965.

——*The Battle for Merger*, Singapore, Government Press, 1962.

LEIFER, MICHAEL, 'Politics in Singapore', *Journal of Commonwealth Political Studies*, Vol. II No. 2 (May 1964).

MALAY LEAGUE OF PERAK, *Hidop Melayu — a Brief Review of Activities of the Malay National Movement*, Ipoh, n.d.

MCGEE, T.G., 'Population: a Preliminary Analysis' in Wang Gungwu (ed.), *Malaysia a Survey*, London, Pall Mall Press, 1964.

MEANS, G.P., 'Malaysia: a New Federation in Southeast Asia', *Pacific Affairs*, Vol. XXXVI No. 2 (Summer 1963).

MILLER, HARRY, *Prince and Premier: a Biography of Tunku Abdul Rahman Putra Al-haj, First Prime Minister of the Federation of Malaya*, London, Geo G. Harrap & Co., Ltd., 1959.

MILLS, L.A., *Malaya: a Political and Economic Appraisal*, Minneapolis, University of Minneapolis Press, 1958.

MILNE, R.S. 'Malaysia: a New Federation in the Making', *Asian Survey* (February 1963).

PALMER, NORMAN D., 'India's Fourth General Elections', *Asian Survey*, Vol. VII No. 5 (May 1967).

PARMER, NORMAN J., 'Constitutional Change in Malaya's Plural Society', *Far Eastern Survey* (October 1957).

PURCELL, VICTOR, *Malaya: Communist or Free?* Palo Alto, Stanford, The University Press, 1954.

RATNAM, K.J., *Communalism and the Political Process in Malaya*, Kuala Lumpur, University of Malaya Press, 1965.

RATNAM, K.J., & MILNE, R.S., *The Malayan Parliamentary Election of 1964*, Kuala Lumpur, University of Malaya Press, 1967.

ROFF, W.R., *The Origins of Malay Nationalism*, Kuala Lumpur, University of Malaya Press, 1967.

ROSE, SAUL, *Politics in Southern Asia*, London, Macmillan, 1963.

——*Socialism in Southern Asia*, London, Oxford University Press, 1959.

SHERIDAN, L.A. & GROVES, H.E., *The Constitution of Malaysia*, New York, Oceana Publications, Inc., 1967.

SILCOCK, T.H. & AZIZ, UNGKU A., 'Nationalism in Malaya' in William L. Holland, (ed.), *Asian Nationalism and the West*, New York, The Macmillan Co., 1953.

Tan Cheng Lock, *Malayan Problems from a Chinese Point of View*, Singapore, 1947.

THOMPSON, V.M. & ADLOFF, R., *The Left-Wing in Southeast Asia*, New York, Institute of Pacific Relations, 1950.

VAN DER KROEF, J.M. 'Indonesia, Malaya and the North Borneo Crisis', *Asian Survey*, Vol. III No. 4 (April 1963).

VAN DER MEHDEN, FRED R., 'Religion and Politics in Malaya', *Asian Survey* (December 1963).

VASIL, R.K. 'Constituency Studies: Batu' in K.J. Ratnam & R.S. Milne, *The Malayan Parliamentary Election of 1964*, Kuala Lumpur, University of Malaya Press, 1967.

——'The 1964 General Elections in Malaya', *International Studies*, Vol. VII No 1 (July 1965).

——'Man for 'any job', *The Dominion*, Wellington, 11 April 1967.

——'Why Malaysia Failed?', *Quest* (Spring 1966).

Wang Gungwu, *Malaysia: a Survey*, London, Pall Mall Press, 1964.

Theses

CLARK, MARGARET, 'The Malayan Alliance and its Accomodation of Communal Pressures, 1952-1962', unpublished thesis submitted to the Department of History, University of Malaya, for the degree of Master of Arts in History, 1964.

MEANS, G.P., 'Malayan Government and Politics in Transition', unpublished Ph.D. thesis submitted to the University of Washington, 1960.

INDEX

225, 227, 230, 272, 278, 288; (1957),
227, 232-3; (1958), 239; (1959),
24, 27-8, 32, 90, 124-5, 128, 131,
190, 191, 196-9, 200, 216-17, 219,
289, 309; (1964), 91, 180, 216, 219,
264-5, 289, 309; (1966), 172; (1969),
309-11.

general: (1959), 8-9, 121, 124-5, 130,
132-3, 134, 175-6, 185, 187, 191,
196, 241, 244, 248-9, 273, 277, 288-
9; (1964), 7, 9, 147-8, 151-2, 180,
187, 210, 212, 213-14, 241-2, 244,
248, 261, 262-3, 277, 284, 285-6,
288-9, 293, 300, 304; (1969), 302,
308-9, 311-12, 313.

municipal: (1952, Kuala Lumpur),
6, 10-11, 13, 38, 54-61, 63-4, 66-7,
72, 80-1, 111, 220, 222, 278; (1951,
Penang), 99; (1953), 270; (1954),
111, 224, 271; (1956), 118, 276;
(1957), 277; (1958), 236, 273; (1959-
60), 143; (1961), 143, 202-3; (1963),
241.

state: (1953), 270; (1954), 86-7;
(1955), 14, 103, 110, 183, 196, 271-2;
(1958), 239; (1959), 24, 90, 131, 176,
191, 196-9, 200, 216-17, 219, 289,
309; (1964), 41, 152, 180, 216, 219,
264-5, 289, 309; (1969), 308-11.

Emergency (1948-60), 99, 108, 109,
111-12, 113, 114, 124, 173-4, 231,
234-5, 257, 278; Regulations for,
167, 194, 234, 235.

Emmanuel, John, 110.

Employment, 6, 16, 18, 134, 135, 136,
142, 145, 148, 243, 259, 264.

English-educated: in MCA, 24; in
Labour Party, 99, 113, 115, 122,
124, 128, 130-1, 140-3, 149, 154-5,
162, 183, 196, 203, 204-5, 214, 215,
220-1; in UDP, 266.

Eurasian Association of Malaya, 76.

Examinations, language for, 27, 135-6,
137, 138, 142, 193-4, 195, 213, 238,
264, 305.

Extremism, 93, 117, 122, 128, 130,
132, 134, 140-2, 143, 144, 145, 153-

5, 168, 171, 182, 254, 280, 309, 312,
313.

FABIAN SOCIETY of PENANG, 106.
Federal Elections Committee, 104,
223.
Federal Executive Council, 77.
Federal Legislative Council, 77, 79,
93, 151, 183, 226, 231, 239.
Federation of Chinese Guilds and
Associations, 17, 19, 20, 156, 229-
30, 233-4, 274, 276.
Federation of Indian Organisations,
76.
Federation of Malaya, reunification
of Singapore with, 174 (see also
Malaysia).
Federation of Malaya Agreement
(1948), 18, 40, 230.
Federation of Malaysia, 3, 307; inau-
gurated (Sept. 1963), 1, 117, 146,
241.
Fenn-Wu Education Report (1951),
149.
Fertilizers, 279, 280, 285.
Fishermen, 170, 175, 194, 282, 286.
Foong Seong, 233.
Foo See Moi, 28.
Foreign troops in Malaya, 108, 114,
195, 286; bases for, 146, 260, 263,
286.
Formosa, 74, 291.

GAN BOON PUAK, 114.
Gan Yong Beng, 114, 115.
George Town, Penang, 14, 80, 84,
94, 95, 99, 111, 118, 248; Muncipal
Council of, 119, 237.
Gerakan Rakyat Malaysia (Malaysian
People's Movement), 300, 301, 303-
5, 306, 307, 310, 312-13.
Government servants, 53, 94, 98, 99,
103, 106 (see also Civil Service:
Public services).
Graduates, 133-4.
Great Britain: Malayan races keep
apart under, 4; protected the Malays,
12, 20, 48, 291; and Malaya's inde-